D1765110

CONTEMPORARY ISSUES IN THE SOCIOLOGY OF DEATH, DYING AND DISPOSAL

Also by Glennys Howarth

LAST RITES
The Work of the Modern Funeral Director

Also edited by Glennys Howarth and Peter C. Jupp

THE CHANGING FACE OF DEATH
Historical Accounts of Death and Disposal (*forthcoming*)

Contemporary Issues in the Sociology of Death, Dying and Disposal

Edited by

Glennys Howarth
Lecturer in Sociology
University of Sussex

and

Peter C. Jupp
Director of the National Funerals College
Institute of Community Studies, London

First published 1996 by
MACMILLAN PRESS LTD
Houndmills, Basingstoke, Hampshire RG21 6XS
and London
Companies and representatives
throughout the world

ISBN 0–333–63862–X

A catalogue record for this book is available
from the British Library.

10 9 8 7 6 5 4 3 2 1
05 04 03 02 01 00 99 98 97 96

Printed and bound in Great Britain by
Antony Rowe Ltd
Chippenham, Wiltshire

Published in the United States of America 1996 by
ST. MARTIN'S PRESS, INC.,
Scholarly and Reference Division
175 Fifth Avenue, New York, N.Y. 10010

ISBN 0–312–12742–1

Contents

Part 3 The Role of Health and Death Workers

Part 4 Social Implications of Legal and Medical Responses to Death and Dying

Foreword

Nothing is more obvious about society, especially about modern society, than that attitudes which make it up are subject to a *zeitgeist*. Nothing is more difficult than to get a grip on, let alone to measure, whatever changes there are in the spirit of the times. It is obvious to any adult not just that technology keeps changing but attitudes do too. People old enough to remember may not be able to put their finger on it but they know that the prevailing mood, both in general and in a host of particulars, is different, say, in the 1990s from what it was in the 1960s. Some of the superficialities can be pinned down. Clothes are different in ways that can be portrayed; music is different in ways that can be heard; food is different in ways that can be tasted.

The temporary culture or sub-cultures of fashion seem to have taken the place of tradition, binding people together not by the re-affirmation of old values but by the multi-faceted requirements of temporary traditions. These requirements are readily obeyed as though they were social imperatives, especially by younger people who would otherwise be the most easily lost in a kind of social chaos. Fashion more than tradition sets the boundaries within which people can strive for freedom, and without which they could be rudderless. Fashion in its broadest sense is to a large extent what holds society together – and this despite, as well as because, no-one can be quite sure what is happening. Control needs a sense of magic behind it to exert itself at all fully.

Death is an example, and a strange one. It remains, and probably will always remain, the ultimate mystery. No-one can ever know whether there is a beyond the other side of the gates, and, if so, what sort of beyond it is. It is even difficult (almost by definition) to imagine oneself dead. But this has not prevented quite endless talk about what cannot be talked about. There even seems to be a pattern to it. Some thirty or forty years ago it was fashionable to consider death a matter of taboo – to be hidden away rather than openly discussed. All that has changed and is certainly still changing fast, partly no doubt due to the media.

The person at home in the middle of an array of knobs and buttons which control his immediate environment can now, with the aid of other robots, summon up at will the most amazing fantasies. The media have added more and more insistently to an immense fairy-story world of death; it feeds the illusion, for adults as well as children, that no-one needs to die.

Artists contribute to this illusion, as they have always done, by imagining how to control time, make it stand still, leap forward or turn back, and their reach has been greatly enlarged by the media. The festival of death has become one of our favourite modern games. No Nero or Caligula was served by as many gladiators as a single child in any industrial country. It has been calculated (*The Times*, 19 October 1971), that by the time an average child in the USA has reached the age of fourteen he or she could be expected to have seen 18 000 people killed on television and we are sure, seen hosts of immortals – as they are called – who are sufficiently immune from death to come through many deaths alive. When all their enemies are slaughtered they re-appear again and again in other equally gripping dramas, and keep re-appearing on the screen of make-believe long after they are themselves reported apparently dead.

Social science has followed the same path. However much death may have been taboo in the mid-century, it is certainly not so as it nears its end. The discussion mounts. This book is an excellent illustration. It takes stock from many angles of the issues as they are presented today. Anyone who wishes to catch up with the views of social scientists about the ever-enduring subject of death is well-advised to start here.

MICHAEL YOUNG

Notes on the Contributors

Stephen Ball is Professor of Sociology of Education in the Centre for Educational Studies at King's College, London. His interests include education policy, post-structuralism and ethnography. As well as continued work on childhood cancer he is currently engaged in a series of studies of education reforms and marketisation.

Sarah Bignold is Research Officer in the Centre for Educational Studies at King's College London. Since 1992 she has worked on projects funded by the Department of Health and Cancer Relief Macmillan Fund into the needs and experiences of families of children with cancer. She is a co-ordinator of the Women in Research Group at King's, and a member of the Death, Dying and Bereavement Study Group.

Mary Bradbury completed an undergraduate degree in social anthropology at the University of Cambridge, and then undertook a conversion course in social psychology. She has recently gained a social psychological doctorate at the London School of Economics. In addition to doing further research in the field of death studies, she intends to train as a psychotherapist.

Alan Cribb is Lecturer in Ethics and Education in the Centre for Educational Studies at King's College, London. He is interested in the social context of health, particularly in relation to health care ethics and health promotion theory.

Christie Davies is Professor of Sociology at the University of Reading. His main research interests lie in the sociology of morality and the sociology of humour. His articles in these areas have appeared in journals such as the *American Journal of Sociology*, *British Journal of Sociology*, and the *Howard Journal*. His work has been translated into Bulgarian, German, Greek, Hebrew, Hungarian, Italian and Polish. His most recent book is *Ethnic Humor Around the World.*

Douglas Davies is Professor of Religious Studies within the Department of Theology at the University of Nottingham. He trained both in social anthropology and theology at Durham and Oxford and has particular research interests in the anthropology of death, and in Mormonism. Apart from numerous papers and book chapters his major books include: *Church and Religion in Rural England* and *Cremation Today and Tomorrow.*

Jon Davies is a lecturer at the University of Newcastle upon Tyne where he is Head of the Religious Studies Department. He is author of *The Evangelistic Bureaucrat, a Study of a Planning Exercise in Newcastle upon Tyne,* and *The Christian Warrior in the Twentieth Century.* He co-edited *The Sociology of Sacred Texts* and *Ritual and Remembrance: Responses to Death in Human Societies.* He lectures on the liturgies, theologies and sociologies of marriage and death.

David Field is Professor of Sociology at the University of Ulster. He has been teaching about terminal care to medical students and nurses since 1976. His initial interest in terminal care developed from this teaching and his latest research project in the area is a study of the experiences of providing terminal care among general practitioners who graduated from the 1979 entry year to the Faculty of Medicine at the University of Leicester.

Shirley Firth lectures part-time in religious studies at King Alfred's College, Winchester, and for the Open University, for whom she also teaches the new course, 'Death and Dying'. She runs regular seminars for MSc courses in health psychology and palliative care at Southampton University on multicultural and religious aspects of death and bereavement. Her doctoral thesis, 'Death, Dying and Bereavement in a British Hindu Community', was accepted by the School of Oriental and African Studies, London University, in 1994.

Jacque Lynn Foltyn, PhD, is an Assistant Professor of Sociology, in the Department of Liberal Studies at the University of Redlands, in Redlands, California, USA. She earned her doctorate from the Department of Sociology, University of California, San Diego in 1989 and is the author of *The Beauty Problem: A Defense, Celebration, and Exploration of Beauty.*

Jenny Hockey is a social anthropologist, currently lecturing in health studies at the University of Hull. Her research interests include the management of death, both socially and institutionally; later life and the lifecourse; and gender and health. She has published *Experiences of Death. An Anthropological Account,* and with Allison James, *Growing Up and Growing Old. Ageing and Dependency in the Lifecourse.*

Glennys Howarth has recently taken up a lectureship in sociology at the University of Sussex. Prior to that she held the T.H. Marshall Research Fellowship in the Department of Sociology at the London School of Economics, where she studied the role of coroners in relation to sudden death. Her primary research interests are concerned with social, legal and medical aspects of death, dying and bereavement. Her publications include *Last Rites: the work of the modern funeral director.* With Peter Jupp she is editor of the journal *Mortality.*

Peter C. Jupp is a United Reform Church minister. He works for the Institute of Community Studies as Director of the National Funerals College. He was Convenor of the British Sociological Association's Sociology of Religion Study Group, 1991–94. His doctoral thesis investigated the development of cremation in England, 1820–1990. He is currently editing three other books of essays: *The Changing Face of Death* with Glennys Howarth, *Postmodernity, Sociology and Religion* with Kieran Flanagan, and *Death: Interpretations and Practice* with Anthony Rogers.With Glennys Howarth he is editor of the journal *Mortality.*

Sewa Singh Kalsi is Lecturer in Sikh Studies at the University of Leeds, where he specialises in teaching Sikhism and the development of Sikh tradition in Britain. He is author of *The Evolution of a Sikh Community in Britain: Religious and Social Changes Among the Sikhs of Leeds and Bradford* and he has published articles on the development of Sikh tradition in Britain. Dr Kalsi was senior lecturer at Bradford and Ilkely Community College, where he taught South Asian Studies to undergraduate students for several years. He is Consultant for the Multifaith Research and Resource Centre, Thomas Danby College, Leeds. He is a member of the English Association for the Study of Religions, and the Punjab Research Group, UK.

Jeanne Samson Katz is Lecturer in Health and Social Welfare at the Open University. She has a MSc and PhD in health sociology, is a social worker and has worked in hospices with dying people. She is presently engaged in research in palliative care and bereavement support. She co-authored the Open University *Death and Dying* course. She has recently published *Easeful Death*, on which she collaborated with a colleague at the Open University.

Margaret Mitchell is the Director of Research at the newly formed Strathclyde Police Occupational Health Unit based at Glasgow Caledonian

University. She is also Reader in Psychology at that university. A major research interest is how death is managed in the community, and she is currently undertaking a study, funded by the Home Office, of how police probationers are trained, both formally and informally, to deal with death. She has published extensively on the psychological impact of the Lockerbie air disaster. A further research interest is how common sense and lay knowledge infiltrates decision making in professional practice.

Demetra M. Pappas holds a JD from Fordham University School of Law and an MSc from the London School of Economics, where she is currently the Morris Finer Memorial Scholar. She is engaged in doctoral research examining comparative approaches and legislative responses to euthanasia and assisted suicide. Prior to commencing studies at the LSE, she spent three years engaged in the practice of criminal law (trials and appeals) and two years clerking to an appellate judge in New York City.

Margaret Robbins trained in social anthropology at Manchester University, obtaining her doctorate in 1985. Since then she has been working in the field of health services research and is currently Lecturer in Medical Anthropology at Bristol University. Her ongoing research interests include the organisation and delivery of palliative care services, and social theory in the individualisation of the body (in death and in life).

Tony Walter is Lecturer in Sociology at the University of Reading. He is author of *Basic Income*; *Funerals and How to Improve Them*; *The Revival of Death*: and *The Eclipse of Eternity*. His current research interests are portrayals of death in the mass media; the care of dying people by neighbours; and the sociology of the afterlife.

Introduction

Glennys Howarth

By entitling this volume of sociological papers on death 'Contemporary Issues', we have sought both to illustrate the range and complexity of late twentieth century approaches to death, and to acknowledge that mortality has long been a concern of sociologists. When we peruse the major sociological texts of this century it is clear that many of these theorists have focused on aspects of death in modern cultures. We might, for instance, consider the work of Emile Durkheim and his study of suicide (1951); the British sociologist, Geoffrey Gorer undertook research into widowhood and patterns of mourning in mid-twentieth century England (1955); Robert Blauner advanced the study of death with an important discussion of its impact on social structure in modern society (1966); Glaser and Strauss (1965; 1968) augmented research on death and developed grounded theory through studies of dying in hospital environments. To this list might be added the insights into death offered by sociologists such as Talcot Parsons (1967), Ivan Illich (1977) and Norbert Elias (1985). One repeated underlying and connecting theme in these and other texts is that the cultural mechanisms surrounding death and dying reveal much about the state of social life and living.

Perhaps the most common assertion of these students of modernity is that the modern 'art of dying' is of a significantly poorer quality than that of an earlier, pre-modern age. The dying, death and disposal rituals of traditional societies are usually perceived as somehow more satisfying and less isolating, and to have contributed to a tightening, rather than a weakening, of community bonds. As a consequence of modernity, traditional communities have become dislocated, individualism has flourished, and medical science has appeared to triumph over nature by extending the duration of life as well as by performing endless miracles in averting death at an 'early' age. To those acquainted with sociological accounts of death in modern societies, these are familiar themes; the verdict is echoed throughout, that the modern experience of death is *isolating, frightening, privatised, medicalised* and *meaningless.*

But are these images still appropriate when applied to contemporary deathways? It appears to many commentators that western societies are undergoing a period of dynamic change in relation to death mores, a period in which there is a manifest rejection of modern scientific and medical rationale. For example, the hospice movement, with its emphasis on a 'better way of death' signals an alternative to the medical model for dying. More people are choosing to die at home – privatised perhaps, but significantly, within a caring rather than a medicalised environment. The creation of such reforming groups as the Natural Death movement is a further indication of dissatisfaction with medical and professional prescriptions of dying and disposal rituals.

Why should this be so? There are many explanations, but the media have played a notable part in increasing our awareness of death. For example, since 1968 they have exploited the political role of death and funerals in Northern Ireland and also in violent conflicts with which the United States, the Middle East, South Africa and Eastern Europe have been involved. The most recent trigger of change and certainly the most widely acknowledged, has been the spread of AIDS, accompanied by a visible and vociferous support movement for sufferers which has, as a consequence, assisted in bringing discussion of death firmly into the public realm. The project of medical science may continue the quest for a cure for all major killer diseases but the spread of AIDS has shaken to its very foundations the popular belief that medical science has won the battle over nature.

It is the animated nature of the discussion of contemporary issues surrounding death that make this volume of papers particularly timely. The present day tension between the discourses of science and nature have fundamental import for the development and significance of a variety of approaches to mortality. Indeed, the theme of science *versus* nature threads its way through many of the following chapters.

Part 1 seeks to locate death in contemporary western society. Jenny Hockey sets the scene with an exploration of the discourse between science and nature. She suggests that in their management of death, western psychologists and bereavement counsellors have drawn upon the work of anthropologists and social historians to construct a more 'natural' paradigm for meaningful death ritual. In the chapter which follows, Douglas Davies utilises empirical research to examine the social facts of death, defined as the attitudes, images and social representations which constitute shared perspectives on our social world. In so doing he considers issues such as AIDS and distinguishes some of the differences between public perceptions of ritual procedures and actual practice. One notable example he uses, is that concerning the conveyor-belt process of crematoria rituals. He points out that in practice, very few crematoria adopt this method for removing the coffin from view; and what is more, few mourners perceived the ritual in this way. Perhaps the view that crematoria committal services are necessarily alienating for bereaved people may be more a rejection of technology and a romanticisation of the past than an accurate reflection of practice or experience.

Sewa Singh Kalsi's chapter completes the opening section by highlighting the tension between the discourses of traditional religion and the pressures of modern secular societies. In a discussion of the dynamics and transformation of Sikh death rituals he illustrates the way ritual requirements respond and adapt to the proclivities of modern western societies. Traditions have had to be adapted to life in modern Britain, but nevertheless, continue to draw upon, and to reinforce predominant ideologies contained within caste and gender divisions. It is interesting to note, as Jenny Hockey encourages us to do, that from a western perspective, ethnic groups which retain traditional religious practices are seen as enjoying more profound funeral rituals. Paradoxically, whilst endeavouring to make our own rituals more meaningful, we have little compunction, as Shirley Firth later illustrates, in coercing others to adapt to the medical, scientific and bureaucratic procedures endemic to modern British life.

Part 2 deals with social representations of dying, death and disposal. It begins with Jon Davies' chapter which makes the intriguing assertion that the doctrine of Purgatory has survived from traditional Christian society into modern secular Britain. He examines the communion between the living and the dead and postulates that despite attempts to rationalise beliefs in Purgatory, 'ordinary people' still find ways of continuing relationships with their dead. In suggesting that the doctrine of Purgatory has not been lost, he cites the *in-memoria* pages of local newspapers as the modern form whereby families publicly attempt to intercede with god on behalf of their relatives – a medieval tradition truncated, transplanted and transformed to give succour to people in a modern society.

It is hardly possible to discuss contemporary sociological approaches to death without contemplating social aspects of the corpse. Indeed, many of the chapters here touch on its social relevance within both the public (for example medical) and the private setting. There are two chapters in this section specifically devoted to the neglected area in the study of the sociology of the body, namely, the sociology of the dead body. The first is Christie Davies' chapter which traces different approaches to the treatment and disposal of the corpse manifest in Britain and the United States. He argues that the distinction between these two western countries (the former preferring cremation and the latter favouring embalming and burial) has developed in response to different ethnic traditions. Preoccupied with hygiene and cleanliness, in the United States dirt and decay must be seen to be abolished, and this, he suggests, forms the cultural basis for the widespread nature of embalming. By contrast, in Britain we could perhaps suppose that pursuit of rational, scientific methods, coupled with the premium on burial space, has contributed to the adoption of cremation as a method of disposal of human remains. It is interesting that in the United States, and to some extent in Britain, death industries are utilising the pseudo-scientific techniques of embalming in an attempt to present a more 'natural' looking corpse that appears to retain human qualities.

Jacque Lynn Foltyn augments this examination of the dead body with a sophisticated analysis of the relationship between beauty and death. When death is visited upon beautiful people, such is the social power with which beauty is imbued that it is not only the individual that is mourned but also the passing of beauty. The preservation and memorialisation of beauty become ends in themselves. Paradoxically, beauty also stimulates a penchant for destruction. The author applies a range of theoretical tools to explore the defacement and destruction of the beautiful; to examine efforts to preserve dying beauty; and to illustrate ways in which dead beauty is memorialised and kept intact.

The chapters which conclude this section consider the concept of the good death. Mary Bradbury's interpretation of the good death, whether traditional, medical or natural, further reveals contemporary views regarding the distinction between science and nature. Developed in more traditional communities and usually premised on entry into an Afterlife, the good death might be expected to disappear in modern secularised societies. In employing Moscovici's theory (1984) of social representations to analyse the findings from her empirical study of the death industry and of widows, Bradbury clearly demonstrates, however, that the concept of the good death is not only extant but has diversified into alternative forms.

Shirley Firth concentrates on the Hindu good death which, in order to be good, must occur at the right time and in the right place. Bad death, by contrast, is prémature, violent or sudden. Relatives have an important role to play in performing rituals which ensure that the death is good. In this chapter the author documents the difficulties they face in trying to facilitate the good death in a British medical setting. In common with Kalsi's earlier discussion of Sikh funeral rites, Firth demonstrates that the criteria which constitute the good Hindu death are being modified accordingly.

The chapters in Part 3 examine the stresses experienced by those who work with dying, dead or bereaved people. The emphasis in this section is on the efficacy of education, training and coping strategies to develop competence and alleviate anxiety. The chapters by David Field and Jeanne Katz respectively, scrutinise the professional role of doctors and nurses in terminal care settings. Field notes that in both medicine and nursing, terminal care is seen as amenable to improvement by the provision of education and training in undergraduate and basic level training courses. Indeed, education for terminal care is now viewed by the General Medical Council as a necessary element of training for medical undergraduates. However, the effectiveness of such education is seriously questioned by Field's empirical studies.

Jeanne Katz' focus is nursing dying people on a cancer ward. In contrast with some of the earlier studies, the findings from her research suggest that long term contact with terminally ill people was not necessarily in itself a source of distress for nurses. Katz explores ways in which nurses conceptionalised their work with cancer patients and shows that more significant triggers of anxiety were the existence of rules pertaining to information control, to behaviour, and to the expression of emotion.

In completing this section, Margaret Mitchell looks at the police response to sudden death and inspects the utility of 'gallows' humour and the concept of habituation in assisting officers to deal with their experiences. Popular perceptions portray the police as steeled to emotional distress. Drawing upon her study of officers attending the Lockerbie air disaster in 1988 she shows that contrary to lay and police beliefs, when faced with sudden or violent death, officers may be deeply traumatised. She suggests that rather than rely on a 'macho' culture, incorporating notions of hardiness, police forces should provide more training and understanding of the psychological needs of their officers.

The fourth and final part of this volume probes the social implications of medical and legal responses to death and dying. Here, discussions of contemporary debates surrounding childhood cancer, euthanasia and organ donation are complemented by the concluding chapter which highlights shifts in attitudes to mortality and characterises the post-modern approach as individualistic.

Stephen Ball, Alan Cribb and Sarah Bignold begin this section by exploring and illustrating the experiences of families with children who have cancer. The discussion revolves around the analytical axis of uncertainty. This uncertainty, partly constituted by the ever present shadow of death, is central to a 'culture of childhood cancer'. By identifying this culture the authors show how the distinctions between lay and professional, 'insider' and 'outsider' are significant for the experience and organisation of care. In this context they offer insights into the ways in which some families find themselves engaged in struggles with professionals for control over their child's experiences.

Demetra Pappas tackles the contentious, and continuing, debate on euthanasia through medical and legal perspectives on the right to die. The guardians of medical science – commonly regarded as the saviours of humankind – wrestle with the moral question of whether it is right, or moreover, whether they have a duty, to assist in ending the lives of those patients who request 'lethal aid'. The issues they face are compounded by parallel debates in the legislature of sanctity of life and individual human rights. This chapter compares developments in the Netherlands, United States and the United Kingdom. By outlining the background to her own interest in these debates the author poignantly reminds us that discussions of death cannot be abstracted from our own mortal existence.

Focusing on organ donation, Margaret Robbins highlights some of the paradoxes entailed in the modern miracles performed by medical science. In discussing the effect on families of organ donors she examines two widely held assumptions about the way in which donation can be a comfort to bereaved people: the 'gift of life'; and the notion that their loved-one may live on in the body of another person. In the quest for ever improved techniques and greater availability of resources (human organs), however, the emotional impact that the decision to donate has on survivors has been overlooked. Transplant surgery may save lives or may prolong life but not without cost.

Concluding this volume Tony Walter's chapter summarises the parameters of the debate. He distinguishes three types of death and, like Mary Bradbury, points to the fact that each of these is present to a greater or lesser extent in the interpretations which individuals give to their own deaths, and to the deaths of those around them. He contends that British deathways are changing and people now demand greater control over dying and after-death procedures and rituals. In post-modern societies, he predicts that individuals will no longer be willing to accept the scientific, medical and professional models of appropriate death and will instead create their own by drawing piecemeal from those known to them. This chapter reminds us of Jenny Hockey's starting point, that in order to make sense of mortality, modern western societies select from the rituals of other communities and periods. This they do because there is a belief that modernity has robbed us of meaningful death rituals and interpretations and that people from traditional societies and earlier historical periods enjoy better and 'more cultural' ways of death.

Together the contributors to this book present a portrait of the contemporary construction of mortality in modern western societies. As such they should assist the reader in understanding something of the deathways which straddle the modern and post-modern worlds. Durkheim's insights into an earlier period of dramatic flux, that between traditional and m societies, can shed some light on the intricacies of our own period in time. For Durkheim rationality triumphed over nature; in the late modern world it appears that nature might yet recapture the hearts and minds of this and future generations. In bringing together the contributions in this, and its companion volume[1], we have offered an insight into the mosaic patterned and multi-layered nature of the discourses which constitute contemporary deathways. In so doing, we aim to illustrate that the sociology of death is at least as complex as the sociology of life.

Note

1. Jupp, P.C. and Howarth, G. (eds), *The Changing Face of Death: historical accounts of death and disposal* (London: Macmillan, forthcoming).

Part 1

Locating Death in Modern Western Societies

1 The View from the West: Reading the Anthropology of Non-western Death Ritual

Jenny Hockey

This chapter raises questions about the way in which accounts of death ritual, enacted at other times and in other places, have been constructed and made use of within frames of reference specific to western discourses. Its focus is the descriptions and discussions of funerary practices initially generated by social historians and anthropologists which have subsequently been drawn upon by psychiatrists and counsellors involved in the management of death within contemporary western societies – an involvement which may be either practical, academic or some combination of the two. Thus, for example, Riley, a bereaved parent and student of child development, states in an article entitled 'The Psychology of Bereavement: a Personal View':

> ... it is felt that old customs and other cultures help the bereaved at this second stage of mourning. The traditional black clothing enables the mourner to give the dead person a central place in her life as before ... while it would appear to the modern view that it is false to impose customs on such an intense and private emotion as grief, the very loneliness of the crisis and the bewildering conflict of feelings cries out for a supportive structure.
>
> (Riley 1984: 180)

An interpretive framework which might be described as therapy-oriented is being used to address funerary material originally presented in more traditional academic terms. Social historians, for example, have highlighted the complexity, the expense and the centrality of the funeral within everyday life during the nineteenth century (Ariès 1981: Gorer 1965; Stannard 1977; Jalland 1989). Psychiatrists and social workers have subsequently interpreted this material as evidence of a 'proper' or 'therapeutic' way of managing death (Hinton 1967; Parkes 1972; Torrie 1981). An example of this process of reinterpretation is to be found in a Help the Aged booklet, *Bereavement*, sponsored by the National Association of Funeral Directors in conjunction with Cruse – Bereavement Care:

> ... in times gone by there was more formality in mourning and the acceptance of ritual expressions of grief were part of the lifestyle of our grandparents. Nowadays with the passing of that formality we may overlook the need to mourn, but it is essential to our wellbeing and our recovery. We need to allow ourselves this time to mourn and to grieve ...

What originated as an 'objective' account of earlier beliefs and practices is now granted a therapeutically prescriptive role. Historians themselves, have adopted various positions with regard to the 'therapy' debates which now surround their accounts.

Well known are the authors who are critical of contemporary responses to death, finding inspiration for a more 'therapeutic' response to death in the past (Ariès 1981; Gorer 1965; Stannard 1977; Jalland 1989). Others perceive this view as at best nostalgic, at worst inaccurate (Cannadine 1981; Richardson 1989).

THE VIEW FROM THE PRESENT

This chapter raises questions about the cultural filters through which the past, the strange and the foreign have been viewed – not only by those whose primary concern is the remedying of the perceived ills of the present, but also by historians and social anthropologists who have provided evidence of other deathways. Taking as my primary focus the ethnography, and the 'therapeutic' appropriation of the ethnography of non-western death ritual, I will argue that certain key themes within western culture during the nineteenth century and now – the themes of 'science' and 'nature' – have underpinned both the construction of the original account as well as its subsequent appropriation by critics of contemporary approaches to death. Whilst these themes gained ascendancy during the social and economic upheavals of nineteenth century industrialisation and urbanisation, they can be traced back to the scientific revolution of the sixteenth century. This revolution saw the natural world, hitherto a domain lying beyond human control, reduced to its quantifiable attributes – shape, number and motion. This development was to underpin an unprecedented control of the natural world, a control which, through time, came to serve nineteenth century western economic interests in previously unimaginable ways. Such is the power of rational, scientific frameworks that society, the body and ultimately the psyche subsequently came to be perceived and experienced in similar terms. Not only the natural world but also human nature itself came to be viewed through the cultural filter of scientific models (Capra 1982).

Nonetheless, alongside the nineteenth century 'civilization' and 'progress' view of a world where 'science' appeared to have honoured its promise of control over nature, Romanticism provided a critique of dehumanised, hostile, urban industrial life. By the late eighteenth century, for example, the Alps, once a troublesome barrier between Northern Europe and the inspirationally civilised world of Italian society, had become in themselves a quite different source of inspiration. Spiritual depths of emotional experience could be found among the solitary peaks of this 'natural' landscape. A tension had therefore emerged between the powerful rationality of scientific models and the intuitive emotionality attributed not only to the 'natural' world but also, by association, to the human 'natures' of those who dwelt in what were seen as more organic 'communities' beyond the constraints of urban industrialised Western society. So powerfully ambiguous was the relationship between 'science' and 'nature' that each took on the depth and resonance of a cultural icon, each one amenable to shifting interpretations. It is the ambiguity of a science-based discourse of bereavement which at times draws very heavily upon shifting notions of 'nature' and the 'natural' which this chapter will examine.

CONTESTING THE PAST

To introduce discussion, debates within social history will briefly be reviewed. Much of the criticism of the contemporary western approaches to death, which has emerged since the mid 1950s, centres around the notion that elsewhere, in the foreign country of the past, or indeed in a foreign country, society's members knew how to respond to death. We alone have a problem with death in that Modernity has gradually robbed us of that knowledge. Gorer, for example, uses his memories of elaborate pre-World War One mourning to ground his critique of post World War Two deathways:

> ...the majority of British people are today without adequate guidance as to how to treat death and bereavement and without social help in living

> through and coming to terms with the grief and morning which are the inevitable responses in human beings to the death of someone whom they have loved.
>
> (Gorer 1965: 110)

Ariès' history of death ritual from the early Middle Ages onwards culminates in a similar critique:

> The beginning of the twentieth century saw the completion of the psychological mechanism that removed death from society, eliminated its character of public ceremony, and made it a private act. At first this act was reserved for intimates, but eventually even the family was excluded as the hospitalization of the terminally ill became widespread.
>
> (Ariès 1981: 575)

Jalland draws on the letters and diaries of upper middle and upper class families between 1850 and 1920 to argue that:

> ...religious belief undoubtedly brought more comfort to the bereaved in the nineteenth century that it does now. Probably equally important was the complex framework of death and mourning rituals, which seemed to comfort the dying and helped to meet the psychological needs of survivors.
>
> (Jalland 1989: 186)

The intellectual framework underpinning this view of the past reflects a contemporary preoccupation with the 'natural'. As a system of editing, it highlights and lends positive value to aspects of bygone universes. The concept of 'nature', as cultural icon, encompasses the notion that ritual, enacted within pre-twentieth century communities, effectively addresses the psychological needs which constitute human 'nature'. Such ritual forms are frequently opposed to the secularised deathways of rootless urban dwellers. Community-based ritual prefigures industrialisation and therefore, by association, lies closer to the more 'natural' way of life beyond the urban conurbation.

Culturally-specific interpretations of the past are of course contestable. Cannadine takes issue with a pervasive association between Modernity and cultural and social impoverishment (1981). He questions the 'therapeutic' view of Victorian death ritual, arguing that, 'the conventional picture of death in the nineteenth century is excessively romanticised and insufficiently nuanced; that it makes assumptions about the functional and therapeutic values of the elaborate death-bed, funerary and mourning rituals which are unproven' (1981:188). What Cannadine highlights are the effects of large-scale first World War death, the public practice of Remembrance Day and the private practice of spiritualism. Referring to a 'massive, all-pervasive pall of death which hung over Britain in the years between 1914 and 1939' (1981:230), he represents contemporary death ritual as more bearable.

Cannadine also refers to 'a bonanza of commercial exploitation' which benefited the undertaker and black crepe manufacturers like Courtaulds (1981: 191); while Richardson (1989) links Victorian death ritual and grave robbery, the practice which enabled a rising medical profession to conduct illegal dissection:

> ... the professionalisation of undertaking and the development of extra-mural cemeteries received strong impetus from public fear of grave robbery for dissection.
>
> (Richardson 1989: 105)

Though the Anatomy Act of 1832 made body snatching unnecessary, paupers' unclaimed corpses could legally be requisitioned by anatomists. It was a proper burial, rather than a secure coffin, which protected the deceased against dissection.

THE PRIVILEGING OF EMOTION

Underlying these debates is a belief that the *emotional* responses of dying or bereaved people should be pivotal to both private and public responses to death. Though Cannadine and Richardson argue that wealth, status or the protection of the corpse can shape death ritual, their work is presented in opposition to a more dominant concern with emotion. Arguably these debates for and against Victorian death ritual as therapy have obscured the question as to why emotion should take precedence over an inheritance system or a cosmology when it comes to the wider relevance of academic studies of death. Richardson argues that contemporary audiences are disquieted by indications that issues other than grief can shape responses to death. Rather, the core question underlying much of this material is how people in the past *felt* when bereaved and how did they manage their emotions? When appropriated by popular literature, such accounts yield a more unequivocal reading. Whatever our forebears or our foreign counterparts felt, it was somehow a healthier or more 'natural' response and authors move on rapidly to ask how we can recapture their 'wisdom'.

While the historical and anthropological literature portrays emotion in accounts of death ritual, it is nonetheless recognised as a problematic endeavour. Diaries and letters provide the historian with autobiographical accounts of grief, but do contemporary frameworks allow a straightforward reading? Similarly anthropologists who witness emotional expression during fieldwork can make sense of it only within the broader context of the society as a whole. As Huntington and Metcalf write:

> Because we know that notions of such seemingly simple things as space, time, and color vary in complex ways from one society to another, how could we assume a constancy for such complicated moods as sorrow, joy, love and hate?
>
> (Huntington and Metcalf 1979: 23)

This theme is echoed in anthropologist, Martins', discussion of critiques of the western medicalisation of death which argue that discourse and meaning have been lost (1983). He notes how critics 'invent' (that is, find or retrieve) death utopias where dying is made dignified through cosmological beliefs and rituals 'even in the social context of underprivilege and, on occasion, of punitive social controls' (1983: x). Only within the 'natural' world of 'primitive' peoples can human nature and therefore authentic human emotionality flourish.

Ethnographic evidence of 'utopian' deathways in the more 'natural' setting of a pre-industrial society is, indeed, less than clear cut. Evans-Pritchard's account of Azande witchcraft, oracles and magic describes farmers and hunter–gatherers who were entirely dependent upon their 'natural' environment yet the concept of 'natural' death was foreign to them (1972 [1937]). While illness or accident represented the physical cause of death, Azande cited witchcraft as the social cause of death in that it precipitated the illness or accident. Even death in old age, the most 'natural' and therefore desirable death among Westerners, is believed to result from witchcraft among the immediate family of an Azande:

> When a very old man dies unrelated people say that he has died of old age, but they do not say this in the presence of kinsmen, who declare that witchcraft is responsible for his death.
>
> (Evans-Pritchard 1972 [1937]: 77)

It might be argued that while this example does not represent an accepting response to the supposedly 'natural' event of death, it does indicate that Azande can give shape to an otherwise inchoate event. It remains questionable, however, whether a desired western response to bereavement might also encompass vengeance, a cultural imperative in a society where 'falling sick', funerals and vengeance represent an inevitable continuum (Evans-Pritchard 1972 [1937]: 441).

The anthropological literature is therefore inconsistent with Jalland's argument that 'the complex framework of death and mourning rituals ... seemed to comfort the dying and helped to meet the psychological needs of survivors (1989: 186). While ritual forms can be shown to express a society's belief systems, those beliefs and values may not correspond to the psychological needs of all survivors. More usefully, we can ask why those emotional needs should take precedence within contemporary enquiries. Ethnographic accounts show the centrality of wealth and status within the rituals of many social groups, over and above our bourgeois nineteenth century forebears. An example is the Native American practice of potlatch, the ritual destruction of wealth during a lavish feast to which competing groups are invited (Boas 1965 [1911]). Another example is the death ritual of the Bororo of South America. Like the Azande, the Bororo have no concept of 'natural' death, viewing it as a violation of culture by nature. Only the vengeance killing of a large animal, representative of 'nature', allows the spirit of the deceased passage to the society of souls. However, while addressing human mortality, a more central theme within Bororo death ritual is the tension between the society's competing sub-groups. Indeed, in Lévi-Strauss's view, death ritual is concerned more with relations among the living than between the living and the dead:

> ... the image a society evolves of the relationship between the living and the dead is, in the final analysis, an attempt, on the level of religious thought, to conceal, embellish or justify the actual relationships which prevail among the living.
>
> (Lévi-Strauss 1973: 246)

Urgent social issues therefore take precedence over individual grief.

Martins' critique notwithstanding, the 'invention' of 'death utopias' by social scientists has nonetheless provided source material for many western practitioners in the field of dying and bereavement. Margaret Torrie, founder of Cruse – Bereavement Care, in a 1981 booklet 'Helping the Bereaved', tells the reader that:

> When we consider the British tendency to hold emotion at arm's length and to encourage a 'stiff upper lip', some of the difficulties surrounding

> bereaved families are understandable. It can be very different in another culture.
>
> (Torrie 1981: 4)

Constructed as culturally variable, bereavement is seen to derive its current difficulties from the nature of western culture. Torrie also refers to 'wise people [who] encourage tears and accept the pain of grief in others and in themselves'. Do these 'wise people' predominate in non-western cultures? Emanuel Lewis of the Tavistock Clinic echoes this point in the *Lancet*:

> Bereavement is always hard, particularly now that we have discarded much of the ancient ritual which promoted the normal mourning and recovery processes.
>
> (Lewis 1976: 619)

Similarly Richard Lansdown, chief psychologist at the Hospital for Sick Children in London, writing in *Bereavement Care*, said:

> The well brought up five year old Victorian was likely to be taught about death, and heaven or hell directly or indirectly. Today the Indian child is taught that we will be reborn; the British child learns, if anything, that our spirit goes to heaven. But the British child may learn that talking about real death is not quite nice.
>
> (Lansdown 1985: 15)

In the post-1950s western bereavement literature, death is framed predominantly in terms of the rational, scientific models of medically trained psychiatrists such as John Hinton and Colin Murray Parkes. However, their medical gaze turns frequently towards a supposedly 'natural' landscape of the emotions, illustrative material being found in ethnographic accounts of those whose lives are believed to unfold in closer proximity to 'nature'. In his widely read work *Dying* (1967), Hinton draws on 'primitive beliefs', referencing them five times in his index. By providing evidence of institutionalised fear of the dead, belief in a continued life, anger and a readiness to blame others among those 'tribal' peoples whose lives unfold within a more 'natural' environment, Hinton reassures the contemporary western reader that their apparently 'irrational' feelings about death are only human 'nature'. An elision is created between 'the world of nature' and 'natural emotion', the emotional experience of the rational urban individual thereby being legitimated. Again it is assumed that, in being pre-Modern, 'tribal' peoples have privileged access to a natural or healthy response to death, one which we may find strange but should nonetheless learn to accept within ourselves.

This view from the West, evident in both ethnographic accounts and contemporary bereavement literature, also emerges within the discourse of practitioners such as clergy. During a study conducted among Sheffield clergy, cross cultural comparison featured in discussion of the management of grief. Thus a Free Church minister said:

> Its very much a cultural matter and I've conducted a Ghanaian funeral and that was a most amazing experience ... because I went through my order of service and did my bits and there were a few Hallelujahs but otherwise nothing much out of the ordinary ... but when we actually got to the graveside there was a great expression of grief and emotion and all sorts of things which in a different congregation you would have called hysteria but it seemed right for them ... and then I went back to the party at the house afterwards and it really was a party ... and I think that worked in that particular culture.[1]

An Anglo-Catholic priest was unequivocal in highlighting the advantages of another culture's deathways:

> I'd advocate the Jewish system of bereavement which I think is a very very healthy system which is that you weep and wail like mad for, is it two days or twenty four hours or something ... and then you stop and then its finished, done ... and I think the Jews have a lot to teach us in this one ... their way of death is very very healthy.
>
> (Hockey 1992: 27)

Thus, despite anthropological caution, we find a consistent focus on the 'healthier' emotional experience of peoples who adhere to more traditional ritual forms. Walter sheds light on the centrality of emotion as a cultural filter in our reading of the death-related behaviour of others in his work on the gradual privileging of affect within Christian funerals (1990). After the Reformation, when the funeral lost its ancient purpose of steering the soul towards God, subsequent Anglican ritual became attenuated for fear of accusations of popery:

> The Anglican funeral service was based on the old medieval rite's final committal to the earth, leaving out the mass in church entirely; this

> turning of the postscript into an entire service is why to this day there is no satisfactory rite for an Anglican funeral in church.
>
> (Walter 1990: 93)

Walter therefore describes a transition from the purposeful funerals of the re-Reformation period where the fate of the soul demanded the prayers of the living, to a secular ceremony which focused on feasting and conspicuous consumption, and finally to a ritual which addressed the therapeutic needs of bereaved people. As he notes, even the Roman Catholic Church has paid more attention to survivors' grief since Vatican II. However, while ousted from the Christian funeral, the concept of purgatory persists in the secular In Memoriam verses where, Davies argues, the living intercede with God on behalf of the dead (see Chapter 4 of this volume).

I would argue that changes in the Anglican funeral have played their part in privileging the emotional responses of the living, such that they now represent the framework through which the death ritual of groups seen to be living closer to 'nature' are viewed. Walter argues that by removing mourners' purposeful participation in the funeral, the contemporary goal of emotional release becomes yet more elusive. However, it is in those funerals of earlier times or more remote places that evidence of the successful achievement of contemporary therapeutic goals is believed to lie.

ANTHROPOLOGICAL 'FICTIONS'

While the ethnographic literature appears to resource emergent therapeutic debates, there remain questions about the view from the West represented by that literature itself. From its nineteenth century roots, anthropology has tended to view non-Western death ritual from a scientistic or positivist perspective, publishing for an audience eager for ethnographies of 'primitive' peoples. As already argued, a respect for 'science' was linked with a preoccupation with the 'natural'. Early anthropological studies therefore gave western society access to 'primitive' peoples whose lives were seen to unfold in close proximity to 'nature' (Tylor 1871; Frazer 1890). Not only were such accounts important features of the social Darwinism of the time; they also fed a paradoxical concern with 'natural', 'unspoilt' social groups, the peasant societies of Europe and the 'primitive' societies which lay beyond the West.

In 1912, Durkheim furnished western readers with an account of death ritual among the native Australian Warramunga. Their wailing and self mutilation, he argued, help maintain social cohesiveness. From a scientistic perspective, this behaviour exemplifies a universal law about social integration. Ritual participation allows society's members to share similar feelings, even those less immediately involved. Durkheim argues that 'Men do not weep for the dead because they fear them; they fear them because they weep for them' (Durkheim, cited in Huntington and Metcalf, 1979). In his view, 'primitive' societies construct rather than minister to the grief of their members, thereby promoting social solidarity.

Huntington and Metcalf (1979) discuss Radcliffe-Brown's interpretation of death ritual among the Andamese Islanders (1964), where the links between ceremonial weeping and the key values of Andamese society are carefully unravelled. Unlike Durkheim, Radcliffe-Brown therefore appears to eschew the positivist injunction to generate universal laws of human behaviour in that he makes the salient point that weeping has a symbolic as well as functional role. However, as Huntington and Metcalf also point out, Radcliffe-Brown then elaborates upon this point to argue, more globally and in accordance with the work of Durkheim, that ritual expressions of emotion promote social bonding and therefore the integration of society. In that these authors drew on scientistic models in generating universal laws, they attracted a readership interested in the more 'natural' lives of tribal peoples, yet committed to an authentically 'scientific' world view.

The fusion and confusion of the cultural icons of 'science' and 'nature' are also evident in more practical discourses surrounding the management of death during both the nineteenth and twentieth centuries.

'SCIENCE', 'NATURE' AND DISPOSAL

During the nineteenth century campaign to introduce cremation, the urologist, Sir Henry Thompson, used clinical and economic metaphors to overcome what he saw as the 'barbarism' and 'superstition' inherent in burial. Of his 'scientific' metaphors, Leaney notes:

> Not surprisingly, the suggestion that the mortal remains of one's nearest and dearest be used as commercial fertilizer was received with mixed horror and disbelief.
>
> (Leaney 1989: 121)

More potent, he argues, was the cremationist language which sentimentalised science:

> Sentimental images of 'mother earth', of 'pilgrimages', of 'reintegration with nature' were given currency as aspects of 'natural science'.
>
> (Leaney 1989: 123)

In the following example of cremationist literature, natural imagery is used to describe the Garden of Remembrance:

> ... the ashes of those who have passed over repose unfettered, kissed by the sun, among the birds, the flowers and the trees.
>
> (Leaney 1989: 122)

As argued throughout this chapter, the western concept of 'nature' can be seen as a cultural icon grounded in the Romantic Tradition of the late eighteenth century. It continues to inform twentieth century therapy-oriented literature, its hegemony manifested in a wide range of practices and social movements – from 'natural' childbirth through to Green politics and the appropriation of traditional healing practices such as shamanism. Nineteenth century cremationist imagery, which transformed disposal through an evocation of the world of 'nature', finds striking parallels in the public face of the 1990s Natural Death Movement. This Movement seeks to de-professionalise the management of death and reassert a more grass roots level of control. Accounts of the Movement's launch (*Observer*, 14.4.91; *Independent*, 15.4.91) describe the interest of its psychotherapist founder, Nick Albery, in the pre-Modern peoples of Tibet and North America:

> Albery has been much influenced by his study of the Tibetan way of death ... and he believes our society could learn much from it.
>
> (*Observer* 14.4.91)

At the Movement's launch, organic, non-Western food and drink was provided. Albery also linked the Natural Death Movement with its 1980s predecessor, the Natural Birth Movement; 'Death is as much a part of nature as birth' (*Independent* 15.4.91). Recently, the Natural Death Movement offered advice about composting the corpse which was similar to that proffered by nineteenth century cremationist Sir Henry Thompson. The *Observer* responded with the headline 'Died-in-the-wool ecologists now babble of green fields' (21.3.93). The press thus make derogatory associations between 'nature', the 'natural' politics of the Green Movement, and an irrational, unscientific airy-fairiness. Nonetheless it is the clinical nature of the composting process, involving autoclaves and slurry production which, the press believes, is most alienating to the aspiring adherent of 'natural death'. Thus the horrified response to Sir Henry Thompson's 'economic' approach to composting 'one's nearest and dearest' is also predicted as the twentieth century reaction to a rational 'scientific' approach to disposal.

The cultural icons of 'science' and 'nature' are therefore evident in the reformist movements of two different centuries. Albery's initiative links the ideas and experiences of peoples seen to live in harmony with the 'natural' world with 'natural' food and the 'natural' life processes of birth and death. A scientific approach to the world of 'nature', evinced in the vocabulary of 'specially constructed autoclaves' and 'biodegradable body bags', does, however, draw the scepticism of the press.

CONCLUSIONS

This chapter has argued that the view from the West, as expressed in both thought and practice, is one which subtly intertwines an enduring loyalty to the world of 'nature' with a responsiveness to 'scientifically' generated insights into universal human experiences. Both 'science' and 'nature' are represented in a contemporary prioritising of emotion, where medically trained psychiatrists explore human 'nature' through reference to the lives of those who are seen to live closer to the 'natural' environment. Developments in liturgical practice as well as a view of the funeral as therapy have contributed to the foregrounding of human emotionality at the time of death. As shown, both academic and therapy-oriented sources draw parallels between Modernity and cultural and social impoverishment, as well as demonstrating a commitment to uncovering universal truths about the nature of emotional experience through cross cultural analysis. While recent anthropological accounts have questioned the imperative to generate universal laws, highlighting instead the cultural and social specificity of death-related beliefs and practices, it is the law-like spirit of earlier works which often surfaces within bereavement literature.

One final example of the complex relationship between the western cultural icons of 'science' and 'nature' is the work of psychologists Rosenblatt, Walsh and Jackson (1976). Their survey of grief and mourning in seventy-eight cultures represents a particularly uncompromising expression of a scientistic tradition. The authors do not view grief and mourning as experiences to be defined only in terms specific to a particular society. Instead they operate from a quite explicit view from the West, offering their (western) definitions of (i) grief – 'sorrow, mental distress, emotional agitation, sadness, suffering', (ii) bereavement – 'the period of time following a death, during which grief occurs, and also the state of experiencing grief and (iii) mourning – 'the culturally defined acts that are usually performed when a death occurs' (Rosenblatt *et al.* 1976: 2). The authors argue that in their survey of seventy-eight cultures:

> ... an ethnocentric perspective has often been productive. Despite warnings ... that American mourning customs and grief behaviour may be peculiar to America, it seems that American practices and behaviours are a relatively safe base from which to generalise about the species.
>
> (Rosenblatt *et al.* 1976: 124)

Their perspective is challenged by the commitment to reflexivity recently developed within the discipline of anthropology:

> We have learned that we must be cautious in attributing particular emotional configurations to members of other cultures.
>
> (Huntington and Metcalf 1979: 23)

The nature of the view from the West therefore emerges as complex in that, as Clifford and Marcus (1986) argue, anthropological accounts need to be read as the 'fictions', in the sense of products, of two different societies – that of the anthropologist and that of their informants. This paper has raised questions about the 'fictions' through which a western knowledge of other peoples' deathways has been constructed. In that those 'fictions' are, in part, the product of a western society they can, if carefully read, reveal to us much that might be useful about ourselves through their accounts of those other more 'natural' peoples who live and die outside the West.

Notes

1. This material is from an unpublished interview transcript which formed part of the material for Hockey (1992).

2 The Social Facts of Death

Douglas Davies

Social Facts

All societies use their cultural values to transform bare biological facts of life including death and emotion into images and motifs representing ideals which sociologists sometimes call 'social facts' (Thomas 1976: 158). In this chapter, three different perspectives are taken towards contemporary British ideas of death and emotion, firstly through the eyes of the media which have given death a high profile, secondly through surveys of people's actual experience, and thirdly through an anthropological analysis of the process of cremation and of grief.

I: THE MEDIA WORLD OF IMAGES

In contemporary Britain the media influence life in new and subtle ways. Television images, viewed in private, help to form public opinion. The question 'Did you see?' emphasises a new kind of media stimulated discourse whose substance always changes and constitutes what is sometimes described as the post-modern world, that is, one lacking any over-arching interpretation of shared reality (Harvey 1989).

There is an interesting paradox here. For, while the media broadcast images which many can share, elite interpreters speak of the fragmentation of all shared values. This justifies Bauman's argument that the idea of post-modernity is more a rallying cry of media elites than a description of popular life (1992b: 94 and 155). With this in mind death may still be the great leveller allowing us neither to assume a total fragmentation of its social significance in a post-modernity of death nor to accept that all believe in a traditionally religious explanation (*pace* Baudrillard 1993: 164).

Death, AIDS, and the media

The loss experienced by some circles of creative artists and media producers, decimated by the ravages of AIDS, has penetrated society at large to give death a higher profile than at any other peace-time period in the twentieth century. If, as Gorer (1955) asserts, death took over from sex as a prime social taboo in the nineteen fifties, AIDS, that fertile combination of sex and death, destroyed it in the nineteen nineties producing what amounts to an AIDS–grief subculture bordering the artistic world. This period of change in the media presentation of the social fact of death is itself worth a brief sketch.

Broadcasting on prime-time radio the morning after the ballet dancer Rudolf Nureyev's death through AIDS, the *Today Programme* (Radio 4, 7 January 1992) sketched this sub-culture. Mark Lawson, a Booker Prize judge for 1992, likened AIDS in the 1990s to the cultural threat of nuclear war in the 1960s. American playwright Larry Cramer spoke emotionally of his life as 'surrounded by the dead and dying'.

The Times newspaper spoke of the 'vulnerability to AIDS of the arts community', mentioning that, 'Every December, members of the New York artistic community hold a "Day Without Art" to raise awareness of the number of artists and performers who are being lost to the disease' (7 January 1993).

In the musical world the influential composer Nigel Osborne reflected the concern in his opera *Hell's Angels*, while the American John Corrigliano (born 1938), produced his First Symphony – recorded by the Chicago Symphony Orchestra under Daniel Barenboim – as an elegy for a friend dead of AIDS. His explanatory notes tell how,

> Historically many symphonists, Berlioz, Mahler, and Shostakovitch to mention a few, have been inspired by important events affecting their lives, and perhaps occasionally their choice of symphonic form was dictated by extra-musical events. During the past decade I have lost many friends and colleagues to the AIDS epidemic, and the cumulative effect of those losses has, naturally, deeply affected me. My First Symphony was generated by feelings of loss, anger, and frustration.

Corrigliano explains how moved he was on first seeing 'The Quilt', an ambitious interweaving of several thousand fabric panels memorializing AIDS victims with each designed by a loved one. He adds that this Quilt, itself the theme of one British television programme, 'made me want to memorialize in music those I have lost and reflect on those I am losing. I decided to relate the first three movements of the Symphony to three life-long musician-friends.'

Cremation on film and television

The visual media too have power to forge vague feelings into specific form, to give prophetic expression to the unvoiced emotions. The James Bond film, *Diamonds Are For Ever*, furnishes a popular cameo in a sequence showing the unconscious Bond placed in a coffin set on a crematorium conveyor belt. Gas jets cover the coffin in flame and Bond regains consciousness to realize his inevitable fate when, the very next moment, the coffin – still smoking and slightly scorched – is withdrawn from the furnace by his captors as the tale takes another turn and Bond is free. This episode expresses a cluster of emotional fears of cremation focused on claustrophobia and being burned alive and has been alluded to by student-aged respondents in the research mentioned below.

An interestingly similar, though ethically more shocking, episode was portrayed in the film *Black and Blue*, by G.F. Newman, shown on BBC television on 27 September 1992. In it, not only is a black local politician cremated illicitly by corrupt police officers, but an undercover black policeman is knocked unconscious, placed on a conveyor belt without a coffin, and sent into the flames. He is saved at the last moment by the crematorium attendant who had also been struck unconscious. The play is fiction. But, in a discussion programme televised the same week, its distinguished playwright hinted at having been told of actual atrocities resembling his play.

These dramas play on the fear of being burned alive, possessed, as our research has elicited, by a significant minority. Both films use the conveyor-belt motif while the second film echoes the popular misconception that bodies are taken out of coffins prior to cremation.

Another film shown on Channel Four on 10 March 1992 as part of Adult Literacy Week, portrayed a different aspect of cremation, one very much closer to people's actual experience rather than to their fearful fantasies. *Homer and His Pigeons*, by Karl Francis, is set in South Wales where Homer, a retired miner, inspires some of his very ordinary friends – one an undertaker – to grasp their human potential. When Homer dies his spirit or ghost appears and discusses their worries about his funeral. After cremation the play ends with Homer's friends scattering his ashes on a mountain where he finds his final freedom.

This is probably the first time that a realistic example of scattering someone's ashes in the open air has been shown on British television. It mirrors those private scatterings which thousands of people are increasingly undertaking on their own initiative as described below. In showing friends disperse the remains, *Homer and His Pigeons* reflects the ordinariness of life rather than the fears of fiction.

By contrast, an entirely humorous face was put on cremation in the comedy *Sitting Pretty* by John Sullivan (BBC1 26 November 1992) when a widow disdainfully poured her husband's remains over his mistress. This comic treatment of human remains expresses the opposite dimension to their profoundly serious nature as a symbol of the once living person. There is a degree of ambivalence towards dead bodies in Britain which is often expressed through coffins as figures of fun. Cremated remains can resemble coffins, in this respect, being almost one step removed from the dead person. Both coffins and ashes represent 'containers' of the person rather than the person as such.

A final example of death's high media profile in Britain came in the one hour prime-time *L.A. Requiem*, focusing on Los Angeles' Forest Lawns Cemetery. This was shown between nine and ten p.m. on Easter Monday 1992. A topic selected by a commercial television station and programmed for viewing on a major public holiday can hardly be regarded as publicly taboo.

II: EMPIRICAL PERSPECTIVES

Leaving these media images, we next consider some empirical research from the Cremation Research Project established at Nottingham University in 1988 (Davies 1991) and the Rural Church Project conducted collaboratively with the Royal Agricultural College at Cirencester (Davies *et al.* 1990).

We begin by comparing people's image of levels of cremation in the UK and the USA with what we know to be the factual case. In a sample of University students studying anthropology about 46 per cent of them estimated UK cremation as being somewhere near its actual rate of 69 per cent, by contrast only 36 per cent of a general public sample came near the correct rate. Even so the majority of both groups did not actually appreciate the high British rate as compared to the United States. Similarly both groups, especially the students, vastly overestimated the USA level of cremation which was actually below 20 per cent at the time. This divergence between popular image and actual practice, suggests that images of funerals were largely fixed on burial in Britain and cremation in the USA. This indicates a culture lag, showing that it takes time for actual social practice to be reflected in public images and hinting at a view of the USA as more modern in technology and therefore more likely to cremate.

Belief in after-life

Turning to the realm of personal belief we focus now on the theme of life after death. Table 2.1 represents a Nottinghamshire sample from the Cremation Research Project (CRP) and samples from Durham, Lincoln, Nottingham, Gloucester and Cornwall from the Rural Church Project (RCP), (Davies *et al.* 1990 and 1991). Representing urban and rural groups they show great similarity with between 42–47 per cent believing in life after death, 28–32 per cent not believing, and 25–26 per cent not knowing. In general the rural population was slightly less inclined to belief in an after-life, but seldom was this difference statistically significant.

As might be expected, what was significant was that active church attenders believed in an after-life more than did the population at large and more than nominal members, especially Anglicans. In the Rural Church Project's interviews with 489 randomly selected attending and non-attending individuals, 'belief' to 'no belief' stood at 69 to 42 per cent. What is particularly interesting is that in these and other surveys we have conducted there is a constant 25 per cent response of those saying they don't know what to believe about an after-life.

Gender

This level of uncertainty is, interestingly, retained when gender is taken as the key variable although men and women are, otherwise, different in their degree of active belief and disbelief as Table 2.2 shows (Davies *et al.* 1990: 223).

Table 2.1 Belief in life after death

	CRP	*Rural Church Project*	
	Gen Pop	*Gen Pop*	*C of E*
Yes	47%	42%	69%
No	28%	32%	10%
Don't Know	25%	26%	21%
Total	100%	100%	100%
Number	459	341	148

Table 2.2 Gender differences in belief in life after death

Belief	*Men*		*Women*	
	Number	%	*Number*	%
Yes	79	38	166	60
No	77	37	46	17
Don't Know	51	25	65	23
Totals	207	100	277	100

This sharp difference between men and women in this sample from the Rural Church Project shows some 60 per cent of women drawn randomly from the community expressing a belief in life after death compared with 38 per cent of men. Only 17 per cent of the women interviewed said they did not believe in life after death compared with 37 per cent of the men. Reasons for this difference are not easily established and reflect the complex debate over sex differences and degrees of piety which cannot be explored here (cf. Batson and Ventis 1982: 36 ff. Lewis, 1986: 27; Christian 1972: 153; Francis 1992: 31).

Another gender difference is that women, usually twice as often as men, expressed dislike and anxiety towards burial. In one group of 146 Nottingham University medical students of practically equal gender mix the difference was highly statistically significant with 42 women and 20 men disliking burial, and 51 men and 34 women not worried about it. Not enough is known about gender and belief to explain this result but, speculatively, it may be related to a cultural sense that female identity is connected with an image of the body more than is the case with men. In which case for a woman to imagine her body rotting is to think of her self-identity as being slowly destroyed. Cremation, by contrast, destroys the body so fast that no slow disintegration has to be imagined. Whatever is the case it may be that this relative dislike of burial by women can go part of the way to explain why cremation came to be so popular in Britain since women tend to outlive men and have to decide which type of funeral to have.

Types of belief

As to the content of belief in life after death we have found that practically all who do believe in an after-life talk of the soul passing on. A resurrection of the body is restricted to approximately a fifth, with a variation in the Rural Church Survey between 19 per cent for the public at large and

24 per cent for those on the church register. Those who accept a future resurrection also think the soul goes on in what amounts to a dual belief (Davies *et al.* 1991: 256).

Beliefs in clusters not systems

One problem associated with surveying beliefs is the western intellectual tendency to classify things into neat categories, a habit reinforced by statistical tables. At least one sociologist argues that statistics have no place in post-modern sociology, concerned, as it might be, with the unpredictability of existence (Bauman 1992b: 192).

Avoiding that theoretical debate, important as it is in connection with death, our task here is to stress that life is not experienced systematically but in 'bits and pieces', a fact which is important for religion in general as for death in particular. Here knowledge is as much experiential as it is learned formally or through the media.

One psychological approach to human learning which does justice to this acquisition of beliefs is called by the rather unflattering term of 'connectionism' (Bloch 1992a: 130). This name alludes to the way each individual's ideas and experiences are interconnected in bundles varying from those of others. In practical terms if we try to explain to someone how we arrived at some decision we probably rationalise things after the event to produce an ordered sequence of ideas instead of repeating the more haphazard jumping between ideas and emotions which really brought us to our final decision.

Similarly, many symbols are understood and linked together by analogy and affinity as argued, for example, by Dan Sperber (1975), and reflected by myself in the case of religious education (Davies 1985). The psychologist Usha Goswami (1992) has demonstrated – against the influential psychologist Jean Piaget – that from an early age children learn to think by means of analogy.

All of which is directly important to death, to after-life beliefs and to age. Except for a few teenagers who experience a close bereavement, most find death unimaginable. The self is perceived as dynamically alive and open to the future. P.D. James sketches this attitude as her Inspector Dalgliesh reflects on the fact that, 'In youth we take egregious risks because death has no reality for us … It is only in middle age that we are shadowed by an awareness of the transitoriness of life.' (1988: 152).

Indeed death is relatively seldom on the school curriculum. In two surveys of student groups at The University of Nottingham in 1989 and 1991, 80 per cent of students drawn from social science and arts departments but studying social anthropology said they did not recall discussing death in school, while 68 per cent of medical students reported the same absence of discussion. Together these students cover an extremely wide band of school subjects but in all cases the majority had no recall of death as part of their formal education.

Awareness of the dead

Still, despite what may be lacking in formal education, life-experience brings its own form of knowledge as for that significant minority who report an awareness of the dead. While some 55 per cent of 62 Nottinghamshire individuals interviewed in one survey, said they had never experienced a sense of encounter with the dead, 27 per cent had possessed some general sense of presence, a further 11 per cent reckoned to have seen the dead person, and 6 per cent said they had heard a voice. These 'visitations' are, as far as bereaved individuals are concerned, quite different from dreams and take place during the waking state and not during sleep. Theoretically speaking such awareness can be interpreted through ideas of attachment and detachment from others.

Detachment from the dead

The social life which binds people together in ways that make them part of each other's identity also causes pain when bereavement brings physical separation. A major study in Holland explored detachment in bereaved people and found that more than a year after their loss a third of family members still found moderate or severe difficulty in detaching from the deceased (Cleiren 1991). The University of Leiden's Detachment Scale was developed to measure this degree of linkage between the dead and survivors and showed that at four months more than 50 per cent felt the deceased still present with them in some way. At fourteen months 30 per cent still talked to the dead either silently or aloud, while 35 per cent still felt the dead person could hear or see them. Slightly analogously, the Rural Church Project showed that both men (36 per cent) and women (38 per cent) attenders at Anglican Holy Communion services reckoned to have gained a sense of the presence of their dead (Davies 1993: 26).

The Dutch views were unrelated to religious convictions, but were age-related in that it was the younger age groups that felt most continuing attachment. Interestingly, while those who lost relatives by sudden traffic accident initially found detachment most difficult this experience then decreased so that fourteen months after bereavement there was no difference in detachment between sudden accidental death, death by suicide, and death after long illness. These findings may contradict some popular images of grief and show the importance of research in relation to some popular 'social facts'.

III: RITUAL AND CULTURAL CHANGE

Some similar disjunctions exist with images of death associated with the rituals of burial and cremation. While this is not the place for a technical discussion of ritual, whether interpreted as a de-codable language or as a behavioural end in itself inaccessible to a code cracking interpretation, it is worth considering some ritual idioms to see how far they reflect actual practice or some abstract idea.

The 'conveyor belt' image of cremation offers a good example of an apparently popular motif describing negative features of cremation as a speedy, impersonal and mechanical process. As far as haste was concerned we found that only about nine per cent of the Nottinghamshire sample of the general public felt that cremation services were too short. In a 1992 survey conducted by the Cremation Research Project for York City Council some 1464 members of their general public were randomly approached; 36 per cent of these, 533 individuals, answered a full questionnaire. Similarly, of these, only 13 individuals thought the cremation services they had experienced had been too rapid. Only 8 individuals (1.5 per cent) talked in terms of the 'conveyor belt' phenoménon.

This suggests that the conveyor-belt motif is less a description of speed and more a metaphorical description of the service itself. This can be explained through the idea 'flow' which Victor Turner described as 'the merging of action and awareness' in ritual contexts, (1978: 103, for the origin of the term). Different societies have their own kinds of flow experience associated with a sense of proper duration and patterns which actions should take. It would seem that the image of the conveyor belt reflects some problem grounded in the ritual even if it is not strictly a problem of time. A historical note may help reveal the problem.

Crematorium design and 'flow'

The nineteen fifties and sixties witnessed a dramatic increase both in the British cremation rate and in the number of corresponding new crematoria. One major planning criterion demanding efficient use of buildings resulted in the 'golden rule' of one door for entry and another for exiting the crematorium chapel. One congregation could leave by a side door while the next funeral party waited to enter by the main door. It was this queue which, I believe, engendered the idea of a conveyor-belt process manipulating people at an emotionally charged moment of their life.

This unfortunate sense of flow was aggravated by the fact that for centuries British churches had only used one major door for entry into and exit from ritual occasions. This tidal flow was linked to the up and down scheme of ritual significance typified in marriage with its movement 'up the aisle' and 'down the aisle'. Modern cremation changed this ritual dimension by fostering a 'going through' from an entrance to an exit. This, in my opinion, initially fostered the sense of being conveyed in an unacceptable way albeit at an implicit level of understanding. People were being told to do something that ran counter to the traditional social flow of ceremonial events.

It could be argued that change should, periodically, be introduced to alter perspectives and shift ethos and mood. Social planners and architects, like theologians and liturgiologists, often see themselves as having the duty to engage in creative reorganization and transform 'ritual-architectural events' (Jones 1993: 207).

With this in mind we could argue that the utilitarian use of one door in and another door out is a perfect symbolic expression of death as a rite of passage from life to eternity. For the mourners who follow the coffin in and who leave by themselves through another door there is a clear statement of the change that has come about in their relationships. This may be true, and over time there may even emerge a cultural sense of flow in association with this practice. Perhaps the low level of complaints about cremation services we have seen in recent surveys marks this change.

As a factual gloss on the conveyor-belt motif we can say that of all British Crematoria surveyed in 1990 (involving a respectable 67 per cent response rate) we found that enclosing the coffin with a curtain was the most usual way of separating mourners from coffin at the end of the service. This was used by 63 per cent of these crematoria. The option of lowering the coffin (18 per cent) was surprisingly popular given the problem of mechanisms which could occasionally malfunction. The dramatically simple procedure of leaving the coffin alone was nearly as popular at 14 per cent, while, to come to the point of this example, the use of actual conveyor mechanisms moving the coffin horizontally, was quite rare at 5 per cent. This shows that the popular conveyor-belt image has little basis in fact as far as contemporary crematoria are concerned.

Cremation as a process

This conveyor belt example shows the need for theoretical analysis of the processes underlying social idioms. Here we use and seek to develop the seminal anthropological contribution of Robert Hertz's early paper (1907, translated 1960) which has already influenced several studies of death and human identity (Cederoth 1988; Huntington and Metcalf 1979).

Hertz argued that for some tribal societies, funerary rites, especially where there was a double ritual, dealt firstly, (through burial or cremation) with the corruptible flesh or the 'wet' symbolic medium of the body, before, secondly, dealing with the bones or the 'dry' symbolic medium of the body.

The first rite dried the skeleton whether slowly through decay or rapidly through fire. Symbolically speaking this phase removed individuals from their given status while the next phase allocated a new identity in a new realm, and may signify this by redeploying the remains.

> This is precisely the meaning of cremation: far from destroying the body of the deceased, it recreates it and makes it capable of entering into new life.
>
> (Hertz 1960: 43)

For Hertz cremation was never a single rite but implied a second which relocated the identity of the dead. I have applied this to traditional Christian views on burial, showing how burial expressed the first stage of the rite; the hope that God would resurrect the dead expressing the second stage. This involves a future directed or eschatological sense of fulfilment of the deceased (Davies *et al.* 1990). In a secularized and individualized context the church may perform the first part of the cremation rites but the relatives are left relatively free, for the first time in modern Christian history, to obtain the remains to use as they will. The private rites may, either exclusively or in combination with a future directed rite, involve a retrospective fulfilment of the identity of the lost partner by being placed somewhere of private significance.

Nobody yet knows how that division of ritual labour might influence bereavement and the part played by the memory of the dead within the continuing identity of the living. The fact that increasing numbers engage in private rites of scattering or burying ashes suggests that such rites are appreciated as a completion of the cremation ritual. They may also reflect the popular view that 'people must have somewhere to mourn'.

Grief, place and health

This notion of a place for mourning is indirectly linked to the therapeutic view of mourning enshrined in the notion of 'recovery'. To speak of recovery is to use illness as the model of bereavement and shows how firmly what might be called the medical model of grief has become established in Britain. Such medical models antagonise issues of existence, indeed the very use of the word 'recover' hides the human significance of bereavement with all its pain, loss and personal transformation.

It is obvious, for example, that some mothers simply do not 'recover' after the death of a child. To speak as though a mother has been ill with some inconvenient malady but is now undergoing recuperation and will, sooner or later, be normal again is to ignore existential and religious experiences at the heart of life and faith. Some events are so influential that people are never the same again. Just how human experiences are interpreted is, itself, an issue that should be open to analysis to prevent partial explanations becoming excessively dominant within society.

Grief and emotion

Following the medical model of grief, some English middle class groups commonly assume that people should express their emotion of bereavement as a way of 'working through' their loss. Emotional display is taken as a sign of coping with death but, as Cleiren's important Dutch research showed, 'the opposite seems to be true' (1991: 257). In his studies, many people showing extensive emotional response at four months after a death were likely to have a similar high level of a negative reaction many months later. In fact for some people the avoidance of such emotional release may be considered healthy and a sound way of coping with death. While this is a delicate area because it contradicts some widely held assumptions, it shows the benefits of large scale research.

Cleiren singled out death after long illness, by suicide and by sudden motor accident, as three potentially significant variables. He found, as mentioned earlier, that there was very little difference in adaptation to bereavement after fourteen months, irrespective of the type of death. He also showed the importance of kinship in relation to the dead, finding, for example, that sisters suffer quite considerably but have been a largely ignored group.

Drawing attention to research on grief, including Kubler-Ross's five stage theory embracing denial of death, protest, negotiation, depression and finally acceptance of death, Cleiren also found that 'in virtually none of the empirical research has there been found evidence for the existence of distinct stages'. He concluded that, 'the concept of distinct stages in adaptation after bereavement seems untenable' (1991: 23; cf. Corr 1993).

This is obviously important for death studies whether in a literary interpretation of grief (Garland 1989: 151), counselling the bereaved, or training in pastoral care. Patterns of grief can be uncritically accepted and then imposed upon others, especially where many young adults lack experience of bereavement and easily accept schemes presented by professionals. Stage theories of grief can bias data collection and analysis in death studies and can also impose a false shape upon bereavement. To a certain extent this is also true of what is sometimes called the Jamesian Theory of emotion, so implicitly accepted in Britain (Solomon 1984: 238). This theory views people as containers full of unhealthy emotion who need to release their pent-up feeling through therapeutic crying. While there may be some truth in this, it too, could benefit from a more sociological perspective giving due weight to the influence of social contexts on feelings and beliefs (Lewis 1986).

SUMMARY

In relating some popular and media representations of funerary rites to actual social practice, this chapter has shown sets of divergences between public beliefs and more empirical facts of funerals.

Acknowledging the complex and non-systematic nature of beliefs associated with death, funerals, and the after-life, we have drawn attention not only to the importance of sex differences but also to the cultural lag between people's assessment of cremation rates and the actual level of cremation in the United Kingdom and the United States of America.

In particular, we have argued that popular theories of grief and emotion need to be subjected to analysis lest folk-models be confused with rational and professional theories used in therapeutic contexts. In complex societies caught up in social change, where images are constantly in process of flux, critical analysis has a particularly significant contribution to make in interpreting popular folk-idioms, always remembering that, when it comes to the topic of death, both folk and theoretical discussions inevitably involve the profoundest reflexivity.

3 Change and Continuity in the Funeral Rituals of Sikhs in Britain[1]

Sewa Singh Kalsi

This chapter examines the processes of change and continuity in funeral rituals of the Sikhs in Britain. It is my thesis that the Sikh funeral rites are one of the fundamental instruments of transmission of traditional cultural values. The central aim of this chapter is to demonstrate how the roles of participants in funeral rituals are closely linked to the power relationships in the Sikh social structure, that is, rules of inheritance of property, status and the differential position of men and women. Analysis of the process of funeral rites also provides new insight into the working of caste, religion, kinship networks and the social orientation of Sikh religious beliefs, *vis-à-vis* the transmigration of soul, *mukti* (salvation/liberation) and *awagaun* (cycle of birth and death). In the following pages I shall consider the social and religious significance of funeral rites; the position of women and specifically of widows, in relation to rites of passage; the impact of the Sikh reform movement on mortuary rituals, and the consequences of Sikh migration on traditional funeral rituals.

Death is perceived as an ultimate truth by the Sikhs. At the mourning sittings a number of phrases are applied by the participants to describe the death of a person: *pura ho giya* (completed his/her span of life), *surgwas ho giya* (has taken abode in heaven), *sansar yatra puri kar giya* (has completed pilgrimage of this world) and *rab da bhana* (Will of God). In order to console the members of the grieving family, incidents of death in other families are talked about, emphasising the mortality of human life. A close examination of these conversations clearly demonstrates the way ordinary Sikhs make sense of human existence and its ultimate destiny. They express their world-view concerning the complex issues of life and death in the most simple terms.

In Punjabi villages a cremation ground is called *sivey* and the burning pyre *siva jalda*. The terms *sivey* and *siva jalda* have close association with the Hindu god Siva who is regarded as the god of *bhut/pret* (ghosts). He is also seen as a symbol of the regeneration of life. The cremation ground is believed to be the abode of Lord Siva. According to Basham, 'Lord Siva lurks in horrible places such as battle fields, burning grounds and cross-roads, which in India, as in Europe, were looked upon as very inauspicious. He wears a garland of skulls and is surrounded by ghosts, evil spirits and demons. He is death and *Mahakala*, which destroys all things' (Basham 1967: 310). The dead are believed to have become ghosts belonging to the profane world. But after the performance of the ritual of *agni bhaint*, the male dead person acquires the status of *jathera* (husband's male ancestor – the term applies to one, who being deceased, is an object of worship) (Hershman 1981: 87). At every auspicious occasion like a wedding or birth of a boy, special ceremonies are conducted to worship the family *jathera*. It is through the performance of these ceremonies that a newly married bride is incorporated into the lineage of her husband.

The term funeral is too narrow for comprehending the meanings of pre- and post-funeral rites. There are series of ceremonies which are an integral part of the funeral ritual called *antam sanskar* (literally the last rite). These ceremonies are: *dharti tey pauna* (lifting of the body from the bed on to the ground), *antam ishnan* (last bath), *modha dena* (participating in carrying the bier), *dhamalak bhanana* (breaking of the earthen pot), *agni bhaint* (ritual offering of one's body to the god of fire), *phul chugna* (collecting ashes), *pagri* (ritual transfer of paternal authority) and *akath* (ritual feast). The ritual of lighting the pyre is called *agni bhaint* (*Agni* is a Hindu god of fire and *bhaint* means ritual offering); it symbolises the making of an offering of one's body to the god of fire. Thus, death is not conceived as the abrupt end of life, but as a gradual transition from earthly existence to life in heaven.

SOCIOLOGICAL SIGNIFICANCE OF MORTUARY RITES

The beliefs and ideals of different civilisations are often formulated in their rituals more explicitly than in any other cultural trait (Bhattacharyya 1975: vii), and the performance of rituals is a clear statement of the deeply held values of a society (Uberoi 1975: 502). In India, Sikhs and Hindus observed the same set of life-cycle rites. Indeed, there was much sharing of cultural traditions between Hindus and Sikhs in the Punjab. They observed the same rules of social organisation, caste and rites of passage. Commenting on the social and ritual practices of Sikhs in nineteenth century Punjab, Macauliffe writes that, 'Notwithstanding the Sikh guru's powerful denunciation of Brahmins, secular Sikhs now rarely do anything without their assistance, Brahmins help them to die, and help their souls after death to obtain a state of bliss' (Macauliffe 1909: vii). In his study of a Sikh village, Tom Kessinger notes that for more than three hundred years, *Jat* Sikhs have regularly visited Hardwar to deposit the ashes of members of their families in the river Ganges (Kessinger 1974). No wonder that in the 1855 Census of Punjab, the Sikhs and Hindus were lumped together in many districts of the province (Marenco 1976).

Let us now consider in some detail the social significance of the series of rituals which together constitute the *antam sanskar* or last rite.

Dharti tey pauna (lowering the body to the ground)

At the time of death the first step is the performance of the ritual of *dharti tey pauna.* In the case of a death in the evening the body is kept in the house – a lamp is lighted near the deceased and the doors are kept open so that the soul is not trapped inside the house. A number of family members, including some members of one's *biradari* (caste) stay in the room.

This ritual consists of two components: religious and social. The religious part is linked with the belief in *dharti mata* (mother-earth). The significance of this belief is beautifully depicted in the Punjabi proverb: *maan chon aiye tey maan wich jana* (born of mother and going back to mother). Reflecting on the significance of mother-earth, Guru Nanak writes, '*pavan guru pani pita, mata dharat mahat*' (Air is the *guru*; Water the father and Earth the great mother) (*Guru Granth Sahib*: 8). Discussing the concept of earth goddess in Harappa culture, and the figurines of the Mother Goddess found at the site of Mohenjodaro, Bhattacharyya notes,

> Stuart Pigot rightly observes that they are a grim embodiment of the Mother Goddess who is also the guardian of the dead – an underworld deity connected alike with the corpse and seed-corn buried beneath the earth.
>
> (Bhattacharyya 1975: 111)

The social aspect of the ritual of dying on the ground is linked with the concept of care of the deceased. Death on a bed is talked about as a symbol of neglect of the deceased person. It is expressed in a satirical form in a Punjabi phrase '*manjey tey mar giya*' (died on a bed). The *biradari* members would say, 'Look, there was nobody with him/her at the last moment; the poor man/woman died on the bed'. Dying on the bed is not only a social stigma but it is also regarded as a most inauspicious occurrence both for the deceased and the family. Where this occurs, the ritual of *gati* is prescribed for the release of the deceased's soul. This ritual would be performed at the town of Peoha. Usually the bed is either burnt or given to the family *chuhri* (sweeper's wife) who receives ritually polluted articles. One Sikh informant said,

> When my wife died in India I could not arrive at the funeral on time. Reaching home I learnt that she died on the bed as there was nobody with her at that time. I was told by the members of my *biradari* and other relatives that her ashes should be deposited at Hardwar and after that I must go to Peoha for her final *gati* (release of soul).

Antam ishnan (last bath)

In Punjab, preparing the body for cremation is done by the family and members of one's *biradari*; it is given a ritual bath before it is dressed in new clothes and prepared to be placed on the bier. The *antam ishnan* is symbolic of ritual purification of the body before it is presented as an offering to the god of fire. There is a structural relationship between *antam ishnan*, *agni bhaint* (offering made to the god of fire) and the offering made to God at a *gurdwara* (Sikh place of worship) or a Hindu temple. Although the dead body is regarded as highly polluted, the ritual of the last bath is perceived as transforming the deceased from being polluted to being ritually pure.

The death of an old person is usually regarded as a symbol of good fortune for the family and the deceased. His funeral becomes like a festive occasion; the family hires a brass band to lead the funeral procession and there is no crying or wailing by the women. After the body has been ritually prepared and placed on the bier, all members of the family pay last respects by touching the feet and sometimes leaving money on the bier. The deceased is treated like a minor deity. At the death of a *Natta* (great great grandfather) a ritual of *soney di pauri* (golden ladder) is performed. A tiny ladder made of golden wire with five steps is placed on the body which is covered by an expensive shroud. This ritual signifies the belief in the climbing of the soul into heaven. Before lighting the pyre, the golden ladder and the expensive covering are removed; they are received by the family barber as a ritual gift. During the journey to the cremation ground the great grandchildren of the deceased throw coins and rice over the bier. The coins are collected by the village poor. In the case of deaths of newly born boys in a family, a coin collected at the funeral is placed around the neck of another newly born boy. These coins are believed to be endowed with good fortune and are symbols of long life as well as protection against evil spirits.

Modha dena (participating in carrying the bier)

Modha dena literally means offering one's shoulder as a symbol of respect for the deceased and sympathy for the family. Only the male agnates of the deceased are eligible to take part in this ritual, female family members are forbidden to participate. Usually the bier is carried by sons or brothers of the deceased and led by the chief mourner, the eldest son. The mystery of this gender divide is shrouded by the traditional rules of inheritance. As a matter of fact the rite of *modha dena* is closely linked to the rules of inheritance of the ancestral property. According to *Mitakshra* (Hindu law of inheritance) only male descendants of the deceased are eligible to inherit ancestral property while women are barred from inheriting property from their husbands or fathers. This in part explains the wish of Sikh and Hindu parents to have a son who will carry their bier, perform mortuary rites, and thus continue the name of their lineage.

Dhamalak bhanana (breaking of the earthen pot)[2]

When the funeral procession arrives near the cremation ground the bier is lowered to the ground. Starting from the head, the chief mourner makes an unbroken circle around the bier with water poured from an earthen pot. As soon as he completes the circle, he throws the pot onto the ground with such force that it breaks into several pieces; this is regarded as a symbol of the release of the soul. It is the sacred duty of the eldest son to perform the ritual of *dhamalak bhanana*; in his absence a younger brother or a paternal uncle may perform this ritual.

Women are again excluded from taking part in the ritual of *dhamalak bhanana* because they are not eligible to inherit ancestral property. In the case of a person dying without sons, the ritual of breaking the earthen pot is performed by one of his male agnates. Although Sikh women accompany the funeral procession, they are forbidden to go beyond this spot and to enter the cremation ground. Indeed, the ritual of breaking the earthen pot is a mark of the different status of men and women in Sikh society.

Agni bhaint and *phul chugna* (lighting the pyre and collecting the ashes)

After *dhamalak bhanana* the bier is carried to the cremation ground where the son performs the ceremony of lighting the pyre. In India, the ashes are collected three days after the funeral by male members of the household and *biradari*. They are then taken to Hardwar to be deposited in the river Ganges with the assistance of the family Brahmin who receives a ritual gift of a set of clothes, utensils and some cash. One eighty-five year old Sikh informant said,

> The ashes were neatly wrapped up in a white cloth and the bundle was left in the cremation ground tied to a tree. The ashes were never brought back to the house because it was like bringing the dead body home. On the journey to Hardwar, ashes were collected from the cremation ground by the son who would shout, 'now *bapu* (father) come with us – we are taking you to Hardwar.' He will keep shouting these words until he is out of the boundary of his village.

Customs of *pagri* and *akath* (ritual transfer of paternal authority and ritual feast)

The ritual of *pagri* (literally 'a turban') is an ancient Indian custom performed thirteen days after the funeral. It is an integral part of the ritual feast called *akath* (gathering of relatives and members of one's *biradari*). It is through the performance of the rite of *pagri* that, as chief mourner, the eldest son succeeds to his father's status as the head of household. At this gathering he receives a turban from his maternal uncle; he wears this new turban and discards the old one. If he is a married man, the turban is supplied by his wife's parents. This is symbolic of the recognition of his new status, not only by the members of his *biradari*, but also by his in-laws. Thereafter, senior members of his *biradari* remind him of his new status and responsibilities. Having been ritually accepted as the head of his household he joins the elders of the *biradari* for a communal meal.

The social function of the rite of *pagri* is to facilitate the gradual incorporation of the son into the role of his father. It is argued that the role of the chief mourner in the funeral rites is implicitly linked to his eligibility to inherit his father's status as well as the ancestral property. Killingley rightly remarks that,

> In Hindu society, and indeed in South Asian society as a whole, one of the factors differentiating ritual procedures is the status inherited by the principal or principals from their parents.
>
> (Killingley 1991: 2)

POSITION OF SIKH WOMEN AND WIDOWS

In Punjabi society the birth of a girl remains a quiet affair, whilst the arrival of a son is celebrated with great pomp and show. Moreover, the festival of *lohri*[3] is exclusively celebrated on the birth of a male child. Olivia Stokes's informant Rukmani, a village midwife, reported that, 'Her fee for the boy baby is four annas, two and a half kilos of grain, one old *sari* and one blouse. Female babies cost half the price.' (Stokes 1975: 222) According to the rules of Hindu law of inheritance, Sikh women, like their Hindu counterparts, had no right to inherit property from their fathers and husbands until the passing of the Hindu Succession Act in 1956. Moreover, it is the daughter who is given as *kanyadan* (ritual gift of a virgin) at her wedding by her father to receive religious merit. The principle of patrilocality confirms her transient status in her natal home. After the wedding she joins her husband's household where her major role as a wife is to produce son(s) who will be her husband's heir(s) to continue his lineage.

The status of widowhood condemns a Sikh woman to the state of perpetual *sutak* (ritual pollution). In Punjabi, a widow is called *vidhwa* or *randi* (*randi* literally means a prostitute and is used as a term of abuse). Hershman reports,

> A woman without a husband is not a proper person and indeed Punjabis often say that it is fortunate if a woman dies before her husband because then she is not left a widow. Widows are considered inauspicious people and, for example, to meet one in the early morning or at the beginning of a journey portends ill fortune.
>
> (Hershman 1981: 189)

Her participation in wedding rituals is also regarded as inauspicious. After the death of her husband she remains excluded from family chores for thirteen days. She discards her colourful clothes and jewellery and wears a white scarf which signifies her state of mourning. The ritual of *bura pauna*[4] is performed on the thirteenth day after the death of her husband. She is given a ritual bath; her old clothes are discarded and she wears a new set of clothes provided by her natal family. Interestingly, there are no such prescriptions for men after the death of a wife.

Sikhs practise widow remarriage called *kreva/chadar pauna*. Traditionally, the groom marries the widow of his brother by placing a sheet of cloth over her head in the presence of relatives and members of the *biradari* (Hershman 1981: 181). A widow is not entitled to the religious wedding ceremony as she cannot be given as *kanyadan* (ritual gift of a virgin), but there are no such restrictions on a Sikh widower. A Sikh woman dreads the state of losing her husband either through divorce or death. A divorced woman is called *chhadi hoi* (literally discarded); she is regarded as a stigma on her natal family's honour. Discussing the significance of the concepts of *suhagan* and *duhagan* in the Sikh scripture, Nikky-Guninder Kaur Singh notes,

> While *duhagan* is the unlucky woman who has been deserted by her husband or has lost him, *suhagan* is the fortunate one who enjoys union and the love of her husband.
>
> (Singh 1993: 79)

In view of the stigma placed on the *duhagan* it is the ritual wish of a Sikh or Hindu woman to die as a *suhagan* (married woman). At her death a married woman is dressed as a bride; it is the symbol of the fulfilment of her wish to die before her husband. Examination of the contents of an advertisement by the *Guru Nanak Nishkam Sevak Jatha* (a prominent Sikh religious organisation in Britain) is useful for understanding the status of Sikh widows. It reads: 'Mrs Charan Kaur, wife of *Sant* (holyman) Puran Singh, died on 22nd January, 1978 after completing her pilgrimage of this world. It was her sincere wish to die in the arms of her husband; by God's grace her wish was fulfilled' (Punjabi *Weekly Desh-Pardesh*, Southall, 22nd January 1993). She, like other Sikh and Hindu women, dreaded the state of widowhood. Her last wish was to die as a *suhagan* (married woman).

Interestingly, a Sikh widow is not forbidden from taking part in religious activities at a *gurdwara* (Sikh place of worship). For example, she participates in the preparation of *langar* (communal meal); distribution of *karah parshad* (ritual food); and reading of the *Guru Granth Sahib* (Sikh scripture). In Britain, many Sikh widows take part in the *kirtan* (religious singing) and reading Sikh scripture; they also hold women's *satsang* (religious singing sessions) at the *gurdwaras* and Sikh homes. Their participation in religious activities demonstrates the ambivalent attitude of Sikh society towards their social and religious domains. Whilst the presence of widows at wedding rituals is perceived as inauspicious, their cooked food is gladly accepted at the *gurdwaras*.

Having examined Sikh funeral rituals and discussed the differential position of women and men (widows and widowers) in relation to the ceremonies surrounding birth, marriage and death, I will now consider the impact of the Sikh reform movement on these rites of passage.

ROLE OF THE SIKH REFORM MOVEMENT

In the 1870s, one of the most important Sikh reform movements, the *Singh Sabha*, emerged in the Punjab; it was led by the English educated elite whose main objective was to create a monolithic and distinctive Sikh identity. In order to achieve their goal, they set out to reform the life-cycle rituals of the Sikhs. Commenting on the impact of the *Singh Sabha* movement, Oberoi writes,

> Eventually, in 1887 when one of the *Singh Sabha* leaders, Kahn Singh Nabha, proclaimed through a vernacular tract that *Ham Hindu Nahin* (We are not Hindus), he brought almost four centuries of Sikh tradition to an end. Until then the Sikhs had shown little collective interest in distinguishing themselves from the Hindus.
>
> (Oberoi 1988:136)

Apart from inventing a new Sikh wedding ceremony, the reformers prescribed changes in mortuary rites. They preached that a dying person should not be lifted off the bed to be placed on the floor and no lamps should be lighted near the deceased. They strongly condemned the ritual of breaking of the earthen pot before cremation. They also forbade Sikhs from depositing ashes in the river Ganges at Hardwar – a ceremony which required the services of a *Mahabrahmin*. Instead the Sikhs were advised to deposit ashes in a river without performing any ceremony. One Sikh informant said,

> Although most Sikhs in rural areas still take ashes to Hardwar, some families have started depositing ashes in a river at Kirat Pur. They make their traditional offerings of clothes, utensils, and some cash to the *gurdwara* at Kirat Pur. But the *granthi* (custodian of the *gurdwara*) does not accompany the family to the river. Nowadays, members of the deceased's family may record the details of deaths and births in registers kept at Kirat Pur *gurdwara*. It is similar to the ancient tradition of registers kept by the Brahmins at Hardwar.

Yet, the impact of the Sikh reformers on funeral rites was minimal. This is evident from the fact that it was not until 1945 that the *Shiromani*

Gurdwara Parbandhak Committee (Supreme body of the Sikhs constituted under the Sikh Gurdwara Act, 1925) approved the *Rehat Maryada* (a guide to the Sikh way of life). Moreover, the social customs of the Sikhs remained entrenched in the centuries old traditions which they shared with the Hindus. The codified rituals did not bring structural changes in the Sikh social structure, and the rituals of *pagri*, *agni bhaint* and *modha dena* remained exclusively male-dominated. The *Rehat Maryada* is conspicuously silent concerning equal rights for women despite the advocacy of the ideal of equality of humankind by Sikh Gurus.

THE SITUATION IN THE SIKH DIASPORA

Sikhs have been living in the United Kingdom for more than forty years; their number is over 350 000 (Ballard 1989). In the 1950s large numbers of Sikhs came to Britain directly from the Punjab; they were mainly *Jat* (agriculturists). In the early 1950s, these migrants from South Asia lived in male-dominated households. The concept of the myth of return was one of the determining factors for their pattern of settlement. There were no demands on these pioneers to celebrate life-cycle rituals. Commenting on the first funeral of a Sikh migrant in Leeds in the early 1950s, one Sikh informant said,

> Mr Singh died in the hospital; we did not know anything about organising the funeral. The doctor told us to contact a firm of funeral directors in Albian Street. They assured us that they will take care of all the arrangements and inform us about the date of the funeral. When the hearse arrived at our house everyone of us was shocked to see the sight of the *dabba* (coffin). We never used coffins in East Africa and India. When you put the body in a coffin, the soul gets trapped inside the coffin. In India, when a person died all the doors of the house were kept open till the funeral. The body was always carried on an open bier so that the soul of the deceased leaves the body freely. We had never heard of the firms of funeral directors; it seems to be a good business. But how one could make money by disposing of the dead; it is beyond my comprehension.

This first funeral of a Sikh migrant provides valuable insight into cultural differences and processes of adaptation. The requirement of a death certificate and the role of funeral specialists were unknown to the early migrants. A radical change in the traditional journey to the cemetery has since emerged in Sikh funerals. It is the Indian tradition to carry the bier to the cremation ground straight from the home. This practice was strictly observed by the Sikhs in East Africa. Commenting on the British practice of bringing the coffin to the *gurdwara*, one founder member of the *gurdwara* said,

> The practice of bringing the coffin to the *gurdwara* was a practical necessity in the early 1960s when more Sikh migrants arrived in Leeds. At the death of a *Jat* Sikh in 1962, we realised that his house was too small to accommodate everybody, so we asked people to meet at the *gurdwara* before proceeding to the crematorium. The arrangement was a practical solution to invite everyone to the central place. We Sikhs, like the Hindus, do not take the bier to our place of worship neither in India nor in East Africa. In 1962, the first coffin was brought to the *gurdwara*; it was placed in the verandah outside the main entrance. It had no religious significance whatsoever. Nowadays it has become a custom. As soon as the coffin arrives at the *gurdwara* it is opened for public viewing for a couple of minutes, followed by *ardas* (prayer) by the *granthi* invoking God's blessing for a safe journey to the crematorium. The Sikhs do not approve the practice of taking the coffin into the main service hall; *gurdwara* is a *pawitar* (undefiled) place.

It is interesting to note that the followers of *Baba* (holyman) Puran Singh Karichowaley insist on taking the coffin into the main hall of the *gurdwara* for the recital of religious singing before leaving for the cemetery. At their *gurdwaras* in the United Kingdom, the practice of taking the coffin into the main hall and the recital of religious singing has now become an integral part of the funeral proceedings. This practice can be described as the invention of a ritual as well as the adaptation of local customs such as the use of a coffin, funeral specialists and so on. Taking coffins into the main hall for the recital of religious singing by this group is strongly disapproved of by other Sikhs.

In the 1960s and 1970s more Sikhs, including women and children, arrived from East Africa and the Punjab: their presence resulted in the life style of Sikh migrants becoming increasingly adapted to more traditional Sikh values. The presence of family units enhanced the celebration of life-cycle rituals which required the participation of wider kinship groups and members of one's *biradari*. In contrast to the Sikh migration from the Punjab, the overwhelming majority of East African Sikhs belonged to the artisan caste of carpenters, blacksmiths and bricklayers – collectively known as *Ramgarhia* Sikhs (Bhachu 1985; Kalsi 1992). They brought with them the experience of conducting life-cycle rites in an urban-industrialised environment.

In East Africa, Sikh patterns of settlement and employment had fundamentally changed from their traditional status of being village menials to that of urban industrialised skilled artisans. They established their own caste-based *gurdwaras* and *biradari* institutions. They also employed full-time professional *granthis* who were responsible for conducting their religious and social ceremonies. They also established their own cremation grounds. The pattern of disposal of the dead continued to be traditional except for a few changes. In East Africa, as a result of the presence of *granthis*, Sikhs discarded the ritual of lowering the dying person to the ground and of breaking the earthen pot. The most significant change was the replacement of the traditional intermediary, the Brahmin with the *granthi*. It became the ritual duty of the *granthi* to recite the *antam ardas* (last prayer), to perform the ritual reading of the Sikh scripture and to receive offerings from the deceased's family. All other traditional mortuary rites were strictly observed by them.

Sikh funerals in the United Kingdom are now attended by a large number of relatives and *biradari* members who come from all over Britain. Sikh women, like Hindu women, accompany the funeral procession. As soon as the hearse arrives at the crematorium, male relatives of the deceased, led by the chief mourner, carry the coffin inside the chapel; it is symbolic of the ritual of *modha dena* (participating in carrying the bier). Sikh women, contrary to tradition, go inside the chapel and sit separately from men. The chief mourner, accompanied by close male relatives, stands next to the coffin. At this stage, the *granthi* recites the last prayer. As soon as the curtains are drawn around the coffin the chief mourner, along with a few male relatives goes down to the furnace room to push the coffin into the cremator. This is symbolic of the ritual lighting of the pyre by the son.

In Britain, the post-funeral rites are conducted at the *gurdwaras*. All mourners wash their hands and faces before entering the main service hall; this symbolises the continuity of the centuries old Indian tradition of bathing after the funeral. At the *bhog* ceremony (culmination of the reading of the Sikh scripture) the deceased's family makes offerings of a set of clothes, bedding, utensils and some cash for the peace of the departed soul. The *granthi*, like the Brahmins in the past, receives these articles. During the recital of *ardas* the *granthi* prays that the merit of the reading of the *Granth Sahib* and the donation of articles should pass on to the deceased's soul. Finally, the ritual of *pagri* (the ritual transfer of paternal authority to the son) is performed in the presence of relatives and *biradari* members. All mourners eat *langar* (communal meal) provided by the family of the deceased, before leaving the *gurdwara*.

CONCLUSION

This chapter has sought to show that Sikh funeral rites are one of the fundamental instruments of transmission of traditional values. Although the form of some rituals has outwardly changed, the content remains traditional. The chanting of Brahminical hymns has been replaced by readings from the Sikh scripture; the role of traditional intermediaries like Brahmins has been taken over by the Sikh *granthis*. These developments are obvious measures of the process of the formation of a distinctive Sikh identity. I have also shown how the Sikhs in Britain have adapted local customs, for example, in their use of a coffin and the services of funeral specialists.

Finally, I have argued that the exclusion of women from important mortuary rites such as *modha dena*, *dhamalak bhanana*, *agni bhaint* and *pagri*, is a clear statement of their differential status within Sikh society. As Uberoi states,

> The obligatory and oft-repeated social performance of a body of rites serves to give definitive expression and form to a people's collective life and their ideas.
>
> (Uberoi 1975: 503)

It is also contended that the role of participants in the death rituals is indirectly linked to the rules of inheritance and the ritual transfer of paternal authority.

Notes

1. The data for this chapter were collected over a four year period from 1980–1984 and updated recently by in-depth, unstructured interviews with twenty-five East African Sikh migrants. The methods employed fall into two categories: participant observation and unstructured interviews. Participant observation was the main technique without which the data could not be interpreted objectively.

2. The term *dhamalak bhanana* is a corrupted form of *ardh marag* in Sanskrit and *addh marag* in Hindi. According to the Punjabi Dictionary (Maya Singh 1885), *addh marag* is the ceremony of breaking of the earthen pot by the eldest son amid most doleful cries, halfway towards the cremation ground.
3. *Lohri* is a traditional Hindu festival – it is celebrated by Hindu and Sikh families exclusively on the birth of a son; sweets are distributed among relatives and *biradari* members.
4. According to *Mahan Kosh* (Encyclopedia of Sikh literature), *bura* means clothes, jewellery and cash received by a widow from her natal family at the *bura pauna* ceremony.

Part 2

Social Representations of Death

4 Vile Bodies and Mass Media Chantries

Jon Davies

> By one man sin entered into the world and death by sin: and so death passed upon all men for all have sinned.
>
> *(Romans 5,12)*

Since the end of the last Ice Age about ten thousand years ago, one hundred billion people have died. Death would therefore seem to be fairly common and indeed benign, because life on earth would be somewhat crowded and fractious if all of those billions had insisted on living. Yet Christianity, as the introductory quote from Saint Paul shows, has never been able to regard human death as normal (let alone benign!) and has placed the death of the individual right in the middle of great doom-laden cosmologies and fates, of dread myths of Origin and primal Offence, of the exploding end of worlds and of the small, unique and solitary littleness of each individual man and woman. Christians can no longer simply *die*. The very act of dying is seen as proof of sin and as the occasion of particular vulnerability to judgment and punishment for sin: original and shared, personal and acquired. A religion in which the inevitably indeterminate stories and theories of Origin and End, Death and Creation, Innocence and Corruptibility (stories which are indeterminate enough on their own, never mind when all mixed up together!) are so deeply interrelated, not surprisingly produces a view of individual death characterised by the mobilisation of terror, anxiety and indeed, of anger and violence.

It is of course true that Saint Paul had other things to say about death. It would appear that in the *early* Christian centuries the expectation of the immediate return of Jesus, and of the related salvation of His followers (if not of those who rejected Him) provided a surety of post-mortem happiness (a *dies natalis)* which perhaps compensated for the misery implicit in the association of death with sin, original or personal. Saint John Chrysostom, for example, forbade excessive mourning at funerals because it might indicate a lack of faith in the resurrection. The dead Christian, he wrote, is merely going on a journey: 'Honour for the dead does not consist in lamentations and moanings, but in singing hymns and psalms and living a noble life', as the departed person goes on his way in the company of angels (quoted in Rowell 1977: 22). As the expected Second Coming receded into a distant future, and (more crucially perhaps) as Christianity became part of established States and governments, the cheerful, millennial liturgy took back stage. By the Middle Ages things had changed in the direction not only of a more dire view of death but also of making such a view part of the day to day life of Christian communities: *Memento Mori* and the *Dance of Death* formed the iconic scenery of the Roman church. The early medieval, and the reformed Roman liturgy of 1570 *and* the liturgies developed by the Protestant churches all stressed the penal nature of death and its association with pain and suffering and the corruption of the body – the *dies irae* of the Lord and his judgement on each and every one of us. Christians, unlike Buddhists and Hindus, have only one definitive life and therefore only one definitive death; and a perilous one at that.

Much of the theological and liturgical controversy of the Reformation centred on the role of the death rite in the business of the Church. The furore about the sale of indulgences was perhaps the 'presenting symptom' of the broader issue. In England the reformed liturgy drew heavily on the more frightening aspects of death. The *Anglican Order for the Burial of the Dead* of 1662 assures us that 'Man that is born of woman hath but a short time to live and is full of misery. He cometh up, and is cut down, like a flower.' The same *Order* tells us that

> After my skin worms destroy this body ... Verily everyman living is altogether vanity ... Thou makest his body to consume away, like as it were a moth freting his garment .. [we are] a vile body ... Of whom [asks the Priest] may we seek for succour, but of thee, O Lord, who for our sins art justly displeased?
>
> (*The Book of Common Prayer of the Church of England*, undated: 326–334)

It is perhaps not too much to say that the fully developed Christian theology and liturgy of death (crucially, the insistence that death is the result of [original] sin) have, to the ordinary problems of finite life and physical decay, added (1) the expectation of an unavoidable post-mortem Judgement; (2) an existential anxiety about its outcome in the hands of a 'justly displeased' and all-powerful Deity; and (3) a terror of a very possible or most likely perpetual post-death eternity of pain, misery and suffering. No ordinary Christian, well instructed and aware that Pride is the first sin, can really be sure that s/he is good enough to go to Heaven, and certainly not by virtue of his or her own endeavours. Equally, most

Christians can at least hope that they will avoid Hell. As an epitaph in Saint Peter's church, Stourton, has it, 'In the doom of death I entered the world. In the hope of life I leave it.'

In the control of the calculus of *post-mortem* salvation lay much of the power of the established Christian church. Much of the dialectic of liturgical and theological dispute and controversy throughout the Christian centuries can perhaps be understood as an attempt by 'ordinary' people to take some control over their own salvation out of the hands of the ecclesiastical authorities. On occasion, such attempts appear as major uproars or conflicts in history. These are documented as great disruptive battles between heretical or reforming movements, such as those involving the Cathars or the Lollards, in which the established priesthood and the reformers found themselves in fundamental and often bloody confrontation. As Eamon Duffy (1992) so wonderfully describes, however, the clergy/laity relationship more often involved acts of popular day to day compromise between community and church: the working-out of systems of mutually acceptable 'arrangements' between the guardians of the 'official' liturgy and the popular versions and manifestations of it. This was no doubt true of other rites of passage such as weddings. But in the management of death rituals in particular, priest and prayer book would be most likely to find themselves under pressure (if, indeed, that is how they saw it) to leave as large a space as possible for the vernacular theologies of their community.

There is a very long tradition of lay involvement in burial rites. Jewish synagogues, under the Roman empire and now, maintain a *Chevra Kadisha,* a 'Holy Brotherhood', responsible for burials. The early Christian communities, for some centuries at least living in a diaspora as perilous as that of the Jews, also ran their own funerals with a high degree of communal control. As Duffy shows, alongside the increasingly formal burial rites of the medieval church there developed a whole array of 'secular' rites and traditions. Sometimes (as now!) these offended the sensitivities of the local priest or bishop, but generally reflected a sensible division of labour in the matter of death and burial.

If there is a trend in all of this (and accepting for the purposes of this short chapter a degree of simplification) one might suggest that the formal ritual of the church tended to move in the direction of claiming for the liturgy a monopoly for God and church over the business of the dead. For their part, the laity sought to define and defend, and if possible to extend a ceremonial role for themselves in the matter of death and in the continuing vitality *of the deceased* for the community of which s/he was a part. In part these popular activities can be construed, as many of the Reformers so construed them, as survivals of popular superstition and folklore. Such a tension between the official and the popular is, of course, a theme well to the fore at other times and places, such as in Biblical Judaism's struggle with various forms of 'Baalism' or in the later Christian confrontations with both sophisticated and simple forms of 'paganism'.

For the Protestant Reformers, the medieval Catholic church had fallen victim to the very superstitions against which, in their view, Christianity had set itself. The *Articles of Religion* of the Anglican Church, promulgated in 1571, denounced all claims for priestly intercession for the dead as 'blasphemous fables and dangerous deceits' (*Article Thirty One, in The Book of Common Prayer*: 607–628, for all the Articles). In particular, the Reformers attacked the doctrine of Purgatory. The Anglican *Prayer Book* anathematises this doctrine in *Article Twenty Two* of the *Articles of Religion* with the following:

> The Romish Doctrine concerning Purgatory, Pardons, Worshipping, and Adoration, as well of Images as of Reliques, and also invocation of Saints, is a fond thing vainly invented, and grounded upon no warranty of Scripture, but rather repugnant to the Word of God.

Purgatory is indeed, for many Protestants, the *locus classicus* of their distaste for Catholicism. Essentially, Purgatory is that place in the Afterworld to which are sent all those humans about whom the Almighty has yet to make up his mind. In the story of the evolution of the theology of the Afterlife, over hundreds of years, there have been many varied representations of the Afterworld. At one extreme it is an undifferentiated, rather indistinct place to which ALL the dead go, in a very final manner, and simply because they are dead. The other end of the spectrum is well exemplified in commentaries as far apart in time as the Egyptian *Books of the Dead* and Dante's *Divine Comedy*. Here death is a moral event, eliciting Judgement, and as a corollary eliciting also a differentiated afterworld, containing either the punishment of Hell or the reward of Heaven. Such a bi-partite Afterworld could be, and was held to be, as 'unfair' as the morally neutral 'Sheol' of the Sadducees. There was no more justice in one place for *all* the dead (Sheol) than there was in basing the decision of 'Heaven or Hell?' simply *on the evidence of one short life*. As Jacques Le Goff puts it,

> Purgatory was an intermediary other world in which some of the dead were subjected to a trial that could be shortened by the prayers, by the spiritual aid, of the living...Belief in Purgatory implies, in the first

instance, belief in immortality and resurrection, since something new may happen to a human being between his death and resurrection. It offers a second chance to attain eternal life. Finally, belief in Purgatory entails the belief that immortality can be achieved in the life of a single individual. Religions such as Hinduism and Catharism, which believe in perpetual reincarnation and metempsychosis, cannot accommodate the idea of a Purgatory.

(Le Goff 1984: 4–5)

Le Goff shows how the elaboration of the idea of Purgatory (an elaboration which received official sanction at the Council of Lyons in 1274) derived in part from Augustine's fifth century writing, the *City of God.* In this work he divided the human race into four: the godless, who at death go straight to Hell, with no second chance; the godly, especially the martyrs and saints, who go straight to Heaven; and then those who are not altogether good and those who are not altogether wicked. By the Twelfth Century this moral calculus had become transformed into the fully developed doctrine of Purgatory, of which Duffy says:

Charity is the life of Purgatory...All who entered Purgatory were ipso facto redeemed and, however prolonged their probation, certain of salvation... Being beyond the reach of love, *the dead in Hell* were beyond the reach of prayer... By contrast, a recurrent motif in treatments of Purgatory is the centrality of both natural and supernatural bonding between the living and the dead. The souls in Purgatory were part of the church of the redeemed, and prayer for the dead was one of the principal expressions of the ties that bound the community together... Friendship and kindred, therefore, are constantly recurrent notions in the cult of Purgatory, for the souls there were 'your late acquaintance, kinred, spouses, companions, play felowes and frendes'... The dead in Purgatory continued to care for their families on earth... [while] ties of blood gave kindred both the obligation and the power to discharge the penances of the dead.

(Duffy 1992: 384; 353)
(emphasis added)

Le Goff provides much of the textual analysis, and Duffy the empirical data on both the logic and the social function of the doctrine of Purgatory. While Le Goff inclines to the view that the doctrine suited the interests of ruling elites, Duffy shows how, in pre-Reformation England, those interests were not in conflict or incompatible with the interests and piety of the ordinary Christian. The Reformation may well have stamped out such piety in the name of stamping out superstition, while the more thorough-going doctrines of Predestination logically resulted in a liturgical nullity: if everything, including the fate of the dead was planned by God, what is the point of humans busying themselves at the graveside? The compromise *Prayer Book* of 1662 did not go as far as some of the Protestant Reformers might have wished, but the Anglican and other Protestant burial liturgies left, and leave, much to be desired. In the eighteenth and nineteenth centuries much of the vernacular funeral practices of ordinary people operated with a degree of tension with the 'new' practices of the established church. As soon as some element of political freedom and economic capacity was achieved (in the nineteenth and early twentieth centuries), burial became massively re-ritualised (re-catholicised?). Above all, the war memorials and war remembrance practices of this century, in their absolute insistence on the continued vitality of relationships between the living and the dead, demonstrate the persuasive power of a view of the afterworld which provides precisely for the expression of that relationship (Davies 1994; cf. Wilkinson 1995).

As far as the modern funeral rite is concerned, it seems to me, that it will survive if it is able to re-root itself in some version of the idea of Purgatory. From van Gennep (1960) we have derived the schema of Separation/Liminality/Reincorporation as the three main subdivisions or stages of rites of passage such as funerals. Heuristically – that is to say that it enables us to ask a question but not to give an answer – this schema has been very useful, but as with all such devices it begins to lose its simplicity on application. There are problems with the actual *subject* of the analysis: if for example the *corpse* is the subject, into what, and how, is it reincorporated? The three stages are themselves not so clear-cut, and begin to fade and shade into one another. There is, though, some logic in this fading and shading: *it is generally in one direction, that is, towards the liminal, towards the indeterminate.* Both the Separation and Reincorporation phases collapse into the Liminal, maximally expanding it so that the period of indeterminacy becomes the central meaning of the rite. The rite is now seen as an indeterminate process. Funeral rites have no end: or, to put it more accurately, *the end is beyond the rite.*

It seems reasonable to postulate an elective affinity between the indeterminacy of the funeral rite and the indeterminacy of older and more Catholic Christian pre- and post-mortem theology, in particular the idea of Purgatory. Both leave the question open, whatever the question is.

In leaving the question open, they also leave open the question of *who* decides the answer: questions of power and influence. Heaven is full of God and Goodness, Hell is full of the Devil and Wickedness. Both are fixed and final destinations in which there is neither room nor requirement for continued human action or reaction. Purgatory is a sociable place and a sociable doctrine, keeping open the possibility, indeed the necessity of continued communication between the living, the dead, and God. In purely secular terms, society itself is based on such a communion or covenant: the founding social contract between the living and the dead. The theological penal calculus of Purgatory complements this covenant or communion by balancing the two concerns of Charity and Justice. It is these concerns that can be understood to govern the relationships between the generations and between the living and the dead. Only in the idea of Purgatory can the ordinary realities of day-to-day life be addressed. People who are not really Sinners pray for the souls of their dead who are not really Saints. We all appeal for Justice when Charity is too generous and for Charity when Justice is too severe.

My general theme, then, is that a Christian theology of death (in contrast to Buddhism and Hinduism) in which the human being is seen as having only one life, one death, and one resurrection, cannot at the same time ground its funeral *liturgy* in a fixed and final form. The doctrine of Purgatory recognises this, underpinning a view of the funeral rite as indeterminate in itself, and a view of death as a mere reordering, rather than a sundering of relationships between the living and the dead. In this purgatorial way, community between the living and the dead is retained and given enhanced significance by requiring persistent human participation in death management, thereby enabling the dead and the living to transcend the divide. It must not be supposed that this is a cosy community: an analysis of the funeral liturgy as an act of recognised sacrifice demonstrates quite clearly that the living, in order to cope with death, require the dead to be quite indisputably dead. Funerals are occasions for killing the dead. Maurice Bloch (1992b) demonstrates how much violence is necessarily bound up in ritual assertions of human vitality such as death rituals. Likewise, the references above to the Anglican *Order for the Burial of the Dead* show how hostile liturgy can be to the dead. Purgatory softens such hostilities.

This chapter will continue with an analysis what I call 'Mass Media Chantries': the *In Memoriam* notices which appear every day in all local newspapers and which, I suggest, represent the continuation of the purgatorial tradition in the vernacular mode.[1]

MASS MEDIA CHANTRIES

Practically every local newspaper of any standing has an *In Memoriam* page. This is a kind of populist, market-provided mass media chantry in which the dead and the living converse with one another and in which

God appears as an occasional fellow-conversationalist or general-purpose audience. The *In Memoriam* notices which follow are taken from Tyneside or Wearside newspapers between 1992 and 1994 and are typical of British local newspapers. The entries, which generally take the form of an unsophisticated or even banal type of blank verse, are paid for by the relatives and loved ones of the deceased. Some are either wholly or partly written by the relatives, whilst others are provided in a rather pick-and-mix way by the Classified staff of the newspaper or chosen from a standard list obtainable at the reception desk.

Some of the poems are combinations, the particular permutation being negotiated with the mourner. In the case of the *Newcastle Evening Chronicle*, the mourner may subsequently receive a reminder of the funeral anniversary which s/he paid for when placing the original funeral notice. Whatever the balance of influence between customer and newspaper, mourner and editor, or willing buyer and willing seller, it is clear that these notices are far removed from the authoritatively prescribed, fixed, formal rituals of an established liturgy.

The origin of these *In Memoriam* notices is not altogether clear. Ancient Egyptian mortuary architecture provided for a libation stone and a stone table on which letters to the dead (written on bowls, shards or papyrus) could be left. Early Christian sepulchral graffiti may have had a similar communicative function. In more modern times, funeral directors and monumental masons will have a set of 'word packages' ready prepared for funeral and monumental texts. Some of these have a long tradition: the language and phrases of the Bible continue to provide a source of familiar and consoling words. Some of the wills quoted by Duffy have the same style or sense about them, as the will-maker endeavoured to leave behind a form of persuasive and amicable conversation to surviving kin. Many epitaphs of earlier centuries also carry the conversational and direct address style used in these *In Memoriam* notices. They seem to me therefore to have a fairly ancient pedigree.

In purchasing these notices and in choosing their own way of addressing the dead, the mourners are able to avoid the petty restrictions of graveyard-owning vicars and cemetery-controlling local authorities. For example, in 1994 the consistory court of the Blackburn diocese ruled that the word 'Grandad' was unsuitable as part of a headstone inscription. The Bishop of Peterborough, commenting on the rejection, felt that the family concerned 'may well feel that they can go to a corporation cemetery, which might suit them better' (*Daily Telegraph*, 10 August 1994). While all that was going on, the *Evening Chronicle* had no difficulty with notices such as the following: 'Grandad we just want you to know that we still love you and miss you so'.

It is the very directness of such notices, as well as their insistent and acceptable use of familiar endearments, which characterises these latter-day mass media chantries. The *In Memoriam* page of the *Newcastle Evening Chronicle* is, a sub-editor told me, the most popular page in the newspaper, read by tens of thousands of people. It appears six days a week and whether prompted by commercially-inspired reminders or out of a more spontaneous feeling, every day lots of ordinary people write in to greet their dead. This they do in a public way and in a public place. By so doing, they advertise *that fact* both to their dead and to the living who read the entries. In these entries the living are talking to the dead in the face of the living. They seem to want everyone to know that they are in direct communication with their dead.

The notices are usually short. Like the inscriptions on war graves and graves in general, they have to be paid for by the word and line. Like all such 'lapidary texts' they are terse but, in most cases, not epigrammatic. They are literal and direct in tone and usually in some kind of blank verse or simple rhyme, that is, they clearly aspire to something other than mere utilitarian conversation. They express, and advertise, the particular, personal virtues of the deceased. They often insist, in phrases such as 'never forgotten' or 'always in our minds', that the dead are not dead; and they frequently invoke as proof of that, the range of living kinship of which the deceased IS (not was) a member. Duffy's sixteenth century Christians would recognise the style and appreciate the sentiments!

These are not the formal *encomia* which we find, for example, in the Obituary columns of *The Times* or *The Guardian.* Rather, they are conversations with the dead, who are often enough seen as located in Heaven, (seldom in Hell) and in a Heaven to which the survivors feel able to look forward as the location of re-meeting. Most people are virtuous, or have at least some virtues, but few are complete Saints or complete Sinners: just human beings, remembered as if in life, and mostly for their good points. They are remembered by people whose evident sorrow at their death is in itself an intercessionary mediation. The style of the notices presupposes the continuing reality of the relationships between the living and the dead and they expect the dead to remember the nature and complexities of familial and communal life.

> Memories grow dearer as time travels on when you long for a voice and a face that is gone. Deep in our hearts you are still living yet, we loved you too dearly to ever forget. Today, tomorrow, our whole lives through, we will always love and remember you. Sadly missed husband Peter, mam and dad, brothers Dick and Fred.

> With every day that passes, I seem to find a way, to wander back and meet you on a road called yesterday. There is so much I want to tell you, I don't know where to start, so I'll just say I love you from the bottom of my heart. Love you always.

Note the present tense of these notices; they presuppose the presence of, and active listening by, the dead. The notices ask the dead to be active in responding to the expressions of memory and love.

> We loved you so much, Freddy, why did you have to go?

> So build that house in Heaven, dad, just for you and me, but never lock the door I have not got my key.

The dead are simply assumed to be in loving communion with the living.

> A year has gone since I watched you die, you hung on for me, so you could say goodbye. I felt your pain, and your fear, I held your hand, so you knew I was near. Every day I see your face, I hear your voice, and it makes me weep, for the father I loved so very much, who was always there when times were tough. Oh dad the hardest thing of all is living with the pain every day. I might laugh, I might smile, but only you know how I feel inside.

> God must have needed an Angel, and when he picked you, Susan, he picked the very best. Love you lot's and always will.

God is addressed very directly, given clear instructions, and gently told off.

> Two years ago God took you away and left us with broken hearts, we feel that we've been cheated. We're forever asking why. We feel our beautiful Helen was too young to die. But the parting cannot be forever and our prayers cannot be in vain. For we're trusting in Gods promise that one day we will be with you again.

Another notice seeks contact with and love from the departed.

> Two years ago you left us, our lives had to change but living life without you is really very strange. Your loving and your kindness really means a lot and so our memories of you will never be forgot. From mam, dad, and all the family, and grandad and grandma.

The same sense of unity, either side of the grave, is expressed in,

> There will be fresh flowers by your photo today nana as there always is, but I wish you were still here to give them to. Till we meet again as know we will we will love you lots.

God is treated as friendly and available, as in the above request for some after-death compensation for a sad life on earth. As we have seen, he is occasionally rebuked or complained about. He is also, in a very familiar way, told what to do.

> Dear Lord up above give our mam a birthday hug and when you see her loving smile, hold it for a little while and on that face we dearly miss, gently place a birthday kiss.

The power of the relationships between the living and the dead is addressed without in any way denying the fact that death has deconstructed and then reconstructed them.

> Since you left me, home has never been the same, all the world would be like heaven just to have you back again.

Time and time again the writers spell out their highly particular, familiar and familial relationships with the dead, stressing the centrality to their own lives of the continuing vitality of the dead.

> Billy, a much loved husband and father. We loved you more than words can say. God broke our hearts when he took you away, your smile, your face we remember still. We loved you darling and we always will. Mary, Maureen and Greta. Dear Grandad you never ever knew me but if you ever did, I'll know one thing for certain, I would have been your little Toon Army kid, love Georgie.

> It broke my heart to lose you but you did not go alone, for part of me went with you the day God called you home. My thoughts are always with you, your place no one can fill. In life I loved you dearly, in death I love you still. I know you walk beside me and when my life is through, I pray that God will take my hand and lead me straight to you.

These notices, of which on any one day there must be thousands appearing in our local papers, demonstrate the continuing validity of the three underlying premises of the 'doctrine' of Purgatory. First, Purgatory denies or ignores the dreadfully divisive doctrine, most coldly enunciated by Calvin, of being *predestined* to be either a Sinner or a Saint: fixed in those categories by an all-powerful God, out of human time and therefore beyond human influence. Embedded in the *In Memoriam* notices is the tacit understanding that the human race is *not* divided into Saints and Sinners; that few of us ever meet such creatures; there is even the suspicion that fully-fledged Saints are as alien to the living as are Sinners. Most of us fall in between: and here Purgatory is a reasonably egalitarian idea.

Second, Purgatory provides those of us who temporarily remain in this world with a feeling that we retain an intercessionary competence for the people now in the next world: a world in which we will join them, and a world in which the fate of our loved ones remains of concern to us. This intercessionary interest in our relatives and friends in the next world is both valid and potent.

Third, deceased people in the next world have, and value, an intercessionary interest in their people in this world. This interest partly bears witness to, and partly reinforces, the idea of communion between the living and the dead. Death, while terrifying and painful, does not divide.

Thus, by contrast, modern Purgatory, while it assumes an after-life that commences immediately after death, contains no element of purging: the process of judgement has, likewise, been evacuated. Nor is there any indication that the place occupied by the dead is in any sense a penultimate location: it is Purgatory and Heaven combined. Furthermore, the vehicle of this modern Purgatory is an entirely *secular* one: only in Roman and Anglo-Catholic churches in the United Kingdom is there a *religious* structure for communication between the living and the dead.

For all that, the modern version of Purgatory, as represented by the newspaper columns, is a very practical idea. It is probably more believable and believed in than Heaven or Hell. It gives space for the continuance of relationships between the living and the dead. It alone makes possible a proper, human, active, mutual remembrance of, and conversation between, those who live in these various worlds. It avoids a major flaw in Christian death theology: the placing of so much fate-governing emphasis on *one* life, *one* death, and *one* judgement. It retains a useful amount of indeterminacy. It is only in, and with, an indeterminate rite of burial that Christians can face the fact of one death, one life. Otherwise God's Judgement will be experienced as more of an unjust threat than an act of proper mercy – an unfortunate outcome for so important a matter.

Note

1. For an extended treatment of this aspect of death see J. Davies (1994) *Ritual and Remembrance: Responses to Death in Human Societies* (Sheffield Academic Press).

5 Dirt, Death, Decay and Dissolution: American Denial and British Avoidance

Christie Davies

In the past in both Britain and America, bodies were buried directly in the earth, enclosed in coffins whose shape reflected that of the corpse. The decay and dissolution of the earthly remains of the deceased were obvious and taken for granted. However, in both countries beginning in the latter part of the nineteenth century and accelerating in the twentieth, major changes have taken place in the way the remains of the dead are disposed of. These distance the living from decay, dissolution and indeed death itself. What is striking, though, is that these changes should have taken such a very different form in the two countries, with the Americans choosing to *deny* death, decay and dissolution through the disguise of embalming, while the British *avoid* them by means of cremation.

In Britain, cremation first became legal but not popular among the educated upper-middle classes in the late nineteenth century with fifty-three cremations being performed in 1889 and 795 in 1908 (Leaney 1989). Jennifer Leaney (1989) has argued in relation to the growing popularity of cremation that:

> At the base of cremationist thought, and underlying the sanitary and economic motives for advocacy of this means of disposal, was a feeling of intense loathing for the physical remains of the dead... Even within the grave hidden from sight, the corpse was felt liable to give offence to the living.
>
> (Leaney 1989: 189)

In Britain, cremation has become more and more common during the twentieth century. In 1967 there was, for the first time, an equal number of cremations and burials and the proportion of cremations has now reached a stable plateau with about seventy per cent of the population being cremated (Jupp 1990; Walter 1993).

By choosing cremation the British have been able to avoid and hide away death and dissolution. Most people die in hospital and are cremated in the seclusion of a high-tech furnace. 'At a western cremation, mourners – unlike Hindus in Asia – never witness the consummation of the body nor do they participate in its destruction' (Walter 1993). Cremation is not a denial of death but an anonymous technical method for speeding up the dissolution of the body into a few pounds of featureless ashes, so that the process impinges less on the perceptions and imagination of the living. Death and decay are not denied but avoided.

By contrast only fifteen per cent of deceased Americans were cremated in 1986–87. Americans of today are buried, not in a corpse-shaped coffin, but in a rectangular casket, which is in turn enclosed in a metal or concrete vault. The vault shields the casket from all contact with the earth. William E. Phipps has noted that the switch from coffin to casket was promoted by the Stein Casket Manufacturing Company during the last two decades of the nineteenth century.

> The Stein manufacturers decided that it would be easier to sell their product if it were called a casket rather than a coffin. Up until then the word *casket* generally had referred to a jewel box. A big design change in the burial box was introduced at this time.
> Realising that a body-shaped coffin was a gruesome reminder of the decaying remains within, the burial container was disguised as an enormous gleaming treasure chest. Stein funded a journal entitled The Casket to publicise the new creation.
>
> (Phipps 1987: 117).

It should be noted, though, that Stein did not and could not have created the values and preferences that lay behind the demand for his product: he merely exploited them to turn a potential market into actual sales (see Huntingdon and Metcalf 1979). In addition to being casketed, Americans are also likely to be elaborately embalmed, for American custom demands the 'presentation of ... the dead in the semblance of normality ... unmarred by the ravages of illness, disease or mutilation' (Mitford 1963; see also Huntingdon and Metcalf 1979; Phipps 1987).

Both cremation and embalming involve a turning away from the realities of decay and dissolution, but the option of embalming, chosen by a large majority in America, involves a strong denial of the realities of death, which the usual British choice of cremation merely tries to hide and avoid. Embalming restores and preserves the features of the deceased long enough for the body to be displayed in an open casket, that is, on the front stage, as a tangible statement that decay has (apparently) been defeated. By contrast the hiding away of the body and its incineration in a furnace in Britain are backstage operations and involve an admission that the individual has been reduced to formless fragments. The contrast between American and British funeral practices is part of a much broader cultural difference between the two nations in the way dirt, decay and death are perceived and avoided. This in turn is based on differences in the way national identity is constructed in Britain and America and in the extent and nature of secularisation in the two countries.

Americans are often seen by foreign observers as being obsessed with personal hygiene. Likewise, for Americans, the individuals who make up other nations do not pursue cleanliness and physical perfection with sufficient vigour, and are shamefully indifferent to the impression that their unsanitised and uncorrected imperfections make on the senses of others.

Horace Miner's mock anthropological analysis of the 'body ritual of the Nacirema' (like Dylan Thomas' Llareggub it is spelt backwards) treats the American bathroom as a shrine where sacred rituals are performed to ward off disease and debility. Significantly, it has been published in a book of essays on American culture and society alongside an empirical study of an American town by the Bengali anthropologist Surajit Sinha (Spradley and Rynkiewich 1975). Sinha gives a central place in his analysis to the peculiar American preoccupation with hygiene, which he sees as part of a general 'rational' orientation, within which such virtues as cleanliness, punctuality and thrift, all fit together.

A further indirect piece of evidence that demonstrates the American view of hygiene as both an expression of rationality and a distinctively American virtue may be deduced from the marked contrast between American ethnic jokes about stupidity told about Poles and Italians and the British and French stupidity jokes told about the Irish and the Belgians respectively. Ethnic jokes about stupidity are a well-nigh universal phenomenon told about local butts in most of the countries of Europe, Latin America, the Middle East and South Asia and in Australia, New Zealand and Africa as well as the United States (Davies 1990a). What is striking about the American jokes in *contrast* to those invented and told in other countries such as Britain and France is how many of them depict the butts of the jokes as being dirty as well as stupid; for the Americans, and for the Americans alone, being dirty is a form of stupidity (Davies 1990a).

What is the riskiest job in the Polish quarter of Chicago?
Riding shot-gun on the garbage truck.

(Collected by author in USA 1965)

How do you get a Polack out of a swimming pool?
Throw a bar of soap in.

(Collected by author in USA 1965)

Did you hear about the Italian businessman who went broke?
He imported 200,000 cans of underarm deodorant to Italy – and didn't sell a single one.

(Wilde 1975: 55)

Jokes like these are rare in Britain and France and indeed, one deliberate attempt (see Hornby 1978, Macklin and Erdman 1976) to import American jokes about 'filthy' Poles into Britain and pin them on the Irish totally failed, because such jokes cannot be fitted into the standard British ethnic stupidity script, which does not include dirtiness (Davies 1990a). In British jokes the Irish are merely shown as incompetent in relation to the means for attaining cleanliness and hardly ever as rejecting cleanliness in the manner of the equivalent American ethnic jokes:

An Irishman went into a shop and asked for a bar of soap.
'Certainly, sir', said the shopkeeper. 'Do you want it scented'?
'No, I'll take it with me'.

(Collected by author in Britain, 1982)

Irish baths have a tap at each end, so the water will be level.

(Chambers 1979: 89)

Ethnic jokes about dirt are, though, only found in *modern* America. In the nineteenth century, the Americans told ethnic jokes about stupidity in relation to Irish people, but there were no jokes about the Irish being dirty, even though Irish immigrants in America lived in very squalid circumstances. American jokes of the nineteenth century treated dirt as a comic but ordinary and unremarkable aspect of everyday life in America and not as an un-American characteristic of foreigners from Europe (Davies 1990a).

One of the links between hygiene and rationality is health, an obsession the Americans share with the many other modern societies. The Americans, however, go beyond the optimal level of hygiene needed to ensure good health, in order to ensure an ultra-clean appearance that will influence the way other Americans perceive them, and to maintain their own self-image. We can see this from international comparative market-research data concerning the use of soap and deodorants (Heron House 1979: 328–9).

If we look at soap purchases, there is only a small difference between Britain, America, France and Belgium. Only the Irish come out grubby, with over a quarter of the population never using soap, but the British either have not noticed or are indifferent to Irish soaplessness. In consequence they do not invent or tell jokes about the 'filthy' Irish in the way Americans do about Polish and Italian Americans, who almost certainly conform to the obsessive norms of cleanliness of their fellow Americans. The *key* statistic, though, is the one revealing the much greater use of deodorants in America, and especially by men, than is the case in Britain, France and Belgium. It is doubtful whether this is merely the result of the hotter American summers, for none of the other differences in deodorant use seem to be related to local climates. Rather, Americans are more concerned *not to appear dirty* to their fellow citizens, than is the case for the British, the French and the Belgians.

For Americans it is as important in life as in embalmed death to suppress all body smells and to achieve a sanitised odourlessness. The greater use of deodorants in America is an expression of the need to appear to be

Table 5.1

	USA	*UK*	*Ireland*	*France*	*Belgium*
percentage of household who buy soap (1977)	97	99	72	91	91
percentage of men who use a deodorant/anti-perspirant regularly (mid 1970s)	80	41	N.A.	29	26
percentage of women who use deodorant/antiperspirant regularly (mid 1970s)	90	73	N.A.	70	73

clean, and is not in any sense a means for ensuring good health. Indeed, if anything West Europeans are healthier than Americans. Health *is* important to Americans but the *appearance* of health and youth is just as important *in its own right.* Indeed physical fitness is less important to them than attaining and displaying a trim figure. By contrast the Poles and Italians of American jokes are portrayed as shapeless bulky folk, nourished on shapeless bulky foods and are depicted as such in cartoons and illustrations (Davies 1990a). The sin of America's substantial fat minority is not merely that they are growing old visibly and gracelessly, but that their bloated shapelessness is a reminder of the ultimate dissolution of the human form which takes place at death. No doubt some tedious ideologue will in time proclaim that fat is an anti-ageist and anti-racist issue, but, until s/he does, Americans will continue to see a fat person as contained within a disordered, unstable and uncontrolled body boundary and as an unwelcome, waddling *memento mori.*

The distinctively American pursuit of the appearance of physical perfection may also be seen in the importance of the American orthodontist, who fits braces on young Americans' teeth, so that they will be able to display a straight and regular set of teeth to the world as adults. Such a procedure is normally adopted in Britain only if a person has seriously deformed or divergent teeth, and in general it is taken for granted, even by parents who can afford to pay an orthodontist, that human beings tend to have irregular teeth and that this is an acceptable imperfection. The need for American teenagers to conform to arbitrary standards of physical perfection, and the compressing of their middle aged into the trim shapes of youth, culminates in the attempts by the old to retain their youthful features, through wrinkle-removing face-lifts for American women or the use of hair-dye by Ronald Reagan when President. Americans more than other peoples seem to live in a world of appearances and of surface perfections. They spend $250 million per annum on suntan lotions (a healthy-looking tan is worth the risk of skin cancer) and 'more on the care and maintenance of (their) hair than (they) do on mental health, more on general grooming of (their) faces and bodies than on books of all kinds' (MacAndrew 1988: 171). It would be a pity to throw all this away just because you are dead. Why not take it with you?

We are now in a position to see how the distinctive American preference for embalming and rejection of cremation fits into a much more general pattern of cultural values and preferences. Embalming preserves, or appears to preserve, the body's appearance, shape and odourlessness, which Americans have spent their lives cultivating. Indeed, one Washington mortuary is reported to have distributed pin-up calendars proclaiming 'Beautiful Bodies by Chambers' (Phipps 1987: 122). The point is well made in William E. Phipps account of American embalming:

> Restoration' is the name morticians give to their masking of reality ... Most of the attention is given to moulding the face into a desired appearance. 'Tissue builders' are injected to enlarge shrivelled parts, cottonwool is used to puff cheeks, and a 'healthy' tan is provided by cosmetics. On the presumption that age lacks dignity, the restorers remove ugly wrinkles, subtracting visible years from the corpse being prepared for viewing.
>
> (Phipps 1987: 122)

In Britain the proponents of cremation, also used notions of hygiene and sanitation in their campaign to promote cremation as against burial. Cremation does after all avoid the slow and dirty process of decay and dissolution in the grave. However, it does so in a way that is incompatible with the lifelong American battle to attain and preserve a youthful perfection of appearance. Where embalming slows down and postpones the process of dissolution, so that decay is hidden for the time during which people may wish to, or are expected to, view the body, cremation speeds it up. An urn full of dry ashes to be kept or scattered back to nature is clean in British terms, but it is also *formless* and for Americans would be a statement of the ultimate failure of their efforts to attain and preserve a clean, well-formed, youthful appearance against the attacks of dirt and decay. Cremation avoids the grave but at the price of admitting its victory.

The modern American denial of death is thus more total than that of the modern British, even if much of it is only skin-deep. Through cremation, the British transform the corpse into a formless unrecognisable ash. In this way they consciously avoid confronting an unpleasant process which their ancestors took for granted, while fully recognising the reality of death and dissolution as 'dust to dust, ashes to ashes'. By contrast, the Americans are in one sense more traditional in that they view and bury the corpse, rather than hide and destroy it. Yet at the same time, they have changed the meanings of what is happening by changing the appearance of corpse and of burial. Just as elderly Americans must be made to look young, the unfit to look fit, the marred to look flawless, so too the American dead are made to look like the living. It is a more subtle and complete denial of death, dirt and decay, perhaps summed up in the American attempt to avoid contact with the unclean earth not only for the person being buried, but even at times in the Christian ritual itself. The ritual action that accompanies the words 'earth to earth' can now be conducted by proxy, 'with a mere flick of the wrist with the Gordon Leak-Proof Earth Dispenser. No grasping of a handful of dirt, no soiled fingers' (Mitford 1963: 76; See also Walter 1993: 46).

The divergence in customs relating to death and dirt between Britain and America may be further related to differences in the construction of national identity and in the pattern of secularisation in the two countries. In Britain, as in much of Western Europe, there has been a decline in religious observance in the twentieth century (Wilson 1982; Davie 1994) and many people admit to being irreligious. In America, levels of church adherence and attendance have remained high (Finke 1992) and most Americans describe themselves as religious. This can be seen from the public opinion data (Heald 1982) from the early 1980s shown in Table 5.2. In answer to the question 'Independent of whether you go to church or not, would you say you were a religious person?' the various peoples of America and Western Europe answered as follows:

Table 5.2

	USA	*Great Britain*	*Europe (Average)*
Yes, a religious person	81%	58%	63%
Not a religious person	16%	36%	24%
A convinced atheist	1%	4%	5%

The rise, noted earlier, in the ratio of cremations to burials in the twentieth century in Britain correlates well with the decline in religious observance and the growth of secular attitudes. Indeed, Peter Jupp (1990) has noted that 'in certain respects, the replacement of burial by cremation in England can be interpreted as a classic instance of secularisation' (Jupp 1990:27–28). It is also striking that in those few American states where cremation is popular (see Walter 1993: 24), adherence to traditional Christianity is weak: notably in godless Nevada with its casinos, fly-in brothels and quick divorces (fifty-six per cent cremation); Hawaii with its large oriental population and hence alternative religious traditions (forty-nine per cent cremation); and the relatively secularised states of the North-West Pacific coast. By contrast, godly Alabama has only two per cent cremations, and bible-belted Tennessee, 2.5 per cent.

In America as a whole there has been no drastic switch from burial to cremation, nor has America experienced the marked fall in church adherence and in attendance at religious services that has taken place in Britain during the twentieth century (Brown, C 1992; Finke 1992). Whether the greater tendency of Americans to describe themselves as religious is genuine or is done to conform to an approved image, it still indicates a major, cultural difference between Britain and America. In America, mainstream religion has survived better and flourished longer than in Europe by means of free competition between denominations in a religious market place (Martin 1978), and through the use of the organisational techniques and advertising strategies of a business corporation. However, this has been achieved at the cost of inner secularisation, for the original aims and values of American religion have been transmuted into more secular and material forms (Lipset 1964; Luckman 1969; Martin 1978; Wilson 1969). In this way purity has become hygiene and sin has become dirt. It is significant in this context that Rokeach (1973) has found that there exists in America a good correlation between rating cleanliness relatively high on a scale of values and membership of a denomination that stresses personal salvation. Thus, Baptists rank cleanliness higher on a scale of values than Congregationalists, who in turn rate cleanliness higher than Methodists, Lutherans and Roman Catholics. Those who give the relatively lowest ranking to cleanliness are the Episcopalians, Presbyterians and Jews and those having no religious affiliation (Rokeach 1973: 117). Rokeach also showed that, compared with slogans and images used to sell competing products, the American advertising slogan, 'Ivory is 99 and 44/100 per cent pure', used to sell Ivory soap and detergent, appealed more to the salvation – clean-minded than to other groups. The trade name Ivory originally came as an inspiration to Harley T. Proctor of Proctor and Gamble while he sat meditating in church, as the pastor read from Psalms 45: 8: 'All thy garments smell of myrrh and aloes, and cassia out of the ivory palaces, whereby they have made thee glad' (Flood 1985: 29). Both Proctor's time of inspiration and the differing denominational responses to the fruits of his profitable meditation, again illustrate how religious ideals and impulses have been turned into a fervour for cleanliness in America. Church going behaviour and the institutional structure of religion remain intact, much as with burial, but the meanings have been secularised. A concern with essence and with the purity of the soul, has been refocussed on the cleanliness of the surface of the body and a secular concern with appearances.

Surfaces are also boundaries (Douglas 1966) and the fashion for embalming began at a time when Americans felt that the huge influx of alien immigrants in the late nineteenth and early twentieth century was threatening and contaminating the essential identity of America (Gorer 1948). Whereas British identity is regarded by most people as a primordial quality inherited from a taken for granted past, those who had chosen and struggled to go to America and had built a new nation there, saw America as a sacred place in which a new and virtuous social order had been created. Furthermore, because America is a sacred land attained through the struggles of one's ancestors, it is necessary to be buried there. When Americans die abroad or are killed on distant battle-grounds, great efforts are made to bring their bodies back to America for interment. In contrast to British historical practice the Americans have clearly indicated that some corner of a foreign field is not the best of places to be buried (Walter 1993: 45). It is not America and likewise cremation is not American.

The influx of new immigrants from Southern and Eastern Europe into America in the late nineteenth and early twentieth centuries (the same peoples who later, when they had been successfully and safely integrated, became the butts of jokes about dirt) was at the time a challenge to the boundaries of Americaness. Among old-stock Americans it was feared that the new arrivals would fail to adhere to the established ways and patterns of American society, which would, in consequence, become formless and incoherent. One of the ways in which this diffuse fear expressed itself was through an anxiety that they might fail to conform to proper American expectations of hygiene and cleanliness. It was at this time that the older sense of a new and sacred America, free from the corruptions of the Old World, began to take a material form, such that Americanism came to be identified with soap and plumbing, in contrast to the unwashed teeming refuse and huddled masses outside, who sought to enter (Gorer 1948; Jones 1960). It is tempting to see the growth of embalming in America as part of this process of defining America the clean. The descendants of the last and threatening wave of European immigrants have, of course, also adopted it as one more way of being American, and as a mode of being permanently planted in the blessed country their ancestors struggled to reach. It may seem both unfair and ironic that these peoples who have become good, clean, conforming, loyal Americans, should in the latter half of the twentieth century be the butts of jokes that state what an American is not:

> Why are there only two pallbearers at a Polish funeral?
> There are only two handles on a garbage can.
> (Collected by author in USA 1965)

> How does an Italian wedding differ from an Italian funeral?
> For the funeral they turn the headlights of the garbage truck on.
> (Collected by author in USA 1965)

It is not the case that Americans take the scripts of these jokes seriously. They do not believe that Polish-Americans and Italian-Americans are dirty or less than 100 per cent American; rather they are accepted as fully American, but only *recently* so. Such jokes were *not* told in the past when these groups really were the subject of anxiety and hostility. Only now, when they are familiar and accepted, can they be fitted into this particular pattern of joking (Davies 1990a). However, the jokes do tell us what it is to be American by making fun of what is un-American, by creating an antithesis between a funeral (the careful and ceremonial placing of a properly treated, enclosed and protected body in a sacred place) and garbage disposal (the dumping of unwanted dirt in an undesirable place). There are, of course, jokes and urban legends in Britain concerning cremation, but they do not take an ethnic and dichotomous form (Davies 1990b). Cremation is not a distinctive part of the British national identity.

CONCLUSION

It would be a mistake to assume that the contrast between America and Britain is an absolute one. Some Americans are cremated and for a minority of British people American style embalming and viewing of the embalmed body is becoming more popular (Howarth 1992). In both Britain and America there is a strong and growing concern with being healthy, as indicated by the very rapid decline in cigarette smoking in both countries, relative to other nations whose citizens are content to remain smelly and breathless. Also the American concern with the victory of fitness over fatness has spread to Britain, together with jogging and salads.

Quite possibly there is a degree of convergence here, based on trends common to most Western industrial societies. It is difficult though, to see how this could properly be assessed. It is more fruitful to contrast two similar societies that differ in certain crucial respects, as has been done above, for it is then possible to discern contrasting configurations of social facts and to infer some kind of causality from them. Here it has been argued that the American preference for embalming, as against the British choice of cremation, is part of a much stronger emphasis in American culture relative to that of Britain on being seen by others as conforming to a well managed ideal appearance: clean, odourless, well formed and free of the blemishes of nature, including those caused by increasing age. It is a pattern that is affirmed even after the individual's death. This pattern is related to two well established, though not entirely compatible, American traditions: namely, a concern with purity in a sinful world and an optimistic view of America as a special created nation, free of the corruptions of the Old World but potentially threatened and contaminated by them. These themes are expressed at the end of life, through the production of an apparently uncorrupted body, whose well-groomed surface seems to deny the pessimistic reality of decay in death. It is then buried in, enclosed but undamaged by, the sacred land of America.

In Britain, secularisation has been far more drastic than in America, and the religious concern with the struggle against sin (perhaps never as powerful as in America in the first place) has evaporated, rather than being transmuted into a struggle to preserve purity of form against the forces of personal decay; in consequence cremation is far more acceptable in Britain than in America. Cremation avoids the disagreeable and dirty processes of decay and dissolution. It takes place out of sight but it does not deny that death involves a reduction of the individual to formlessness, a process more acceptable in a society that lays less emphasis in life on presenting a well-formed appearance to others. In Britain, a country with a taken for granted primordial identity and without a founding mission, there is neither a special way of life to be protected from moral contamination, nor a sense of living in a promised land to which the body must be returned intact.

Note

I wish to thank Glennys Howarth and Tony Walter for their helpful comments on earlier drafts of this paper.

6 Dead Beauty: The Preservation, Memorialisation and Destruction of Beauty in Death

Jacque Lynn Foltyn

'Death is the mother of beauty', wrote the American poet Wallace Stevens in 'Sunday Morning'. Indeed, some of the attributes of beauty – stillness, calm, repose – are attributes of death (Bronfen 1992). For Freud (1952), death and beauty share a hidden identity; representations of beauty can articulate an anxiety about and desire for death and may be viewed as an aesthetic substitution for it. For Lacan (1986) this means that a function of beauty is to guide us to our own deaths, to present death as a dazzling sight.

Though the association of death with beauty is a common one, it remains an uneasy one, at least in Western civilisation where death is thought to be the body's most polluted form, the antithesis of beauty, something to deny and to disguise. Death, after all, is about decay, the shattering of aesthetic harmony and is ultimately about human failure. Beauty, on the other hand, is about the balance of form and is usually thought to represent health, vitality and power. As such, beauty contradicts death.

In this chapter I will examine this duality, the alignment/disalignment of beauty with death, and explore the visual aesthetic as a dynamic force in the processes of mourning, death, dying and disposal of the dead. My intention is not to provide an exhaustive analysis but rather to present some poetic possibilities of the dead body. My position is that beauty mediates the grief caused by death; elevates the territory where life and death meet; and reorders nature. Through beauty's functional equivalents appearance and adornment, we aesthetically transform the dead into memory and ourselves into mourners, and so transgress, if you will, the boundary of death itself.

About transition and duality, beauty is also about paradox. The social power with which the beautiful body is imbued creates a dilemma: to some extent beauty may be split off from the actual person as an abstract aesthetic category. The preservation, memorialisation and destruction of beauty may become ends in themselves.

My approach is multidisciplinary. I draw on psychoanalysis, sociology, anthropology, neurophysiology, history, religion, philosophy, cultural criticism, and art history. Throughout, I will show the historic continuity in aesthetic practices in connection with death, using examples from antiquity, cultural anthropology, the visual and narrative arts, popular culture and in-depth interviews.

THE BEAUTY IMPULSE

The beauty quest is a personal quest, a fundamental human trait and imaginary process that moves us from nature to culture. We cultivate beauty to transcend our bodies, to create identity and to tap into the figurative realm where artifice and gesture allow us to be more than who we inherently are. Nothing in the human world exists naturally. We participate in a symbolic universe of language, signals and signs; in this world the body was made to mark and adorn (Baudrillard 1990). From this perspective, artifice comforts those who live, and, from some perspectives, those who are dead.

A primordial, genetically encoded urge that thrills and disturbs us, beauty is nature's aphrodisiac, a biological weapon in the human battle to survive, a defense against death. The ability to derive aesthetic pleasure is encoded in the immense labyrinth of the human brain and has a neuronal basis, an art drive tied to sexual releasers that set up resonance in the hedonic brain centres (Klopfer 1970; Rensch 1984). We wield beauty to attract and to reproduce; to affirm and to celebrate life; to combat and to deny death; and to console the dead and the living, with the reminders of the beauties the dead have left behind. Even Neanderthal humans infused death with beauty when they buried carefully placed flower bouquets with their dead. The life impulse, beauty is a vast ground and reminder about what makes life worthwhile and helps us to transform the living into the dead and the dead into the living.

BEAUTY AS METAPHOR

As a metaphorical conceptual category, beauty is a potent, 'sexy' concept imbued with the tension of paradox. Enigmatic and slippery, beauty is good and bad, truth and illusion, power and powerlessness. For each myth we have about beauty we construct a counter myth to cancel it (Lakoff and Scherr 1983). The structural anthropologist Claude Lévi-Strauss (1958) was convinced that the human brain must operate in this binary manner and suggested that all myth-making is a method of neutralizing potentially destructive anxiety. Conflicting metaphors allow us to experience beauty's various aspects, for like another topic that is frequently the target of muddling, interdiction and fascination – death – the facts of experience demand an attitude of 'both-and' rather than 'either-or' (Bowker 1991). This shared tension makes beauty a natural bridge between life and death, for like these two states a major belief about beauty is that it is a transitory state, something that is temporary.

TRANSITIONAL BEAUTY

The connection of fertility with cycles of death, rebirth and resurrection is probably the most widespread of all ritual associations (Napier 1986; Bloch and Parry 1982). Rite of passage ceremonies, involving birth, puberty and death, usually involve beautifying the body in some way. Cross-culturally, the corpse body is marked for passage into another world and transformed into the cultural body, aesthetically displaying a group's common values, customs, social roles and social relations (Brain 1979).

Nowhere is the importance of beauty in such cycles better illustrated than in the ancient Greek flower myths which go back to the seventh or eighth century BC. Created to explain the origins of wild flowers like the narcissus, hyacinth, chloe and anemone, these myths explain the cycles of nature and designate beauty as something worthy of preservation (Hamilton 1942; cf. Goody 1993). The Anemone/Adonis story is illustrative. Cut down in the Springtime of life in a hunting accident, the bleeding corpse of Adonis, beloved of Aphrodite, nourishes the earth and has a flowery resurrection each Spring in a blood red blossom, the anemone. Desire, inspired by beauty, revives the lifeless. The Anemone myth illustrates the lack of boundaries between concepts such as death-birth and birth-resurrection; such stories reconceptualise death as the return to a symbiotic unity (Bronfen 1992).

THE LIVING DEAD AND THE DEAD LIVING

On a mythic level, this transitory quality makes live and dead beauty in some sense interchangeable. In the Pygmalian story the statue of Galatea is a substitute for a live woman and then becomes a living one. Such a replacement is also seen in Pliny's account of the 'Knidian Aphrodite', 'Praxiteles' sculpture of the goddess about to step into her bath. The statue's beauty was an element of its sanctity and inspired passion in male pilgrims who spoke to it exactly as if it were a living woman of overwhelming beauty (Clark 1959). The nineteenth century sculptor Antonio Canova's neoclassical marbles were said to produce a similar effect (Barbieri 1992). As an aesthetic replacement for death, lifeless beauty, no matter how frigid, can be a surrogate for life.

A common complaint voiced by physically beautiful people is that they are treated as if they are 'dead' (Foltyn 1989). 'I hate being treated as public property', says Leslie, twenty-one, a university student whose long naturally platinum blonde hair and huge blue eyes really do make her look like a porcelain doll. This view is shared by Errol, aged twenty-four, a gay model, who is distressed by lovers who will not let him be anything but sculpturally beautiful. 'It feels like necrophilia.' The essence of the complaint of these people is that while they are both beautiful and erotically stimulating, they wish neither to be touched nor to respond against their will.

THE JUXTAPOSITION OF IMAGES OF DEATH AND BEAUTY

The juxtaposition of life and death is a familiar motif in religious and secular art. Voluptuous life size funerary statues of beautiful young women and men decorate tombs in ancient Egypt, Greece, Rome and India and populate Victorian cemeteries such as Highgate. Sensual dead beauties also appear in the contemporary vampire novel and film. The convergence of death and beauty is seen in the Antonio Canova and Georges de la Tours versions of the repentant Mary Magdalene. Sculptor (Canova) and painter (de la Tours) reject the usual iconography of the repentant prostitute with the mortified flesh and present Mary as a luscious beauty. Physically untouched by her penance, she holds a skull in her lap, a *memento mori* rather than a living child (Carter 1992).

Artistic representations such as these are aesthetically pleasing, but also disquieting. When photographers like Weegee, Arbus, Mapplethorpe, Gardino, Avedon and Witkin couple death with beauty, they evoke a confusing mixture of fear, violence, anxiety, the aesthetic and the erotic. In Flor Gardino's photograph 'The Woman', a beautiful woman holds a 'necklace' of dead lizards at her neck. In a series of paired photographs, Richard Avedon juxtaposed the fashion model Dovina with his dying father. In 'Still Life, Marseille', the photographer Joel-Peter Witkin has arranged an aptly named *nature morte* as beautiful as any eighteenth century fruit, flower and fowl study that on closer inspection reveals the decapitated head of a man, posed as a flower-filled vase. In the drama of death, Bronfen (1992) claims that such representations are viewed aesthetically, precisely because we know the image is not life.

Making the dead beautiful is nothing unusual; this practice underlies embalming procedures that make the deceased socially presentable sights, a topic I will return to later. But making horror beautiful is another matter. Speaking of Witkin's work, curator Germano Celant notes that its 'references to decadence and ecstasy, to the body decomposing and being transformed in a theatrical way', are designed to disturb (Woodward 1993: 194). Witkin, himself, wonders whether he is 'healthy' or a 'psychopath with a keen aesthetic sense' (218).

Dead beauty can be both contradiction and fetish, as Dijkstra (1983) demonstrated in his study of *fin désiecle* misogynist art that connects woman with such passive states as death, sleep, sickness and decay (for example, Millais' 'Ophelia'). Distinct biological and existential conditions have caused people cross-culturally to place woman closer to birth, death and dirt (Beauvoir 1974; Douglas 1966; Bloch 1982); it should therefore, not be surprising that the three should sometimes mix in the aesthetic and the erotic. Still, the erotic corpse is not woman's exclusive iconographic domain, though one stream of feminist criticism would have us so believe. As a male colleague observed, 'my first nude was the erotic body of the dead Christ'. Artistic renderings of the Crucifixion, Deposition and Resurrection by painters such as Ribera, Pontormo and Michelangelo feature a sensual, decomposing Christ. The iconographically attractive St Sebastian, shot full of arrows, has long been a cult idol in homosexual circles; indeed, Oscar Wilde was so taken with the saint that he used Sebastian as his alias and compared him to John Keats in a poem about the poet's grave (Ellman 1988). Other standard images of dead male beauty are: the broken body of Icarus; the mortally wounded hero (for example, Achilles, Lord Nelson); and the male suicide (for example, Goethe's Werther, Henry Wallis' Chatterton).

DRESSING THE DEAD

Ceremonial burial coincides with the beginning of human social and aesthetic life. Mesolithic and neanderthal humans painted their dead and buried crowns, ornaments, flowers and pots of body paint in their graves

(Trinkhaus and Shipman 1993). By making the grave a domicile, they provided the dead with creature comforts to aid them in their transition to another world; alternatively, they were attempting to make them stay put (Jaynes 1976; Grainger 1988).

And so it has been since. Much of Egyptian, Assyrian, Sumerian, Hittite, Babylonian, Mayan and Inca art originated in funerary cults and rituals enacted to preserve life after death. The Egyptians embalmed the body and then restored its beauty by stuffing and painting it, paying particular attention to the face and hands, the parts that give us a distinctive identity and that most need a natural, tranquil appearance (Crichton 1976). Impalancing the mummy, they did everything possible to create a hospitable situation for the soul to return to its body. Such rituals are about life and beauty as much as about death; as Phillipe de Montebello (1983), Director of the Metropolitan Museum of Art, observes about ancient Egyptian funeral art, 'there is little that is funeral' about it.

In an increasingly appearance oriented world, how we look in death is also increasingly important for many. In an article published by the *Los Angeles Times*, 'Date with Destiny', celebrities talked about their burial attire. Socialite Ivana Trump will be buried in a black silk frock from Madame Gres of Paris; *Cosmopolitan* editor-in-chief Helen Gurley Brown vows to go to her grave in a Pucci minidress; and the designer Mr Blackwell will wear jeans, Reebocks and a t-shirt (Warrick 1993). In an effort to preserve the body, some people buy 'worm insurance'; others have themselves (and sometimes even their pets) mummified or freeze dried; and still others seek preservation through cryogenics, in the hope that future technology will see them reanimated.

THE EFFIGY

While an embalmed body is in some sense a work of art and may even appear statue-like (Bronfen 1992), there is no denying that all corpses will eventually rot. For this reason some cultures developed the practice of using an idealized stand-in for the living, usually a statue or a portrait. Mourners better cope with their distress by constructing such likenesses for they allow them to aesthetically redirect their grief outside of themselves (Jaynes 1976; Kristeva 1989). An effigy can be dressed, caressed, visited and even given offerings of food, music and companionship. In some cultures, such doubles acquire a life of their own. The Egyptians, Greeks, Romans, Incas and Mayas believed that life could be imposed by the gods onto a statue of incorruptible beauty. Such beliefs continue today.

Roman Catholics in some parts of the world venerate weeping statues of the Virgin Mary; others bathe, dress and incense idols of Jesus Christ and the saints as if they were living beings.

THE ENCASED BODY AND THE FUNERAL MASK

But what if the dead body is a real, rather than a symbolic, body? Herodotus speaks of ancient peoples who gilded the heads of their dead leaders and sacrificed to them, believing the skull had supernatural properties. In seventeenth century Bavaria, Roman Catholics rejected the dogma that humans forsake their bodies when they die; they believed that some parts of the soul remain in the cadaver and have grace bestowing properties. To conceal and nullify the body's decomposition, they bejewelled skeletons and dislocated body parts and entombed them in glass coffins. By using an aesthetic ritual to abolish death, they supported a cultic economy of the saints and other corporeal relics (Quattrocchi and Harvolk, 1987).

'Death should dazzle when you stare at it', said the aesthete Giovanni Pascoli (Quattrocchi and Harvolk 1987), and so it is when we gaze upon the funeral mask of Tutankhamen, a Mycenaean King, an Inca warlord or a Mexican peasant on the Day of the Dead. The sepulchral mask marks the transformation from life to death, attests to an awareness of the ambiguities of appearance and testifies to a proclivity toward paradox emblematic of transitional states (Napier 1986; Bloch & Parry 1982). When we mask death, we transform it; the mask itself, becomes a sexual, reproductive symbol, a revivifier of the dead (Needham 1986). Because the embalmed and cosmetised face of a dead person can appear mask-like and even more beautiful in death than in life, it too, may be viewed as erotic; the pain of grief and the pleasures of beauty are conjoined in the adorned dead.

REDRESSING THE DEAD

Whether in the past or the present, such funerary practices would horrify Jessica Mitford, the author of *The American Way of Death* (1963), an exposé of the entrepreneurial greed underlying the funeral industries' commercial exploitation of the grieving. According to Mitford, restorative arts that strive for idealized artificiality deny the reality of death.

In a different analysis, Ariès (1974) discusses the historical changes that have made death 'embarrassing', 'forbidden', the 'failure of a cure'. For Ariès, the illusion that we have eternal life has become a social obligation in many western cultures, a spin-off of capitalist optimism and the medicalisation of death. As Christie Davies has shown us in Chapter 5, the American response for this purpose is embalming, the British one, cremation. Using Gorer's (1955, 1965) work to explain why death in contemporary times has become taboo, Ariès contends that from time to time, sex and death reveal themselves to be similar phenomena and exchange positions as forbidden subjects. In 'The Pornography of Death', Gorer (1955) argues that the more sexually liberated societies become, the more they reject things having to do with death.

Psychoanalytically speaking, we attempt to deny our own mortality when we make the dead look alive; in this one sense the restorative arts are sublimation. But our analysis must go deeper than this for funerary rituals are always a reflection of earthly states and concerns and are invested with enormous psychological significance for the living (Jackson and Vergara 1989; Geertz 1973). 'The art of living well and the art of dying well are one', said the ancient Greek philosopher Epicurus.

To survive, humans must make prohibitions about death. When mourners aesthetically grieve and dispose of the dead, they protect themselves from possible contamination through the cleansing of the corpse but also utilize a psychic defense that allows them to get on with the business of living. By making the corpse presentable for viewing, the bereaved release a familiar body into an unfamiliar world, a world they may hope one day to join; in so doing they make death less ugly and frightening. Even if the passage is viewed only as a symbolic one, observance of the transition through beauty culture is as much a recognition, as it is a denial, of death, a way to honour the deceased and to console and to heal the living. Analysts like Mitford discount the psychic importance of such motivations and ironically, practice the very denial of death they criticise. To beautify death is to acknowledge it.

PRESERVING, MEMORIALISING AND DESTROYING BEAUTY

'The body dies; the body's beauty lives', wrote Wallace Stevens in 'Peter Quince at the Clavier', yet another poem whose sub-text links death and beauty. What are the implications for the living and for the dying about the relationship among beauty, life and death? How do people who live beauty, experience the loss of their looks to the process of dying? How do those who live the beauty of another, experience that loss? Why do we celebrate dead beauty in popular culture? Why do some people seek to defile or destroy the beauty of the human face, of nature and of art?

Earlier in this chapter I discussed how the beautiful may be viewed by others as works of art. Highly prized, beauty can be split off from a person as an abstract aesthetic category. In death, this may mean that the passing of beauty is mourned, as well as the expiring of the individual. An AIDs patient, who modelled for Calvin Klein, lamented his lost looks and comforted himself with photographs of his model perfect self. According to his caretaker, family and friends stayed away from him, not only because they feared his disease, but because they did not want to face the transitional ugliness that preceded his death.

Preserving beauty can go beyond maintaining a memory and can become an end itself. In Greek mythology, the beautiful are rarely destroyed by angry or meddlesome gods; instead, as we have seen, their beauty is transformed into an aesthetic substitute. The Associated Press (4 February 1981) reported that a kidnapped child, a seventeen month old girl, was found stuffed into a gift-wrapped box, unhurt, after her abductor telephoned her parents and told them that she was too pretty to kill. When I interviewed physicians I learned the discomforting truth that hospital personnel may give the beautiful better care. In the United States, the beautiful are more likely to get away with murder and are less liable to receive the death penalty (Hatfield and Sprecher 1986). In times of war, the beautiful are less apt to be executed. During World War II, beautiful Jewish women were often delivered from the gas chambers in the Nazi concentration camps and used as whores. A former mistress of the notorious Dr Mengele, Eva, sixty-seven, told me that her gorgeous sixteen year old body saved her from certain death when it caught Dr Mengele's eye.

THE SUICIDE

On a profoundly personal level, being beautiful can also affect the decisions of the actual or potential suicide. Actress Gene Tierney (1979) stopped herself from jumping off a building by the thought of looking like scrambled eggs in her casket. Brigitte Bardot acknowledges that vanity figured in her unsuccessful suicide attempt. 'I took pills because I didn't want to throw myself off my balcony and know people would photograph me lying dead below' (Goodman 1992: 57).[1]

For those who do away with themselves, the choice of suicide site may be an aesthetic one. Those looking for a stylish way to go have given San Francisco's Golden Gate Bridge the dubious distinction of number one suicide shrine in the western world (Warren 1993). That something as tragic as suicide can exist in the midst of remarkable beauty is one of the vastly contradictory and paradoxical aspects of life (Jamison 1993). Mishima respected and mocked this paradox when he filmed his suicide.

'I died for beauty', wrote the poet Emily Dickinson in poem '449' (1862). 'I want to live fast, die young and have a good-looking corpse', said the actor John Derek in an early film role. A patient of the controversial American practitioner of euthanasia, Jack Kevorkian, had her hair done before her appointment with 'Dr Death.' 'You'd never imagine she was getting all fixed up to *die*', said one of her neighbours (Warrick 1993: 2).

THE CULT OF DEAD BEAUTY

Once dead, the beautiful may become more famous in death than in life and have a cult-like following that keeps them 'live', that is, visually intact and lucrative. Images of dead celebrities (for example, Marilyn Monroe, James Dean, Elvis Presley), at their youthful best, are often more popular than those of living luminaries. *People* magazine has published commemorative issues celebrating the life, looks, style, careers and deaths of two recent dead beauties, Audrey Hepburn and Jacqueline Kennedy Onassis. In 1993, the most popular postal stamp in America depicted the young, lean, beautiful Elvis Presley; when put to a public vote, it won in a landslide against a stamp that featured Presley as a bloated, middle-aged, Las Vegas habitué.

DESTROYING THE BEAUTIFUL

But such aesthetic attachment can be the impetus to destroy, as well as to preserve beauty. Consider the case of the serial killer. In an interview with Robert Ressler (1992), founder of the FBI Serial Killer department, I learned that a desire to control the beauty object inspires murderers who prey on particular archetypes of male or female beauty. Transformed into something lifeless, beauty is something the sociopath can possess. In John Fowles' *The Collector* (1963), Fredrick Clegg, an impotent, obscure clerk and collector of butterflies, decides to 'net' his finest specimen, twenty year old Miranda Grey; when Miranda dies, Clegg discards her corpse only when it becomes unaesthetic.

'He was so beautiful that I wanted to slap him.' 'Her beauty makes me want to do violence to it.' Such responses to beauty from seemingly normal persons can help us to understand why the beautiful victims of sociopaths are sometimes mutilated. Anna, a psychologist, fled her volunteer job at a mental hospital when an inmate said: 'You have such pretty green eyes; I would like to poke them out.' Alexa, an English model, survived an acid attack from a disgruntled former lover. Defacement became an international news story when New York model Marla Hanson was the victim of a brutal razor slashing, commissioned by a rejected would-be suitor. On a continuum from normalcy to pathology, the disturbing behaviour of the notorious necrophiliac-necrophagist Jeffrey Dahmer becomes more comprehensible. A beauty hunter, Dahmer transformed his alluring young victims into fetishes; profoundly nostalgic and driven by an art drive, he dismembered their bodies and spray painted their skulls, and arranged these souvenirs of his monstrous desire into Witkin-like 'still lifes' (Oates 1994). For Dahmer, amorous possession and annihilation of the beauty object become one (Freud 1952).

Beauty inspires cultural reverence and awe, but also ambivalence, fear, anger, envy and anxiety. In their comfort or discomfort around the beautiful, people reveal attitudes not only about beauty, but also about self-development. Some people are unable to relate to the beautiful except through a morass of fear, accusation, projection and fantasy, and their discomfort about people or things being beautiful can turn ugly. Psychoanalysts, anthropologists and even historians of human sacrifice have noted the human attempt to equalize those with superior gifts. The Aztecs feted a beautiful young man as a god for an entire year before tearing out his heart and eating it, symbolically incorporating the power of his beauty into their culture. In an essay about Marilyn Monroe's death, Diana Trilling (1973) argued that Monroe was sacrificed by a society that couldn't handle the power of her biology, a power which Trilling viewed as a savage force that was a danger both to Monroe and to society. The public call for such sacrifice is reflected in the tabloid press pattern of adulation and then attack on public figures.

There is a cut-off point of attributes considered beneficial in a culture; too much beauty may be too much of a good thing and cannot be contained well in society as we know it. Nietzsche valued this subversive aspect of beauty and noted that when it comes to beauty there is always a debt to be paid. The Navajo, a people who organise their lives around aesthetic pursuits, weave an imperfection into their weavings to avoid paying that debt; for them, flawlessness is hubristic, a challenge to the gods.

Beauty's complex character soothes but also provokes. Those deeply conflicted about the beautiful may defile, deface and destroy it, transforming it into something impotent, ugly, pitiable, worthless, 'dead.' This may help to explain why certain works of art – Bottecelli's 'The Birth of Venus', Da Vinci's 'Mona Lisa' and 'Saint Anne', Michelangelo's

'David' and 'Pieta', the British Museum's 'Portland Vase', have been the regular targets of art assassins. But when the latest maniac takes a hatchet, hammer or canister of paint to a monumental work of art or a knife to the face of a fashion model, something more profound than a Nietzchian politics of resentment is also at work. Freud (1952) theorised that a repetition-compulsion exists in psychic life, a death instinct that propels us to an earlier condition of non-existence. Freud argued that this drive to death, figures in sado-masochism practice and fantasy; I believe it also figures in the destruction of the beautiful. 'Everything living dies from causes within itself, and returns to the inorganic', said Freud, remarking that 'the goal of all life is death' (1952: 652). Death is the mother of beauty, but also its offspring.

Note

1. Of course, this does not address how being beautiful may have figured in either Tierney's or Bardot's desires to die.

7 Representations of 'Good' and 'Bad' Death among Deathworkers and the Bereaved

Mary Bradbury

When I think about my own death I know I want to die when I have had time to prepare myself and when I have said goodbye to those I love. In this activity of contemplating my ideal death, I am sub-consciously drawing upon social representations of the good death. Representations of good or bad ways of dying are common to many different cultures. The quote given below, for example, describes the good death for the Lugbara people in Uganda.

> A man should die in his hut, lying on his bed, with his brothers and sons around him to hear his last words; he should die with his mind still alert and should be able to speak clearly even if only softly; he should die peacefully and with dignity, without bodily discomfort or disturbance; he should die at the time that he has for some days foreseen as the time of this death so that his sons and brothers will be present; he should die loved and respected by his family.
>
> (Middleton 1982: 142)

SOCIAL REPRESENTATIONS OF GOOD OR BAD DEATH

In this chapter I will be drawing upon research findings from a recent study of death and bereavement in the London area (Bradbury 1993a). Rather than focusing on attitudes, opinions or beliefs concerning the good or bad death I will look at social representations of death. The theory of social representations was developed in France, although there are publications in English (notably: Moscovici 1984; Farr 1987, 1993; Jodelet 1991). This theory emphasises the social process whereby we attempt to understand our world through discourse and certain patterns of behaviour. We 'represent' the world to each other through our talk and through our actions. When someone dies, orderly life is dramatically disrupted and there is an urgent need to re-present reality. Efforts are made to represent the death as the survivors discuss the quality of the deceased's death. Mortuary practices not only reflect or emphasise the label applied to that death but also serve to produce further representations. Thus, creating representations of death can be seen as a means of gaining some kind of control over a potentially chaotic situation.

A CROSS-CULTURAL AND HISTORICAL PERSPECTIVE

The discipline of anthropology has made a significant contribution to our understanding of mortuary rites and the social representations that surround them. Bloch and Parry (1982) discuss the way in which many non-industrial and pre-industrial cultures assert that death leads to birth, just as night leads to day. These beliefs are constructed and maintained through participation in ritual.

The manner of death is closely associated with the perceived regenerative power of that death. Deaths that are orderly are called good; they give the survivors some sense of being in control. In contrast, bad deaths are uncontrolled; they happen at the wrong place, at the wrong time. Good deaths lead to a positive rebirth, bad deaths do not.

Parry (1994) describes the Hindu good and bad death. The good death is one in which the dying person prepares for the event, materially, socially and physically. The dying should offer their body as a sacrifice to the Gods. The ideal place to die is in the sacred town of Banares, in North India. Certain deaths (the young, or deaths which are unexpected and/or violent) preclude the chance of making such a self-willed sacrifice. There is a clear link between the manner of the death and its form of regenerative potential, as positive or negative. While those who die a good death can look forward to a new life, those who die a bad death remain stuck – as malevolent ghosts – in the world of the living.

While Ariès' (1974) medieval 'tame death' would appear to be a fine example of a western pre-industrial good death it would make sense to presume that our representations of death have undergone changes since the industrial revolution. Bloch and Parry (1982) suggest that one would not expect to find strong beliefs regarding the rebirth of the dead in contemporary western societies. They suggest that in such an individualistic society a person's death poses less of a threat to the social system than would the death of a person in a highly integrated society. In short, the deceased can afford to be mortal as there are many other people who can fill their social roles. So, one would expect to find that current western representations of death would not emphasise rebirth and, possibly, would not need to make use of the good/bad dichotomy.

Related to this hypothesis is Mulkay and Ernst's (1991) work on the 'social value' of elderly people. They note that a low respect for elderly people can result in a 'social death' prior to physical death. If someone has suffered a social death one can imagine why there would be little need to talk about the relative merits of their eventual physical death. Given that western death rates are concentrated among these 'invisible' or 'redundant' elderly, then it would not be surprising to find, as Bloch and Parry imply, that our representations of the good or bad death will be poorly articulated.

Perhaps this paints a rather grim picture of contemporary social representations of death. I was interested in finding out about our current death practices and, in particular, about our social representations of death. Do we believe in the good or bad death? If we do, does the good death have regenerative potential?

A LONDON STUDY

Rather like an anthropologist in the field, I wanted to know how people behaved at the time of a death. So, I needed to gain access to the 'natural settings' where death can be found, such as the hospital, the funeral parlour, the registry office, the crematorium and the cemetery. I therefore carried out a multi-site study, visiting the various places where we treat the dying and the dead. I observed deathwork professionals in their day-to-day work and talked to them about their experiences. Many people are involved with death on a professional basis: nurses, doctors, patient's affairs officers, the police, registrars, coroners, funeral directors, the clergy and, of course, cemetery or crematoria staff. While these deathworkers are involved in very different activities they do have a common goal in achieving the social organisation of death. They are also paid for their services.

Of course, this is only one side of the story. I also needed to gain the perspective of those who had lost someone they loved. Presented with the ethical problem of whether it is right to disturb newly bereaved people, I chose to hold in-depth interviews with a small sample of women, aged thirty to sixty five, who had lost their spouse some months previously. The women came from a variety of socio-economic backgrounds. They were nominally members of the Church of England. The interviews were relatively unstructured, although at one stage I focused upon the woman's categorisation of her husband's death as good or bad.[1]

It soon became clear that social representations of good or bad deaths are in constant use. I found that any talk about a death was full of references to its relative goodness or badness. However, as one would expect in a complex industrial society, the representations of good or bad death are somewhat different from the examples given earlier.

GOOD AND BAD DEATHS: SACRED, MEDICAL AND NATURAL

In the course of my fieldwork I did not identify a single, all-embracing, definition of a good or bad death. Instead, I discovered an enormous range of descriptions of what made a death good or bad. People appeared to exercise a great deal of choice when considering the good death: apparently, one can die young, one can die old, one can die suddenly, one can die slowly, and any of these deaths can be labelled as good. On closer analysis there appear to be three broad types of good and bad death – the sacred, the medical and the natural (Bradbury, 1993b). The brief discussion below will not attempt to define our various social representations of death. It is simply that these three theoretical constructs help to explain some of the apparent contradictions that arise when people come to explain why a death is good or bad. All three types are closely related and interwoven. Indeed, they were usually presented in combination in an ever shifting kaleidoscope. Significantly, no one appeared to think that some deaths were neither good nor bad – it appears that the neutral death does not exist.

The sacred good death

The first type of good death has much in common with both Aries' medieval 'tame death' and Bloch and Parry's (1982) descriptions of good death. This is the ancient representation of death as a source of regeneration, in which a good death results in the rebirth of the dead person. I have called this the sacred good death. This kind of good death is commonly associated with the deathbed scene. It is a familiar image: family and clergy in attendance at the bedside, while the dying person says his or her farewells with a display of resignation and dignity. This art of dying well is still described in the arts and the media (see Douglas Davies' chapter in this volume). Indeed, the continuing existence of this representation should come as no surprise when we consider how universal this ideal was, just a few generations ago. For those who believe in the afterlife this representation continues to be vivid.

The medical good death

Porter (1989) discusses the way doctors began to appear at the death bed of the elite during the eighteenth century. The use of opiates meant it was possible to die without pain and, perhaps for the first time, deaths could frequently be likened to 'falling asleep'; indeed, this rapidly became the dominant analogy for death. The promise of a pain-free death meant that the doctor soon came to usurp the clergy at the moment of death. The doctor thus became the new 'manager' of the death. These changes represent the turning point in our definition of good death.

> He has got cancer and he is not going to live for very much longer – but, we can control the pain.
>
> (Owen – doctor)[2]

Contemporary medical practices can provide the optimal conditions to manipulate the process of dying. Not only can we control the location of a death at home, hospital or hospice, but with the use of drugs we can also have some say in the timing of the death. Ironically, medication that renders the patient unconscious or semi-conscious prior to death can give the illusion that they have stopped fighting for life and have accepted their fate. This giving up of life resonates with the definition of a sacred good death. However, unlike the ancient good death from which it grew, the medical good death is not regenerative or sacred, but profane.

Currently, the medical good death dwells in the hospital and, to a lesser extent, in the hospice. It is the dominant representation of our culture. While the prevalence of the representation is perfectly understandable – nobody wishes to die in agony – the absence of other factors as contributors to a good death can strike one as bizarre. For example, Owen, the doctor quoted above, did not appear to consider the possibility of saying 'He has got cancer and he is not going to live for very much longer – but we can help him comes to terms with things'. For Owen, such concerns were outside his job description. Like the sacred good death, expressions of the medical good death can be found in the arts and media. Yet, such is the dominance of this representation that it is also expressed in behaviour, that is, in choices of pain killing drugs or in embalming practices where strenuous efforts are made to make the corpse look 'reposeful', rather than dead.

> Embalming restores a much more pleasant appearance... as far as the family are concerned, it gives people a more healthy appearance. One of being at rest, rather than one of being – dead.
>
> (Peter – funeral director)

The natural good death

The third type of good death I have called the natural good death. Talking to the widows I was mystified by their talk of deaths being good because they were natural. This is not what I had expected. In her study of seventeenth century good deaths, Beier (1989) notes that deaths which were viewed as natural, such as death in childbirth, were immediately excluded from the category of good deaths. These natural deaths were commonplace and, while devastating, were met with a sense of resignation. The women I listened to told me about deaths that were good precisely *because* they were natural. It looked as if the very definition of what makes a death natural, or for that matter good, had undergone a change. An explanation for this transformation can be found by referring back to two key elements of the medical good death – its profane nature and the search for *painlessness*.

> I think it was good really. Yes, I don't think he suffered long. To me, he never seemed to be in any pain.
>
> (Sarah – bereaved woman)

If painlessness is now perceived as the single most important factor for the achievement of a good death then a new possibility occurs. Deaths which are painless simply because they are sudden, can, in certain circumstances, be categorised as good. Of course this does not include unexpected deaths (for example, those caused by severe burns) that are patently awful. It is of note that classifications of death as natural are, like medical good deaths, profane. Death does not lead to rebirth.

> It was a good death for Ken. A brilliant death for Ken. Because Ken hated illness. He couldn't stand it.
>
> (Paula – bereaved woman)

Further confirmation of the close links between medical and natural definitions of good and bad death was provided by the launch of the Natural Death Centre in 1991. Drawing upon the name and ideology of the Natural Birth Movement, this new cause aimed to de-professionalise death. It was suggested that more people should be allowed to die at home and that the bereaved should take charge of arranging the disposal of the corpse. Like the sudden and painless natural deaths just described above, the type of deaths which the Natural Death Movement catered for did not appear to be particularly natural; they bore more resemblance to slow, expected, cancer-type deaths. In fact, the natural good deaths described by my respondents and by the Natural Death Movement were not so much 'raw' or 'natural' deaths; they were simply painless, sudden or free from medical intervention.

In these various descriptions of different types of good or bad death one can observe a multi-layered discourse. For example, it appears that everyone has their own idea of what is meant by a 'natural' death. These confusing and often contradictory discussions as to the goodness or badness of a death illustrate the multi-faceted and ever-changing character of social representations. Yet, each of the three broad forms of the good death have one thing in common; they represent different attempts to *control* the potentially anarchic character of death.

CASE HISTORIES

It is useful to refer to case histories. This will illustrate how some descriptions of a good death may coincide with an 'ideal type' of death, while others seem to draw on a mixture of forms. When I first started interviewing I had imagined that the women I listened to would be motivated to claim that their husband's deaths were good. After all, the women must have been acutely aware that they were talking to a psychologist, whose hidden agenda may well have been to investigate their grief reaction. However, such was the women's commitment to their personal representation of their husband's death that several were quite prepared to tell me just how bad their husband's death had been.

Kate's husband died while on holiday in the Caribbean. One glorious afternoon they went for a swim. Watching her husband wading out of the sea from her spot on the beach, Kate saw a huge wave gathering behind him. She cried out but he did not hear her. The wave engulfed him and he was killed instantly. Kate described his death as good, because, as she put it, 'it was natural'. This good death appears to fit the contemporary social representation of the natural good death. One has to remember, however, that in the past, before we had romanticised nature and before we became fearful of excessive medical intervention, such a sudden death would most certainly have been described as bad.

> Oh, I have considered this all the time! This is my greatest source of comfort. My husband's death was an excellent death. He was very happy... and, you know, he just died without suffering.
>
> (Kate – bereaved woman)

Another woman's description of her husband's good death was quite different. Ann's husband had cancer. Together, she and her husband prepared for his death with as much frank discussion as they felt they could cope with. He stayed at home. Finally, they decided he should receive opiate-based pain killers. Shortly after starting this course of drugs he fell into a coma and died in her presence. While this would appear to be a perfect example of the medical good death, this categorisation is tempered by the fact that, in her definition of the death as good, Ann also drew upon the sacred form of a good death. She surrounded her dying husband at his deathbed with his family and made use of props such as candles, music and even a bottle of champagne. A quietly spiritual woman, she was touched when her daughter suggested they open the bedroom window to enable his soul to escape.

Christine and Susan felt their husband's deaths were bad. Both deaths were as different from each other as the two good deaths just described. Christine's husband was diagnosed as having cancer. A few weeks after the discovery of the tumour he went into a coma and died, at home, in her presence. Christine did not feel prepared for his death as she had relied heavily on the longer, two year, life-trajectory provided by her doctor. Susan described a death that seemed to have all the classic qualities of a bad death, such as unexpectedness and a general lack of control. While she was abroad on business her husband, slightly the worse for drink, fell down stairs, fatally fracturing his skull.

There were no set rules as to how to categorise a death. The factors that tipped the scales one way or another could be subtle if not completely idiosyncratic. For example, the context of Christine's bad death sounds very similar to Ann's good death. Both men died of cancer, at home. Yet it is clear that Ann referred to her husband's death as good because she had felt in control of the situation.

It was possible to identify certain broad themes, each of which was linked to the three forms of the good or bad death. The women I spoke to cited the following factors as particularly important to them when deciding whether the death was good: the couple's awareness of impending death; dying at home; the wife's presence at death; the painlessness of the death; and dying in tranquil or beautiful surroundings. Less frequently, the women talked about deaths as being good because the person did not suffer the pains and difficulties of protracted illness or the trials of old age or senility. Finally, several of the women talked positively about the 'dignity' of their husband's good death. On the whole, the inverse criteria were cited as reasons as to why a death was bad.

In contrast to the widows, the deathworkers' criteria for defining deaths as good or bad was altogether more casual because they were less emotionally involved with their clients. For them, the majority of deaths were perceived as good. Rather than emphasise what made a good death good, as the widows did, the professionals usually referred to what would have made it bad. For example, the intervention of the Coroner was a reasonably accurate indication that a death would be a bad one, as the Coroner becomes involved when the cause of death is violent, sudden or suspicious. Other characteristics of a bad death suggested by deathworkers included: the youthfulness of the deceased; the amount of pain experienced; and the state of the body. The condition of the corpse was particularly important to the deathworkers who were involved during the first few days after death.

So, if the death was good, as the majority were, the professional expressed this representation in various ways: they made positive statements about the appearance of the body (both in the hospital and in the funeral director's viewing parlour); they talked about the painlessness of the death, often likening it to 'falling asleep'; and they encouraged viewing of the corpse. Some deathworkers referred to the timeliness of these good deaths. They would sometimes give the next of kin gentle reminders that excessive expressions of grief were inappropriate or unnecessary. If professionals perceived the death as bad, their self-imposed role was that of protector of the bereaved. They believed the grieving client needed to be shielded from things that would 'upset them', for which we could substitute, 'make them unmanageable'. This protection took the form of avoiding talk concerning the manner of the person's death, playing down the pain experienced, and of sheltering them from the 'upsetting' sight of a disfigured body by persuading the bereaved that it was either unnecessary or undesirable to view the body.

The cause of death plays a particularly important role in the decision making process of both the next of kin and the deathwork professional. For example, if a person is diagnosed with a terminal cancer and is told that they have only a few months left, then this knowledge helps to facilitate a state of awareness, painlessness through drug regimes, presence of family at death and, possibly, a death at home. Further, it is unlikely that the Coroner would be involved in such a death, hence the professionals would be more likely to view the death as a 'good' one. In contrast, a heart attack victim is more likely to die in some kind of accident and emergency situation at which the wife, or next of kin, will be less likely to be present. It is also probable that there will be a Coroner's inquest, or at the very least a post-mortem. This is not to say that dying from cancer is good, it is just that certain ways of dying allow for more human intervention than others. Having involvement in the death creates the illusion that the death is within our control; such deaths are more likely to be described as good.

NEGOTIATING THE GOOD DEATH

One can see the contrast between the somewhat straightforward way in which the professionals categorised a death as either good or bad and the more complex and often agonized reactions of the widows. This distinction between deathworker and bereaved client is a reflection of the profound difference in the purpose of labelling a death. The widow's use of the representation is linked to her attempts to re-create order out of a world turned upside down. Deciding whether her husband's death was good or bad provided a structure to the woman's loss; she could then shape her responses to the bereavement to fit this label. Even her grief itself may have been influenced by her social representation of that death as good or bad. In contrast to the bereaved, the deathworker is supported by the medical, bureaucratic or commercial system within which he or she operates. Dealing with death is part of the day's work. Yet, one has to remember that the deathworker's job is an unusual one. Knowing how to deal with both the body and with bereaved people helps to alleviate the anxiety and stress of the deathworker's role.

> It was a perfect death, if you can think of anything more awful. I mean, we had done everything they [the nurses] had suggested...I think they orchestrated it, the nurses...It was almost professional.
>
> (Ann – bereaved woman)

The possession of the corpse empowers the deathwork professional (Howarth, in press). In fact, the almost complete and unquestioned power that the deathworkers gain by keeping the body – for most of the time backstage – meant that the women I spoke to were initially unable to contradict the predominantly medical representations of death presented to them by the professionals. Yet the bereaved had their own back-stage areas, such as their homes, which were peopled by friends and family. In this, usually sociable, domain they came to their own labels for the death. During the week or so that the bereaved family and the deathwork professional had contact with each other, I observed discussions between the two parties regarding the goodness or badness of the death. It is of note that these negotiations did not necessarily end in consensus (Bradbury 1993a).

One could argue that people's good and bad deaths, and the factors people use to justify them, are simply a reflection of their state of grief. For example, those who were doing 'badly' in their grief reaction, would have been more likely to view the deceased's death as a bad one. This begs the question as to why the deathworkers bothered to construct social representations of good or bad deaths. I would suggest that there is more to this phenomena than a person's mood or mental state. It is also a reflection of the personal allegiance of the labeller – deathworker or bereaved – to social representations of life and death as sacred, medical or natural. This helps to explain why deaths that occur in apparently similar circumstances can give rise to very different classifications. It also illuminates the source of clashes of opinion between deathworker and bereaved.

SUMMARY

Categories of good and bad deaths reflect the current discourses about health, illness and mortality in Britain. In this instance, the dominant representation of the medical good death slots neatly into the medical model. This medical good death is not only different from the good deaths of other cultures, but is also represents a departure from the good deaths of pre-industrial Britain. This indicates that our social representations of death are temporally and culturally specific.

Contemporary western society has responded to change and choice by renegotiating both its ancient funerary rituals and its social representations of death. The impetus for renegotiation is to be found in the desire to have some control over death. Currently, we appear to have multiple representations of good and bad deaths, only one of which is connected to the regenerative potential of death. For the majority, the concept of the good death has been reinterpreted – and made profane – to reflect an ideal of the painless, medicalised death. However, the pursuit of a painless death has perhaps taken us to extremes of behaviour which are increasingly being rejected. The dispossession of the dying from their own deaths and of the bereaved from their own grief has led to an upsurge in the number of people who are now wary of excessive medical intervention. Associated with this general rejection of medical science is a belief that certain sudden deaths which bypass both medical intervention and pain can, for the first time in the west, also be viewed positively. Thus, the move away from medical intervention has given rise to the concept of the natural good death.

Meanwhile the professionals continue to use the dominant, medical model of good death and sometimes unthinkingly impose this representation upon the bereaved. This influences the way they talk about the death and the way they treat the body. Yet, the deathworkers' power is only temporary and bereaved people often come to their own conclusions as to the goodness or badness of the death. The definition applied by the grieving relatives not only reflects the context within which the death occurred but also their representations of good and bad death. Once labelled, the perceived nature of the death provides a structure within which the survivors can experience their sorrow.

Notes

1. For a fuller discussion of the methodology see Bradbury (1993a).
2. All the names used are pseudonyms.

8 The Good Death: Attitudes of British Hindus

Shirley Firth

In an introductory section to the new Open University course on Death and Dying, Alyson Peberdy states that 'the concept of "a good death" is highly contentious', and raises the question, good for whom? Is it a quiet peaceful death (perhaps even a sudden or unexpected one) which is without pain or fear for the dying individual? Is such a death good for the relatives who may have a lot of unfinished business and no opportunity to say goodbye? Or is it one which causes the minimum of fuss and upset to relatives and carers? (Peberdy *et al.* 1993: 43). Ariès (1974; 1981) has shown that in the Middle Ages the concept of a good death was linked to the *ars moriendi*, the art of dying, in which the dying individual had an opportunity to review his or her life in the context of a belief in heaven or hell. Mary Bradbury (1993b) suggests that the expression can only be evaluated in terms of particular criteria, and suggests three types of contemporary representations of the good death. These are a 'sacred' good death, with a religious reference; a 'medical' good death, which is pain-free, and in which life may be prolonged as long as possible; and a 'natural' death, with minimum intervention and full consciouness.

THE HINDU GOOD DEATH

The Hindu emphasis is on the sacred good death, which, ideally, is also a natural one. Death is seen as a process of transition, so that there is not just a concern about the moment of death, but about appropriate preparation and the correct performance by relatives, of death-bed and post-mortem rituals. In the diaspora these needs are often difficult to fulfil adequately and a process of adaptation is taking place. This chapter explores the concept of the good death in the contexts of Indian, and of British Hindu societies. The data derives from an interdisciplinary study of a small Hindu community in Southampton.[1]

For Hindus a good death is set in the context of their entire lives, previous lives and the next life, and is thus part of a continuum of life, death and rebirth. It is also firmly embedded in the extended family. There is a right time, a right place and a right way to die, and a good death is marked by certain signs on the body. Although a good death depends on the good *karma* of the dying person, his/her reaching the final destination, the good end, depends also upon the relatives, particularly the son or sons, performing the correct rituals at the time of and after death. This has been likened to your son buying you a ticket and seeing that you get on the right train for your intended journey. In turn, the survivors are affected in the long term by the way in which the death occurs and is subsequently handled. A bad death is a premature, sudden or violent death which has not been prepared for, or an otherwise normal event marked by bad signs such as the wrong astrological time to die or certain physical signs on the body.

The ideal death is one in which a person dies in old age, having lived to see his or her grandson or great grandson. All unfinished business should have been dealt with regarding disposal of property (including gifts to charity); having arranged for the marriages of daughters or granddaughters; made amends for any quarrels; and said good bye to members of the family. A Brahmin priest may be called to facilitate an act of penance, and a cow or calf brought for the dying person to hold its tail. The animal symbolically takes the deceased across the river of death, the *Vaitarani Nadi*, and it may be donated to the priest.

Preparation for death is therefore, not just a last minute affair but should be thought about throughout life. The four *ashramas* or stages of life (student, householder, forest dweller and ascetic) are often cited as an ideal model, several informants saying that from mid-life, one should begin thinking about the third and fourth stages. A Panjabi Brahmin man, aged 45, commented:

> You should start thinking of the journey fifty years before you've got to leave this world. It is as if you started getting ready for a holiday a long time before. On this journey you start renouncing your things in the world and people around you. You have less and less attachment towards the family, towards the belongings of the world, and you do more public service, help the people about you, give things for others' happiness, maybe perform temple service, maybe try to help children in the home or some elderly person or someone sick or do voluntary work. You start living a simple life.

Many older Hindus gradually withdraw emotionally and mentally, if not physically, in order to concentrate on reading the scriptures, prayer and meditation. If they are prepared, then it is easy to relinquish life. A Panjabi woman who had recently lost her husband and her eldest son recognised the importance of detachment as one got older:

> If you are too attached, death is very painful because you know you have to leave everybody and everything behind, whereas if you start giving up things you find a different kind of happiness. You realise the fact that your family and friends are not really what you think they are, they are individual souls, so the stronger the attachment the more intense the pain.

The ideal death is one which is entered consciously. In a sense it should be 'willed'. The person who is spiritually prepared for death may have foreknowledge of the day and even the time he will die (Parry 1982: 82). Carstairs quotes from a Brahmin informant in India, who says of the *bhakta* (devotee) with a controlled mind, that 'he is able to see his death before it comes, and tell his family that on such a day, at such a time, he will die and so it happens' (Carstairs 1958: 233). Parry observes that the ideal death is regarded as preparation for the final sacrifice on the cremation pyre, so the dying person fasts to purify and weaken his body to enable the spirit to leave more easily and to avoid polluting faecal matter:

> Having previously predicted the time of his going and set all his affairs in order, he gathers his sons about him and – by an effort of concentrated will – abandons life. He is not said to die, but to relinquish his body'.
>
> (Parry 1982: 82)

Many of my informants described such a death in their own families. An elderly person may call family members to come to say goodbye, ask for the floor to be prepared, bathe and lie down chanting God's name. Unusually, one Sindhi woman in my sample, sent her son out so that she would not be distracted and then asked her maid to assist her, but most informants spoke of the need for the family to be present to perform the final rituals and to help the dying person think of God.

A favourite book at the time of death is the *Bhagavad Gita*. According to the *Bhagavad Gita* and other scriptures, a person's thoughts at the time of death will influence what happens afterwards, so it is important to die with the name of God on the lips and in the heart. Devotional hymns may be sung, or *Ram Ram, Om namah Shivay,* the sacred syllable *Om*, or the short Sanskrit prayer known as the *Gayatri Mantra* may be chanted.

The good death is characterised by the right place (cf White 1995). The ideal site is on the banks of the Ganges, where all sin is washed away, or on the ground at home rather than in hospital. Because the Ganges is, for most people, an impossible ideal, it is brought to the patient in the form of Ganges water, *gangajal*, which most British Hindus have in a small container at home. This, together with the leaf of the *tulasi* (basil) plant, should be placed in the mouth of the dying person. These have the effect of purifying him/her of sins. According to ancient tradition and scripture, it is important for Hindus to die on the floor, not on a bed and older Hindus in Britain may express a preference for this, even climbing out of a hospital bed to do so (Neuberger 1987). The head should be to the north. This aligns the body with the magnetic currents of the earth, and having no boundaries (such as the bed) enables the soul to be released more easily. The time (*kala*) of death should also be astrologically correct; and certain periods of the moon or sun are considered to be unlucky.

At the point of death a lamp, *diva*, should be lit to show the way to the soul.

> My mother was like a saint and she died in just five minutes at 103. She was able to thread a needle and walk without a stick. She asked for bed on the floor and asked for a light. When a person dies we give a *diva*, like a candle made of flour and ghee – into her hand to show her a way to God... Then my sister's son came and said, 'What's happening, Bibi?' She said, 'O thank God you have come. Come and give me a *diva* on my hand.' And my sister started crying and she said, 'Don't cry, I'm going to God. Don't stop me. Your tears will make a river for me to cross.' He did everything, [then] she said, 'Put my head in your lap, I want to go to God.'
>
> (Panjabi Brahmin; Firth 1989: 70, adapted)

THE BAD DEATH

The bad death (*ku-mrityu*), or untimely death (*akala-mrityu*), is exemplified by premature or sudden death from violence or by accident, or death at any age, from certain diseases such as cholera, suicide and death in childbirth. This is the death 'for which the deceased cannot be said to have prepared himself. It is said that "he did not die his own death"' (Parry 1982: 83). The bad death is an uncontrolled death – whereas the good death implies a degree of control – it is a willed death. Because sudden death takes the person unprepared it may be bad even for those who would otherwise be ready to die. Nevertheless, some of my informants described premature deaths of saintly relatives which they interpreted as God willing the individual to come to be with Him. Some were seen as a reward and other sudden deaths, such as Gandhi's, were viewed as good because God's name was remembered at the point of death.

The physical signs of a bad death include vomit or excreta. They indicate that the soul has left through a lower aperture, whereas the good death is indicated not only by their absence but by slightly open mouth or eyes. It is also considered bad to die during certain phases of the moon. If this happens remedial ceremonies have to be undertaken, or other people in the family will die prematurely. A bad death may be caused by the failure of the family to perform the correct rituals at the time of death. Should there be a bad death, especially a violent one or a suicide, the spirit of the deceased will remain a ghost. S/he will cause problems for the family unless a ritual called *Narayana Bali* is performed to help the unhappy ghost to move on to the next life.

A series of rituals are performed for all deaths (cf Kalsi, this volume). If a person dies before being placed on the ground and given Ganges water and *tulasi*, these can be done immediately after death. Neighbours and relatives are informed and gather at the house to assist and condole. The body is then bathed and dressed by members of the same caste and sex and according to status and age. It is then placed on a bier. The family are now highly impure for ten to thirty days[2] and will touch as few objects as possible. Images and pictures of gods used in worship may either be covered or taken away until the period of impurity (*sutaka*) is over.

The chief mourner, who has responsibility for all the rituals, is ideally a son, or if there is none, a male relative on the husband or father's side. This role is so important that families may adopt a son (often a nephew) to enact the rites when the time comes. In higher caste families the family priest may be called. Five or six balls of rice, wheat or barley (*pindas*) are made as offerings to the spirits at the house and along the route to the cremation ground. The bier is carried to the cremation ground by male relatives of the same caste as a sacred obligation.

THE CREMATION

The prescribed rituals vary with geographical context. In India and East Africa, the cremation normally takes place on the day death occurs, or on the following morning, although in urban areas refrigeration has meant that the cremation is sometimes delayed until overseas relatives arrive. In many parts of India the chief mourner is expected to break the skull of the corpse with a stick as the body burns on an open pyre. This is said to release the soul or to release residual 'airs' in the skull which prevent the soul from moving on.

While the men are at the cremation ground the women remain at home, cleaning the house (cf. Kalsi, this volume). Either on this day, or on the tenth day, any foodstuffs, utensils and clothing used by the deceased are thrown out or given to the poor. Families do not cook during this period so relatives or caste peers provide food. Normally no one eats until after the funeral.

MOURNING RITUALS

For the next ten days the soul of the deceased must create a new ethereal body. This is created ritually, by making offerings of food (*pindas*) and water, although nowadays these rituals may be combined on the tenth day. The rituals on the eleventh day strengthen the body for its journey through the kingdom of *Yama* (the King of the dead), which is said to take a year, before it can become an ancestor. Usually, however, the ritual of creating an ancestor is performed on the twelfth day, this being a symbolic year. Again the chief mourner plays the pivotal role of enabling the deceased to become an ancestor, in a complex ritual called *sapindikarana*. The ashes, which are collected on the third day, may be taken to a sacred river such as the Ganges at Hardwar or Banares and the ancestral ritual may be carried out there. Until these rituals are accomplished, the ghost, or bodiless spirit wanders around and is tempted by unresolved attachments to cling to the family. After it becomes an ancestor there is a symbiotic relationship between the dead and the living, exchanging good fortune and fertility for sustenance.

During this period of ten to sixteen days it is expected that close relatives will come to stay to give moral support. Anyone who knows the family will come to pay their respects and offer condolences. Following the twelfth day ritual, or on the sixteenth day, depending on caste tradition, a turban (*pagri*) may be given to the chief mourner by his wife's family, particularly among Panjabis.

The wife is now a widow and, as Kalsi (this volume) notes of Sikh society, her role has changed dramatically. It is only as the mother of sons that she receives respect. It is now rare for widows to shave their heads but until recently this was customary in many higher castes. Younger widows are often blamed for the death of their husbands, although at another level it is acknowledged that death occurs only because the time is fixed by one's previous *karma.* A few castes allow re-marriage of young women, often to the husband's brother.

DEATH IN BRITAIN

There is a sense in which life in Britain is seen as being very different to life in India or East Africa. The traditional social supports for Hindus in Britain are far less strong. While there are clusters of some caste groups in various cities in Britain, economic and social mobility can lead to the weakening of the religious and caste support system. Thus in many instances, groups are left without a network of older relatives and a family priest who would have provided information and guided the rituals. Often only older informants can remember details of what used to be or should be done in the particular family and caste tradition of the dying person. If there are no senior family members in Britain but there are still older relatives in India, the relatives may telephone for advice. This helps to maintain the umbilical cord to India. Because of smaller houses and mobility in Britain, people are less likely to live in extended families which in India not only cared for the elderly but were also more likely to deal with death in the home, as Indian hospitals often send patients home to die. Where there are three generations under one roof, they are often parents living with a son and his family; other sons may or may not live close by. Sometimes it is the wife or daughter-in-law who cares for a sick relative at home, and she may not be aware of the availability of professional help. If the family have moved away from a caste network they may be isolated at a time of bereavement. One young Brahmin woman graduate from Bombay did not integrate into the local community because she felt she had little in common with them. When her father died in India she received no support from other Hindus in the area.

HOSPITAL DEATHS

In Britain most deaths occur in hospital where it is very difficult to facilitate the Hindu good death (Neuberger 1987). Hindus have less control over the processes of dying and death than they would in India or East Africa. The next of kin have to be present in order to say farewell and take *darshana* (literally, a sight) of the dying person. They have an obligation to read religious books, recite prayers and mantras and aid the dying person. However, hospitals in Britain are not geared to receiving large numbers of relatives, and there may be a conflict between the requirements of the ward and those of the patient and his or her family. In some hospitals familiar with Asian patients, a separate room is made available and, if requested, a mattress is placed on the floor. This gives the family the opportunity to say their farewells and to chant the name of God for the dying person. However, the reluctance of some medical staff in British hospitals to inform patients of their terminal condition also hampers Hindu death procedures. If the dying person and the relatives do not know, and consequently, miss those crucial final moments it can be disastrous. First, the relatives have failed in a sacred duty to assist the dying person. Second, there is the emotional trauma of missing an opportunity to say farewell and to hear the all-important last words. For Hindus there are added complications because there is a belief that unless the rituals are performed properly at the time of death, the dying person will not pass on to the next life but will remain a ghost. This spells disaster not just for the patient, but subsequently for the family, as the unsatisfied ghost can cause illness, bad luck, nightmares and infertility.

THE FUNERAL

After death there is even less sense of control because the professionals take over. Unless there has to be a post-mortem the undertaker removes the body; the thought of paying someone to look after this seems unnatural to many Hindus. The relatives may have to wait as long as a week to obtain space in the crematorium. According to many pandits, this has serious implications for the progress of the soul, which needs to be liberated by an immediate cremation. As in India, the body is bathed and dressed by same sex caste and family members in order to prepare it for the fire god *Agni*. However, if there is a delay, this may be done a week or more after the death and can prove an unpleasant experience. Some families may ask the undertakers to do this for them, and just give the corpse a token 'sprinkling'. It is then placed in a coffin and taken back to the family home for a service. It can be difficult getting the coffin into a small terraced house and so it may have to be passed in through a window.

Once in the home, the coffin is opened and the pandit instructs the chief mourner in the performance of rituals. Certain rituals which in India would take place at the cremation ground, in Britain take place in the home. As a consequence some of these have been adapted. For example, since the mourners are unable to circumambulate the body with fire, symbolic sticks of incense may be used instead. The pandit recites various Sanskrit texts and supervises the making of the *pindas* mentioned above. These will be placed in the coffin instead of on the ground at intervals en route to the cremation ground. One advantage of this change is that women are present for more of the service than would be the case in India. Moreover, Panjabi women, and increasingly, Gujarati women, now go to the crematorium as well. Some, but by no means all pandits in Britain allow daughters to act as chief mourners in the absence of sons. This is yet another area of change.

In Britain, the ritual procession to the cremation ground has virtually disappeared, although male relatives and friends still 'give shoulder' to the body. I observed the breaking of the pot at only one funeral in Britain: timed just as the family were taking the coffin out of the house to the hearse. Kalsi (this volume) comments that, this is common in the Panjab. The mourners and often large numbers of friends and neighbours follow the hearse in double-decker buses. At the crematorium there is a short service which seems to owe as much to Western influence as to Hinduism, with a few prayers and a homily. The chief mourner then presses a button to hide the coffin, and he and a few relatives and friends go down to the cremator to witness its entry into the furnace.

MOURNING IN BRITAIN

For the twelve to sixteen days following the death the family institute mourning procedures. In Britain, unlike India, these have to begin *before* the funeral. If a pandit can be obtained, all the tenth to thirteenth day rituals are normally completed in one condensed ceremony on the twelfth or thirteenth day. If a pandit is unobtainable, the family may arrange for a surrogate to perform the rites in India. Alternatively, the son or widow might travel to India with the ashes and have the rituals performed there as part of a pilgrimage. Several informants have described this as a 'send-off' to give peace to the soul of the deceased, rather than in terms of making a new body to enable it to become an ancestor.

CONCLUSION

For Hindus, as we have seen, death is understood as a transition from one life to another: a journey for which one should be prepared. Given optimum conditions, it is possible to make the transition in a manner which is cognitively and emotionally satisfying for both the dying person and the family. The representations of the good death in Hindu culture, with associated beliefs about the continuity of the soul, do seem to help people approach death in a philosophical way, and to aid the process of recovery for the survivors when such a death has occurred. When, for one reason or another, a death lacks this dimension, the recovery is more difficult. People may feel devastated if they have a sense of failure in the performance both of their own duties and of the appropriate religious rituals. Such experiences, according to Eisenbruch (1984), are common to other expatriate communities. He comments that professionals need to take into account aspects such as, 'the fear of incomplete mourning [which] suggests a vulnerable point in the bereavement practices' (1984 II: 333). On the other hand, if, despite the strange environment, the community can perform the appropriate death and funeral rituals or can find satisfactory adaptations, they can be tremendously useful in coming to terms with the death.

A good death, then, depends not only on the beliefs and attitudes of the dying person and his or her closest relatives, but also upon the support of caste and community; on the appropriate rituals; and on the sympathy and understanding of health-care professionals and provisions. It is therefore important that in the setting of the hospital, hospice or nursing home, the complex needs of Hindu patients are understood. After death, the attitudes of various professionals concerned with disposal of the body also affect the way in which mourners cope. The failure of any of these factors not only makes the death more difficult but complicates the process of bereavement. When handled well, the time of death, says one pandit, is, 'the time when a person should be eager to go back, like a child eager to go back to his mother after school. He has sent us to do certain work and he waits for us'.

There are sometimes conflicts between the older Hindus in Britain and individuals of the second or third generation who may feel alienated from the more traditional aspects of their communities. Younger individuals may feel disorientated at the time of a death if they have not maintained their religious beliefs and practices and do not know what should be done following a death. They may feel uncomfortable with traditional expressions of grief, yet often acquire a sense of cohesion and strength from the community. This is a time when many younger Hindus re-examine their faith, trying to find a new set of meanings which integrate their traditional practices and their particular religious and spiritual insights with their experiences and life-style in Britain. Expectations may also change, particularly for educated women. The changes relating to widows in India have been very dramatic within the life-time of older women. However, in Britain many women have commented that within some of the stricter Gujarati caste communities, there are greater constraints on women than, say, in Indian cities. It will be interesting to see, over the next generation, whether younger educated widows in Britain will be able to find more freedom than their Indian counterparts with respect to social activities, re-marriage and work.

In spite of the changes faced by many Hindus in Britain, the strength and cohesion of the community becomes most apparent at the time of death and bereavement, when strong social bonds and religious traditions provide meaning and support. The good death provides a useful model of a philosophical approach to death. A study of Hindu belief and practice is of value at a time when there is a growing awareness among professionals in Britain of the need to help people to die with dignity and to legitimate the need for adequate mourning. For Hindus themselves, living in an increasingly secular society in which death is highly medicalised, there can be a risk of separating religion from the rest of society. The need to find rational explanations for illness and death in terms of physical causes may lead to a debasing of religious experience and spirituality, as both dying people and their relatives may resist the concept of the inevitability of death and the consequent need to prepare for it. The changes in ritual practice because of delays in cremations and the difficulties of finding suitable priests could also influence beliefs about the progress of the soul: for example, if it is believed that the soul, or some airs associated with it, depart at an immediate cremation, there may be implications for its well-being if there is a seven to ten day delay. The beliefs associated with the complex rituals of the tenth to twelfth days, which enable the soul to grow a new body for its post-mortem journey prior to rebirth or joining the ancestors, may lose their significance without priests to explain them. However, many Hindus retain the umbilical to India through visits to relatives and on pilgrimages; and the rituals, if done in India, are often filmed on video, with knowledge passed on this way. Even with this link it seems likely that Hindus in Britain are going to need to adapt in ways which integrate their traditional practices and their particular religious and spiritual insights with their experiences in Britain.

Notes

1. In Southamptom there ae approximately 2000 Hindus, of whom about 60 per cent are Gujaratis and 40 per cent Panjabis, mainly mercantile castes

and Brahmins. The material for this paper is derived from a PhD thesis, 'Death, Dying and Bereavement in a British Hindu Community', 1994, SOAS. Three months were also spent in India for comparative purposes. Research methodology included semi-structured interviews and participant observation of rituals.

2. The period of ritual impurity varies from caste to caste and according to the degree of relationship. According to the texts, Brahmins are impure for ten days, *Kshatryas* (warriors and nobility) for twelve, *Vaishyas* (merchants and farmers) for fifteen days and *Shudras* (labourers and peasents) for a months. In practice, many British Hindus end the extreme period of purity with the rituals on the twelfth day, and the lesser impurity ends after sixteen days, with further rituals after a month and monthly thereafter.

Part 3

The Role of Health and Death Workers

9 Terminal Care Education for Doctors[1]

David Field

INTRODUCTION

In common with other advanced industrial societies one of the features of modern Britain is the central role played by doctors and nurses in the ways in which death and dying are dealt with. Death and dying have become both institutionalised and medicalised as Blauner and other writers have noted (Ariès 1974; Blauner 1966; Illich 1977; Elias 1985; Field 1994a) and medical and nursing work with people who are dying and those close to them have important consequences for the ways in which members of our society experience the stresses and traumas of death, dying and bereavement. In the 1990s both medical and nursing hierarchies in the UK have seen this area of medical and nursing work as amenable to improvement via education. The Standing Medical Advisory Committee and the Standing Nursing and Midwifery Committee issued a joint report on 'The principles and provision of palliative care' (1993). Its first two recommendations are that all patients needing palliative care services should have access to them and that terminal care services for patients dying from diseases other than cancer should be developed. To achieve its recommendations the report sees education as 'the most basic requirement which must be at undergraduate and postgraduate level in medicine'. The General Medical Council's document aimed at improving the education of medical undergraduates (1993) also emphasises the importance of caring for dying people by including it as a topic in the 'core curriculum' for medical undergraduate teaching.

The inclusion of Terminal Care Education (TCE) as an explicitly taught part of the medical undergraduate curriculum is a relatively recent phenomenon. In medicine, the influential Todd Report on undergraduate medical education (1968) contained no reference to teaching about death and dying and it was not until 1980 that the Wilkes report on terminal care for the Standing Medical Advisory Committee recommended that a terminal care element should be included in undergraduate medical training.

The emergence of the speciality of palliative medicine in 1987 both reflected and gave further impetus to concerns within medicine about the adequacy of care for people who were dying. A working party set up in 1991 by the Association for Palliative Medicine of Great Britain and Ireland provided detailed guidelines for such teaching for medical students, general practitioners and hospital doctors and specialists in palliative medicine (1993). Similar importance is attached to TCE in Nursing education. It is a requirement that terminal care must be covered in both 'core' and 'branch' teaching programmes, but it is left up to each department and unit to decide how to do so. At the post-basic level there is a well established specialist course in terminal care (931) and nurses can gain a diploma qualification in terminal care.

This chapter considers the provision of education for terminal care in the undergraduate medical curriculum. It first outlines what currently constitutes education for terminal care. It then discusses the aims of such education and concludes by asking about the effectiveness of such education.

THE CONTENT OF EDUCATION FOR TERMINAL CARE

There are a number of difficulties in establishing exactly what constitutes education for terminal care in our medical schools. In part this reflects debates within the field about the nature and remit of the medical care of dying people and those close to them. Three inter-related terms are used to describe such care, each with a slightly different but nevertheless important emphasis. The modern hospices were originally developed to improve the provision of *terminal care* (James and Field 1992) – that is, the care of those for whom death is certain and not too distant. Hospice care has been very largely restricted to those suffering from cancer and there has been a long standing recognition of the desirability to expand the scope of hospice care to other conditions (Wilkes 1980). *Palliative care* developed from this focus and incorporates key features of the hospice approach. It can be defined as 'the total (physical, emotional, social and spiritual) care both of patients with life threatening disease and of their families. The focus of care is both the quality of remaining life of the patient and the support of the family and friends' (Higginson 1993). Although in practice still largely focused upon the care of cancer patients, palliative care has a wider remit. In theory at least (although not always in everyday practice) the principles of palliating symptoms in order to maximise quality of life should extend to the care of people dying from chronic respiratory or heart failure and other progressively deteriorating conditions. *Palliative Medicine* was recognised as a speciality by the Royal College of Physicians in 1987 and is defined as 'the study and management of patients with active, progressive, far-advanced disease for whom the prognosis is limited and the focus of care is the quality of life' (Doyle *et al.* 1993). Here too the focus is upon the quality of life rather than simply its prolongation and the intention is to include conditions other than cancers. There is, however, some disagreement about whether such a definition broadens the scope of care too widely and there is some concern that in such a definition the fact of death itself seems to have become less central (Ahmedzai 1993, Biswas 1993, Doyle 1993). There is also concern expressed by some about what seems to be a more active role for doctors (Johnson *et al.* 1990, Biswas, 1993, Field 1994a).

Given these differing definitions this paper takes a broad definition of teaching for terminal care (TCE) as encompassing any teaching about death, dying and bereavement in a medical setting. Such teaching is quite diverse and may be located in a number of departments and provided by a range of instructors within any one medical school. Simply identifying the teachers is difficult, even for those teaching within the same medical school and it is not uncommon for teachers to be unaware of other teachers or of what they are teaching.

A survey of all UK Medical Schools in 1983 (Field 1984) provides some information about how much TCE there was, what topics were covered and what methods were being used at this time. Four schools provided no formal teaching in the compulsory curriculum, although in one of these it was optional. On average just over six timetabled hours were spent on TCE in the other 27 schools. Six topics were reported by most medical school respondents: attitudes to death and dying, bereavement, communication with patients, communication with relatives, the experience of dying (pain, anxiety, etc) and the social contexts of dying. Only seven schools reported teaching physical therapy. The main teaching methods used were lectures and small group discussions. A companion survey of UK Nursing Schools (Field 1986) found that they provided a greater range and amount of teaching than the Medical Schools, that they were likely to cover more topics and to devote more time to such teaching. However, neither survey was able to account for TCE which occurred incidentally to or as part of the students' practical experiences in clinical settings such as hospital wards or GP surgeries and so it is virtually certain that they under-estimate the actual amount of teaching given at this time.

The *preliminary* results of a second survey of all UK medical schools (Field 1994b) suggests that a greater amount and variety of formal teaching was occurring about aspects of death dying and bereavement in 1994.

One school did not respond, and the reorganisation of undergraduate medical education in London has reduced the number of schools since 1983 to 27. Table 9.1 shows that the time spent on teaching about death, dying and bereavement has increased from 1983 to 1994 with nearly 300 hours of such teaching reported in 1994 – more than double the total reported in 1983. As in 1983, these hours certainly underestimate the amount of terminal care education which is taking place in our medical schools. In addition to optional elements undertaken by only some students, there will be adventitious teaching in many clinical firms as students come into contact with terminally ill patients. Relevant issues are also likely to be addressed in teaching about communication skills, especially about 'breaking bad news' (Buckman 1993a) and about general ethical issues (Gillon 1986).

Table 9.2 shows the teaching methods used. The main changes between 1983 and 1994 are in the clinical years with increased use of the experientially based methods of role play and simulated patients and the use of hospices. In two schools, Oxford and Southampton, clinical students spend a week in the local hospice, at Glasgow there is a two-day hospice attachment and at King's College some clinical students also spend a substantial period of time attached to a hospice. This is consistent with Thorpe's study which found that most medical schools have established links with hospices (Thorpe 1991). Schools were also using a slightly greater range of methods in their teaching in 1994 than in 1983.

Table 9.1 Amount of formal teaching about death, dying and bereavement in UK medical schools 1983 and 1994

	Teaching in hours					
	Pre-clinical years		*Clinical years*		*Overall*	
	1983 (n = 20)	1994 (n = 20)	1983 (n = 22)	1994 (n = 26)	1983 (n = 27)	1994 (n =26)
Range of hours taught	0.5–11	1–16	1.5–12	1–76	1–13	2–76
Mean hours taught	2.85	5	5.10	8.00	6.27	11
Total hours, all schools	57	88	112.5	210	169.25	298

NB: Totals do not include optional teaching elements.

Table 9.2 Teaching methods used

	Pre-clinical years		*Clinical years*	
	1983 (n = 20)	*1994 (n = 20)*	*1983 (n = 22)*	*1994 (n = 26)*
Lecture	19	19	13	21
Role Play	4	18	2	13
Simulated Patients	n/a	0	n/a	18
Video/Film	8	13	15	17
Small Group Discussions	11	14	17	22
Clinical Case Discussions	2	4	14	17
Hospice Visit	1	2	5	18
Other Methods	2	1	4	7
Mean number of methods used	2.35	2.75	3.18	5
Range of methods used		1–4		1–8

n/a = Not asked in 1983.

It is evident that UK Medical schools are now undertaking a greater amount of teaching about death, dying and bereavement, covering more topics and utilising a greater range of teachers than in 1983. In both 1983 and 1994 staff from a range of professional backgrounds were involved in the teaching, with a wider range of clinicians and others in the clinical years. In 1983 the main teachers in the preclinical stage were psychologists (14) and sociologists (7) whereas in 1994 although these are still the most commonly involved teachers at this stage (in 10 and 12 courses respectively) there is a wider range of teachers including general practitioners (5), hospice doctors (6) and others with experience of working with terminally ill people. In the clinical years, in 1983 general practitioners (14) and psychiatrists (12) were the most frequently identified teachers. In 1994 psychiatrists are scarcely mentioned (4) and general practitioners (16) are joined by oncologists (20), specialists in palliative medicine (19) and hospice doctors (19) as main teachers. Nurse specialists (11) are also participating in nearly half of the clinical programmes of teaching.

Topics taught in 1983 continue to be taught, with a large increase in the number of schools teaching about physical therapy (Table 9.3). The new topics asked about in 1994 are all suggested for inclusion in the undergraduate curriculum by the Association for Palliative Medicine (1991). In 1983 they were either not mentioned at all or by only one or two respondents. Of these new topics, psychological aspects of dying is a topic addressed by

Table 9.3 Aspects addressed in teaching

	Pre-clinical years		Clinical years	
	1983 (n = 20)	1994 (n = 20)	1983 (n = 22)	1994 (n =26)
Attitudes to death and dying	14	18	14	20
Grief and Bereavement	13	16	16	18
Communication with Dying Patients	14	15	15	22
Communication with Relatives	11	20	16	20
Demographic & social aspects	10	13	7	8
Social contexts of dying	11	14	15	18
Psychological Aspects of Dying	n/a	14	n/a	20
Experience of Dying	11	14	12	16
Religious and Cultural aspects	n/a	7	n/a	12
Physical therapy	1	1	6	22
Team work in caring for the dying	n/a	3	n/a	18
Euthanasia	n/a	2	n/a	7
Ethical Issues	n/a	7	n/a	17
Statutory Regulations	n/a	1	n/a	12
Certification of Death	n/a	5	n/a	13

n/a = Not asked in 1983.

most schools and team work, ethical issues, statutory regulations and the certification of death were addressed in most clinical years in 1994.

THE AIMS OF TERMINAL CARE EDUCATION

What is education about terminal care in the undergraduate medical curriculum trying to achieve? What knowledge and skills are to be imparted? What 'needs' or 'deficiencies' are to be addressed? What personal effects are sought? What moral or ethical issues should be addressed? Scott and MacDonald (1993) identify three broad and inter-related aspects which should be included in medical undergraduate teaching in palliative medicine: the exploration of attitudes, beliefs and values; imparting basic knowledge; and the acquisition of specific skills in order 'to enhance the care of the dying and to improve the general quality of medical care' (1993: 764). They also stress the need to integrate such teaching with other parts of the curriculum. However, it is unclear how many medical schools actually have clearly specified aims to shape and inform the content and style of their teaching in this area and to link it to other elements of the curriculum. In practice there seem to be three main aims: the acquisition of the relevant knowledge and technical skills of symptom management and palliation; the improvement of communication skills; and the bolstering of students' personal coping capacities. One might consider the imparting of knowledge about death, dying and bereavement to be an aim in its own right. Similarly the exploration and understanding of ethical issues could be regarded as a separate aim. However, these are both essentially adjuncts to these three main aims.

The acquisition of the knowledge and technical skills necessary for the control of physical symptoms, including the recognition and management of psychological distress, is an important part of the TCE curriculum. Under the influence of the hospice movement the role of doctors in terminal care is at least acknowledged to be wider than the bio-medical management of physical symptoms. Whether this 'holistic' approach is reinforced rather than contradicted by clinical experience and teaching elsewhere is a matter for concern as in other areas of the medical curriculum a narrower bio-medical model of disease and the tendency to objectify and de-personalise patients persist (Charlton 1992). Within TCE the dominance of the 'cancer paradigm' for terminal care means that pain relief is central and other terminal diseases and symptoms (with the possible exception of AIDS) receive less attention. Over half of all deaths occur among those who are 75 years or older and less than 20 per cent of such deaths are caused by cancer. Although the symptoms experienced may be similar to some extent, the palliative and terminal care of non-cancer patients will be different in important respects (Seale 1991a). In the community (where most terminal care is located) people who die are likely to be ill with long term respiratory disease, chronic heart failure and other progressively worsening conditions which although leading to death take a long time before they become 'terminal'. The management of such conditions in the general practice situation is unlikely to be substantially addressed in the current undergraduate curriculum which is delivered mainly in acute hospital settings.

Communication skills are seen as central (Doyle *et al.* 1993, Buckman 1993b). Hence improving communication skills, especially those involved with the handling of 'Bad News', is another key aim of TCE. Improving communication skills may be linked to the aim of improving personal coping. Although it is now generally accepted that information about a terminal prognosis should be given to someone who is terminally ill (Seale 1991b) *how* to do this sensitively and effectively is a matter of concern among both teachers and students (Buckman 1993a; 1993b; Maguire and

Faulkner 1988, Spencer Jones 1981). Such teaching typically uses small groups and may use video material and role play by students, sometimes with simulated patients (Preston-Whyte 1992). At its worst such teaching can suggest that by becoming proficient at breaking bad news the student can somehow make the news no longer bad and there is the potential danger of focusing too much on information giving and the technical skills of communication with the result that the students may lose sight of the person(s) they will be communicating with. While good communication skills may facilitate acceptance of death by patients and their intimates, students should not be led to believe that it will guarantee it (Maguire and Faulkner 1988).

The aim of enhancing students' personal coping capacities is less clearly articulated. There are two elements here which may be confused with each other: the aim of reducing student anxiety by changing attitudes towards death and dying and the aim of enabling students to deliver good quality care of dying patients after they qualify. A key feature of some TCE – especially in N America – is the attempt to reduce students' anxiety by making them less fearful of death. The assumption is that if students are able to come to terms with death and dying on a personal level this will enable them to perform their professional caring tasks better (Neimeyer 1988, Razavi *et al.* 1988). There are two difficulties here. First, the assumption that students are highly fearful of death (Feifel 1963) seems unfounded. Some students are, but research suggests that most are not (Durlak and Riesenberger, 1991; Sundin *et al.* 1979, Thorsen and Powell 1991). Howells and Field in a five year cohort study of British medical students found that there were no statistically significant differences between medical and social science students in their fear of death although small significant associations were found between fear of death and personality measures (Howells and Field 1982) and that there was no difference between first year (pre-clinical) and fourth year (clinical) students in the intensity of their fear of death (Howells, Gould and Field 1986). Second, the benefits of such teaching for students are equivocal and it is unproven that less fearful or anxious practitioners communicate more effectively and deliver better terminal care (Durlak and Riesenberg 1991). Howells and Field found that in their final clinical year students with 'high' fear of death were more likely to report difficulty in discussing the prognosis with a dying patient and to report experiencing minor psychological difficulties but were not more likely to report avoiding dying patients or to be less open with them. They concluded that while 'high' personal fear predicts subjective disturbance in dealing with dying patients it does not produce different caring behaviour (Field and Howells 1988).

While it is appropriate to enable students to reflect upon and discuss their own attitudes, anxieties and experiences in a constructive manner too much should not be claimed for such exercises.

An aim which is important but which appears to be insufficiently addressed in undergraduate TCE is to improve interdisciplinary care (Calman 1988, Doyle *et al.* 1993, Dent *et al.* 1990; Scott and MacDonald 1993). For example, in the 1994 survey one school with virtually the most extensive range of teaching activity and almost the greatest number of teaching hours comment that they have only just begun teaching about team work in the care of dying people (Field 1994b). Doctors and nurses are not taught together, let alone with other relevant health or community workers despite the centrality of interdisciplinary team work in terminal and palliative care.

THE EFFECTIVENESS OF TEACHING

The effectiveness of undergraduate teaching in improving the quality of care received by terminally ill patients is unclear. This in part reflects the general difficulty of evaluating the effects of education upon future practice. Three general problems exist: establishing what is and should comprise relevant teaching, identifying the best time for this teaching to occur and the technical difficulties of undertaking rigorous evaluation of teaching activities.

One difficulty in establishing the amount and content of TCE is the gap between formal instruction about attitudes and knowledge, often taught in the classrooms, and practical skills training in clinical settings. The former can be readily identified and examined as to its amount, content, assessment and whether it is optional or mandatory for students. The latter is harder to identify, is more variable and uncertain in the exposure to it among the student body and is heavily dependent upon individual circumstances with respect to both the skill and availability of clinical instructors and the students' clinical experiences. The linkage between these two aspects of TCE within the undergraduate medical curriculum seems to be poor and uncoordinated and it may be a matter of chance whether formal instruction is reinforced by practical experience (Charlton 1992). As with so many areas, integration across teaching blocks and resolution of conflicting messages is left to the student. Given these difficulties it is hard to be certain about the full extent of TCE in UK medical schools. What is certain is that not all students receive the same amount of education and training in this area and that not all of the staff involved in TCE are conversant with the full range of relevant teaching in their school and their role within this.

An associated difficulty, again not exclusive to palliative care, is that one cannot easily draw boundaries around some of the topic areas which have been identified as central elements in the training for palliative care. For example, communication skills are high on the agenda of essential topics (Doyle *et al.* 1993, Buckman 1993a; 1993b), but the communication skills required – giving and receiving information, using and interpreting non verbal communication, acknowledging and facilitating the expression of feelings, showing empathy – are not unique to palliative care. While some of the difficulties doctors experience in their communications with dying patients and their intimates are directly linked to the fact that they are dying, others can be traced to poor communication skills. Poor communication by doctors can also cause difficulties for nurses and other co-workers (Davey 1993, Field 1989) as Katz discusses in the next chapter. If *general* communication skills are improved, this will greatly enhance the ability to communicate with patients, relatives and other staff in the area of terminal care. Teaching about communication skills within terminal care 'modules' is increasingly overlapping with and dependent upon teaching within 'modules' on communication skills.

With regard to the most appropriate timing for teaching about death, dying and bereavement there is the argument, which is relevant to all specialities, that only basic knowledge and skills should be taught in the undergraduate medical curriculum as the technical skills of symptom management and palliation for those who are dying are best learnt *after* the student has completed their basic training. This appears to be one of the more important implications of the General Medical Council's 1993 recommendations on undergraduate medical education. At the undergraduate level it may be inappropriate to focus specifically upon the techniques of palliation and sufficient to emphasise the general principles which may or may not be linked to actual student experience with terminally ill patients.

There has been little systematic evaluation of the effectiveness of undergraduate TCE UK medical schools and although many studies evaluating the impact of death education have been published in N America care must be taken in applying their findings to the UK. Not only are there important differences between the societies and their educational and health care systems, but the quality of the research is not high (Durlak and Riesenberg 1991). The great majority of the studies focus upon affective changes such as reduced death anxiety or more positive attitudes towards death and dying. In reviewing this literature Durlak and Riesenberg (1991) suggest that 'experiential teaching' such as role-play and the use of simulated or real patients are more effective than didactic methods such as lectures for altering student attitudes and reducing personal fears about death. Overall, the N American research suggests that death education programmes are only moderately effective.

In Britain, Field (1984) reported that evaluation was mainly ad hoc and qualitative, concluded that TCE in UK Medical Schools was ineffective, and suggested that more rigorous research into the consequences of TCE should be an 'early priority', a conclusion echoed by Mason and Fenton (1986). In Field's 1994 survey respondents were again asked whether they had been able to assess the effects of their teaching in any way. Although most teachers reported positive evaluation of their courses this was almost entirely based upon some form of student evaluation of the teaching and/or examinations. We thus have very little evidence about the effects of TCE at the undergraduate level.

CONCLUSION

It has been argued that the social construction of death and dying in modern society is largely shaped by the medical profession (Ariès 1974, Blauner 1966, Illich 1977, Field 1994a) and within the medical profession the call for more and better training for terminal care continues unabated, not least from those who have experienced the inadequacies of what they have (or have *not*) received (Benton 1985, Hull 1991, Jeffrey 1994). As sociologists we might therefore be interested in examining the role of TCE in shaping the meaning and experience of death and dying in our society and the functions it performs in the socialisation of medical students.

There are two main difficulties in establishing the role of TCE in reproducing and shaping the meanings and experiences of dying and bereavement for members of British society. First, despite the apparent importance attached to providing adequate education for terminal care to our future doctors there is little evidence about the effectiveness of the education which is currently being provided in the UK medical undergraduate curriculum. Indeed one expert, writing with reference to the USA, claims that 'the evidence suggests that the majority of health care workers have not been adequately prepared for giving terminal care. In fact, there is much to suggest that the training in general still emphasises traditional roles organized around a hierarchical model of acute medical care, with little if any attention given to (a) the special clinical skills associated with good terminal care and (b) preparation for teamwork in the context of complex organizations' (Benoliel 1988: 348). Despite the evidence of increased attention to clinical skills and teamwork in medical undergraduate TCE and the emergence of the speciality of palliative medicine there is little evidence to support a contrary view in the UK. In their comprehensive review Scott and MacDonald conclude that 'it is clear that palliative medicine enjoys little emphasis in undergraduate teaching' (1993: 366).

Second, and more fundamentally, the outcomes of teaching can only be seen in the medical practice of qualified doctors – yet how does one separate out the effects of teaching from those of maturation and practical experience? Indeed, it may be that the most important factors affecting the quality of terminal care have little to do with the provision of formal teaching during the student years. Informal learning and 'apprenticeship' on wards and units may be much more important and at best TCE can only be one component contributing to the care of those who are dying. The critical feature of TCE is that it can only *prepare* doctors (and nurses) to deliver terminal care. The quality of terminal care they actually deliver depends upon a range of other factors found in the various organisational contexts where terminal care is delivered (Field and James 1993, Field 1989, Vachon 1987). It is these which facilitate or constrain palliative care work, as any comparison between an in-patient hospice and a busy understaffed general medical ward amply demonstrates. The success of hospice care is not simply the result of its philosophy of terminal care but also stems from the development of appropriate organisational forms in which to deliver it (James and Field 1992).

It could, then, be argued that in terms of the everyday practice of doctors TCE has very little direct effect and that its role in the undergraduate medical curriculum is essentially that of a placebo – a symbolic gesture which acknowledges the importance of dealing with the experiences of death, dying and grief; claims to provide some assistance to students in dealing with the practical, emotional and communicational issues entailed; but which 'works' only in so far as teachers and students believe that it does! In the absence of clearly demonstrable measurable effects of TCE it must be concluded that its increased significance within medical education lies elsewhere. We therefore need to consider the more general functions performed by TCE in the socialisation of doctors in terms of legitimating medical work with those who are dying and as part of a broadening of what is deemed good medical practice. By affirming the importance of the topic within medical practice TCE thereby legitimates for students medical intervention into what is often a very personal and private domain. Second, as Charlton (1992) has noted, it is an area within medical education which runs counter to the more conventional 'bio-medical' model of medical practice. TCE is thus part of an emerging strand within medical education which emphasises a broader and more 'holistic' view of medical practice (Arney and Bergen 1983; General Medical Council 1993) and its position needs to be considered in the light of more general debates and struggles to transform undergraduate medical education.

Note

1. An earlier version of this paper appeared as 'Medical Education for Terminal Care in the Undergraduate Medical Curriculum', *Critical Public Health* (1993) 4/3: 11–18.

10 Nurses' Perceptions of Stress when Working with Dying Patients on a Cancer Ward

Jeanne Samson Katz

INTRODUCTION

Many studies investigating the ways in which health workers interacted with dying people suggested that this activity was experienced as stressful *per se* (Benoliel 1983; Vachon 1987; Field 1989; Davey 1993), especially for nurses who of all health workers have the most frequent contact with dying people. Nurses' perceptions of their work are influenced by the nature of their patients' conditions, and in turn, the quality of patient care is influenced by the ways in which nurses perceive their caring for dying people. This chapter focuses on ways in which nurses conceptualised stress and distress in their work environment when caring for dying cancer patients. The study upon which this is based (Katz 1989) sought to investigate whether nurses did indeed find caring for dying people stressful and if so, to identify particular aspects of their job as stressful. An additional aim was to elicit nurses' views about strategies which might operate as stress alleviators.

Method

The study was carried out on Taylor Ward, the cancer ward in a London teaching hospital. All nurses joining this ward over a six month period were interviewed three times. The first interview took place within their first week, the remaining two when they had completed their allocation, three months later. The first and second interviews were conducted in groups of peers; in the third, respondents were interviewed alone. Staff *in situ* were also interviewed, once alone and once with colleagues of the same grade. Nurses of all grades staffed the ward; this ranged from auxiliaries, first year students on their first ward placement (firstwarders) to trained sisters.

The ward

The ward was managed by oncology trained nurses and had a very low turnover of qualified staff. Its reputation being that of a caring, supportive ward meant that it was sought after for post qualification posts – all the staff nurses had spent time on Taylor Ward as students and requested returning. In contrast to Wilkinson's (1991) study of a similar ward, Taylor ward was reputed to be adequately staffed and to provide a calm, controlled atmosphere conducive to learning.

Nurses divided patients on Taylor ward into three 'medical' categories:

(1) short stay treatment patients
(2) long stay treatment / palliation patients
(3) terminally ill patients

Short stay treatment patients were admitted overnight for chemotherapy and required little nursing care. They had little contact with student nurses, speaking about treatment options and sometimes emotional issues with trained staff. Nurses of all ranks engaged with both the second and third categories. This chapter focuses on the third group, describing how nurses perceived their roles *vis-à-vis* terminally ill patients.

Findings

The findings of this study challenge previously published works of health workers' responses to caring for dying people. These suggested firstly, that caring for dying people is in itself a cause of stress (Quint 1967, Vachon and Pakes,1984, Vachon 1987) and secondly, that most nurses use blocking tactics to prevent patients from discussing their concerns (Wilkinson 1991). However in this and several subsequently published studies nurses reported that they did not find caring for *dying people* to be *per se* stressful. The stresses they experienced related to preventing them from practising what they conceptualised as *good nursing*. Indeed, the job of *nursing dying patients* fulfilled these nurses' criteria of good nursing. Nurses in this study had particular beliefs which related to their identity as nurses and their aim to provide what they termed 'total care' for their patients. Their worldview did not necessarily categorise patients according to their illness, but as to whether they could provide them with what they viewed as optimal nursing care.

For nurses to be able to provide good nursing care certain conditions had to prevail. These related primarily to the way in which the ward was managed and whether there was congruence between the agenda of ward management and that of the nursing staff. Implicit and explicit rules of behaviour prevailed which set clear boundaries which were perceived as protecting nurses as well as patients' interests and which facilitated opportunities to practise good nursing.

There is insufficient space here to address the rules of behaviour in detail and how they operated. To summarise, these conveyed to nurses how they were expected to manage their emotions, deal with information about patients, and how to behave when patients died.

GOOD NURSING

Nurses aimed to practise good nursing. This meant that all patients' needs, whether emotional, psychological, physical, technical or spiritual, were met with quality care . It required that nurses were well supported and that the ward ran smoothly. There were several components to good nursing; this chapter will focus primarily on nurses' perceptions of providing excellent nursing services, and assessing ànd meeting patients' needs. I intend to show how caring for dying people enabled nurses to provide an excellent *nursing service*, rather than being adjuncts to medical colleagues.

1. The provision of excellent nursing services

This is illustrated by the focus on paying attention to details:

> We learned a lot of detailed things like caring for patients, giving them bed baths, having time to do things like that, silly little things, well not silly, simple things, like cleaning their dentures or washing their faces and hands whereas other people wouldn't have time.

> You should make sure they're comfortable, free of pain, clean having their bowels open, getting rid of their waste, excreting. I think that's how one should look after patients on any ward, because everyone has the same needs.

2. Assessing patients' problems and providing appropriate nursing solutions

The style and content of the handover meeting (ward report) where one shift handed over responsibility to the next is the best illustration of how this was learned and operationalised. Ward report was the forum for conveying *expected behaviour* to nurses – nurses joining the ward were impressed by the style of management on Taylor ward and contrasted this with other wards.

On other wards, it was usual for firstwarders and, often, second year students to attend discussion of their own patients only. They played a passive role simply noting 'instructions'. Nurses viewed ward report on other wards as an efficient mechanism to assign nurses work, transmit 'doctors orders' regarding technical procedures and provide qualified staff with succinct information about patients' conditions. *Ward reports elsewhere were simply communication exercises providing the next nursing shift with depersonalised accounts of patients.* Nurses took copious notes in order to avoid the embarrassment of resorting to trained staff for guidance or obviously seeking information in the kardex. Accounts of ward reports elsewhere resembled those described by Melia (1987) where there were tense meetings during which nurses in charge emphasised the priority of *getting the work done*. Even James's (1986) study of a continuing care unit caring for dying people, described ward report in a similar way.

On Taylor Ward, nurses however junior, presented what they perceived as their patients' problems. Senior nurses probed and prompted them until they were satisfied that student nurses had understood the reasons for decisions taken. Thus through emphasising dialogue and teaching, the nurses in charge ratified students 'learner' status. Students were expected to attend ward report, present patient's problems and learn about good nursing practice through observing how *trained staff and other students debated and discussed their work and came to negotiated solutions*.

Patients' needs were always paramount and it was acknowledged that student nurses may lack skill and expertise when dealing with delicate situations. So there were clear directives about how junior nurses should deal with patients' requests for information. Students thus learned that they were protected by, yet accountable to trained staff. When difficult situations arose, students should turn to their nursing superiors who would then advise them how to handle the problem or would take it on themselves. At all times, students were responsible for their patients. If they neglected their duties or abused the privilege of being a team member they could be sanctioned.

Ward report on Taylor ward was the most significant daily nursing event. It conveyed the principle characteristics of nursing ideology on the ward – *good nursing practice and good nursing education*. The high staff to patient ratio on the ward, and the expectations that students would complete their work in good time to ensure attendance at ward report, facilitated a large turn out. Meanwhile a skeleton staff ran the ward. In addition to assigning work, ward report focused on the following areas.

1. Emphasis on patient's complaint

Nurses' discussions concentrated on their patients' complaints. In contrast to the narrow medical interpretation used on other wards, on Taylor ward these were broadly conceptualised.

> I worked on a ward where a lot of patients had cardiac conditions and the wardsister liked the nurses to write down the condition as being the main problem, whereas it states in the nursing process that the nurse should write down what the patient is complaining of. The patient won't say, 'My main problem today is my myocardial infarction.' He might say, 'It's my bad heart', but he's more likely to say, 'I'm breathless or I have chest pain'. Whereas here, we don't say the patient's main problem is his lymphoma – his main problem is whatever he is complaining about – could be dysphagia – the fact that he can't swallow because he's having radiotherapy. So we actually leave it to the nurse to decide what the patient's main problem is. If we do realise that the nurse is having a problem in deciding priorities we will actually point it out, but we won't disagree with her flatly because of course she's doing the assessing and the reporting.

Through observing the processes at ward report, student nurses learned that they could influence the resolution of their patients' problems in two ways: firstly by assessing the problems through observation and discussion with patients and secondly, by presenting these problems at ward report for consultation with colleagues and superiors which in turn would be relayed to the medical staff if appropriate.

2. Talking to patients

This was a legitimate activity for all nurses on Taylor ward, an essential component of 'nursing care', and the primary route of discovering patients' concerns. In contrast to Wilkinson's (1991) findings, nurses in this study maintained that they routinely asked patients how they felt or what was worrying them. The trained staff encouraged student nurses to recognise the emotional implications for the dying person and their relatives of both the illness and a short term prognosis.

> I think Taylor Ward is different in that sense because there is an awful lot of psychological care, just sitting down and talking to the patients or letting them talk to you ... I like to be able to talk to patients, I don't think you can really assess their needs unless you can sit down and talk

to them – on some wards you just haven't got the chance to do that – you may have 10 or 11 patients that want hoist baths so when do you get the chance to talk to them – that's not nursing to me. I mean that's not nursing the way I like it, I like to be able to get to know patients, and perhaps understand them a bit more.

3. Responding to patients' changing needs

Good nursing included a flexible response to changes in the patient's physical condition as well as spiritual, emotional and social needs. As the ward catered for cancer patients at different stages in their illness trajectory, nurses were dealing with a variety of situations. In relation to dying patients, nurses described how they often anticipated deterioration intuitively and tried to plan care accordingly, even if this meant conflict with medical staff.

4. Respecting patients as individuals

Many nurses entered the ward as advocates of patients' rights to information and control. In addition, the ethos of ward meetings conveyed a strong belief in individualised care. The emphasis on respect for individuals as people with rights and feelings can be exemplified by the care provided to dead patients. Nurses extended the same kind of respect and optimal nursing care to dead patients as they did to living people and were affronted by the lack of courtesy demonstrated by other hospital workers:

> It depends on your view of a dead person anyway – my view is that he's still a person lying there and I don't think of it as a corpse now – like when that nurse died, we both laid her out and the porters came to collect her and they take them down in this awful tin thing and when they lifted her body from the bed onto the thing, they wacked her head really hard on the thing and that really got me and when they wacked her head I said, 'God, watch out, be careful, watch her head'.

5. Dying patients are not a nursing failure

In contrast to the nurses described by Davey (1993) but similar to those in Field's (1989) study, dying patients were seen to be the ultimate challenge to providing total care. Assessing needs of dying people was a particularly valuable skill to acquire:

> I think that probably the most important thing on the ward was to keep people out of pain, making sure they get their painkillers on time ... that stands out in my mind as the primary aim – to keep them comfortable.
> *Do you think this was achieved?*
> On the whole, yeah. I remember going to the doctor one day and he said, 'You can't tell if someone's in pain unless they tell you'. So if somebody is very, very sleepy or unconscious it's obviously difficult to tell whether they're in pain *but you just use your own sort of feelings* – the sister will come up and say, 'Do you think she's in pain?' And you can say yes or no.

Nurses felt they were failing their patients when pain was not adequately controlled:

> With some patients I've felt satisfied just making them comfortable but with Mr S I don't think I was ever satisfied with the way he was nursed – he was continuously in pain and I felt that anything I ever did for him on the nursing side of it – keeping him clean and comfortable didn't really help, because he was still in pain.

The nursing of dying people was seen as a *challenge*, rather than a *threat* to nurses competence.

6. Good nursing is a skill that can be taught and learned

Nurses believed that good nursing care was something that they could learn through teaching, as well as emulation (see Field, this volume). Basic nursing, knowing the essentials of nursing practice, for example, good oral care and techniques to prevent pressure sores, was the foundation and the essential ingredient of good nursing care. Without these skills good nursing was not possible. Terminally ill patients provided an opportunity to perfect basic nursing skills, something which nurses on Taylor Ward strove to achieve.

AREAS OF STRESS

When questioned about the pressures and stresses to which they were subjected nurses highlighted not so much the condition of the patient group but aspects of their work, and for students, their status as learners.

Working as a nurse

Simply 'being a nurse' involved compromise and conflict. These centred primarily around nurses' expectations of what nurses are and how they comport themselves. Nurses felt that their uniform imposed constraints on their behaviour. They also suggested that British culture did not tolerate public expressions of emotion. The nursing school also expected them to maintain an equilibrium and not demonstrate emotion in public. Similar to students in Melia's (1987) study they had to 'fit in' – student nurses 'ought to know their place', respect doctors' competence and neither interfere with patients' treatment nor furnish them with information. This was the remit of the medical staff.

Dealing with death and dying

Nurses noted that a quick succession of deaths was a source of stress, not only because this was emotionally draining but because additional formal procedures were required which interfered with getting on with general nursing care. These procedures sometimes placed 'time' constraints on nurses (see the discussion below).

Working within a multi-disciplinary team

Nurses saw their professional interests and the interests of their patients as congruent. Other disciplines have different agenda and when nurses saw these in conflict with their own, they felt stressed. In particular, certain aspects of the conflict of ideologies between nursing and medicine created difficulties for them. Although the doctors on this ward undertook drug trials, the team on this ward, unlike many other cancer wards, was not engaged in high status clinical research; hence Taylor ward was not prestigious within the medical school pecking order. The low priority of research meant less potential for conflict between doctors and nurses regarding the appropriateness of treatment for certain patients. Nurses commended the medical staff for their general willingness to accede to patients' requests for cessation of treatment contrasting this with incidents that they had observed on other wards.

However when conflict between doctors and nurses arose this usually related either to differences in approach to pain relief or to providing patients with information about their condition. Medical staff occasionally refrained from increasing patients' pain relief on the basis of the danger of side effects. Where nurses were of the firm opinion that the patient was moribund, they found the doctor's reluctance to provide maximum pain relief intolerable.

Managing one's work

'Time' and 'Trust' were two themes which nurses frequently referred to – when these were compatible nurses were enabled to manage their work without feeling stressed or compromised.

Time

Nurses conflated stress with pressures of work, in particular the time to do good nursing. This ward usually facilitated ***good nursing*** through more than adequate staffing levels.

> You haven't got the same work as ordinary nurses have – it's very quiet. You don't do nearly the same work – we get lots of afternoons off whereas on other wards they really work hard. Everything is very spaced – it's such a different ward from nursing on other wards. You're just with people all the time that you know are probably dying, whereas on any other ward you've got all the nursing work plus probably that one patient too ... One thing it wasn't, it was never pressurised, never, no. Many patients are so independent in that way I'm so used to just sitting down, chatting to people for about an hour

> I enjoy this sort of nursing – I don't like to be under too much pressure. I did like the aspect where you can have time to get to know people as people and not as bodies – you've got too many things to do in some cases on the surgical wards – you don't tend to look at the patient as a person as a whole – in some cases I began to get myself totally wrapped up in just the technical side of what I had to do to people rather than being able to treat them like people and talk to them – that's why I like this ward especially – you get to know people better and get to know their families.

Nevertheless several situations peculiar to Taylor ward did create the sense of work pressures despite sufficient staffing levels. Student nurses felt under pressure when there was a disproportionate number of high dependency patients requiring frequent surveillance or when nursing care was disrupted by additional drug rounds to provide relief to patients in pain. Adjusting frequently to new patients or new allocations was also time consuming and frustrating when students would have preferred to provide continuity of care to their existing patients. Qualified nurses found management responsibilities restricted the time they could spend with patients. They were particularly stressed when they felt that administrative demands took precedence over patients' needs.

Trust

Nurses emphasised the importance of the trusting relationship between patient and nurse. The different components and aspects of disclosure (informing patients about diagnosis and prognosis) are hotly debated in the literature (James, 1986; Field 1989, Davey 1993; Katz 1993;) and these will not be rehearsed here. Suffice it to say that there was no consistent disclosure policy evident on Taylor ward. Consultants' beliefs and practices ranged from full disclosure to blatant concealment. Nurses found this confusing and initially complained that they were not informed about patients' diagnoses and prognoses. Unlike nurses in Davey's (1993) study, where nurses felt obliged to tow the party line and keep patients in the dark, nurses on Taylor Ward observed a range of disclosure behaviours.

Although most nurses entered the ward believing that all patients had the right to full information on moral grounds, they soon modified their views acknowledging that this was not necessarily always in the patient's best interests:

> Sometimes telling the patient is as traumatic as not telling them, depending completely on the person's character. A patient, for instance, who was told his full diagnosis and realised immediately what it meant, he wasn't going to get better, just went down hill from then onwards and wouldn't speak to the registrar who told him – every time the registrar went into his room, he wouldn't speak to him – he'd done this terrible deed, telling him.

Most junior nurses joined the ward believing fervently that most patients should have as much information as possible to enable them to make decisions about their own lives. However once nurses began to accept that not all patients wanted this information and were comfortable with others making decisions, they no longer viewed non-disclosure as a cause of stress nor feared patients' questioning. In this move away from wanting to empower patients, to the view that 'individual patient's wishes must be respected' – nurses gradually adopted the philosophy of individualisation of care. Their explanation may be seen as reflecting an acceptance of ward philosophy that not all patients want to have details about their conditions but that they require sufficient detail to reassure and motivate them to accept treatment or palliation. As with all other areas of care, decisions were based on the assessment of the individual patient's needs. As long as nurses felt that the disclosure issue did not impede the trust they were building up with the patient, they were willing to accept variations in disclosure practice. In addition, non-disclosure often presented nurses with a strategy for coping with what might potentially have been stressful encounters with patients.

For some younger nurses, the disclosure issue remained a cause of stress throughout their allocation to the ward. They felt that the denial of information to patients, irrespective of patients' apparent wishes, inferred sub-optimal nursing practice. They felt coerced into colluding with deceptions imposed upon them by others.

NURSES VIEWS ON SUPPORT

Nurses perceptions of support usually related to a well managed ward with supportive, non-punitive qualified staff who recognised and tried to meet the students varied needs which included emotional and educational support. Certain extra-mural activities also contributed to their sense of wellbeing.

Nurses often equated support with leisure needs and complained about the lack of facilities. Like nurses in Baldwin's (1981) study they felt the need to 'work off' tensions in a physical sense. Some nurses used the hospital pool before or after work. Others wanted access to a gym with an attending physiotherapist (to treat their back problems). Nurses' emphasis on leisure as providing support can be seen to reflect the same belief system which led to the appointment of a *social secretary* in the School of Nursing. The statement of her duties included arranging sporting fixtures with other nursing schools, in addition to planning parties, theatre outings and suchlike.

Students regarded the provision of leisure time as crucial to coping. Third years felt that studying for impending exams reduced their opportunities for leisure considerably and increased their vulnerability to stress. They suggested that reduced ward responsibilities during the pre-examination period would be a supportive measure.

The concept of psychological support

Most student nurses believed that the provision of specialised psychological support would be inappropriate. A great deal of suspicion surrounded psychology and psychologists. Even those who viewed positively the concept of imported support were divided over how it would best work on Taylor Ward. Students with previous geriatric or psychiatric experience were more positive about the concept of imported counselling. Like nurses in Baider and Porath's (1981) study, they felt group discussions at work were helpful but not essential. Student nurses who had not experienced previous group discussions were hostile to the idea.

Some trained nurses reported that they had previously benefited from formal support groups. At her first interview the new sister said she planned to introduce these. However three months later she believed that regular formal sessions would not be appropriate for this ward.

> One day things on the ward were pretty heavy-going and we decided to all sit down and talk about how we're coping but we went right off at a tangent, we had an absolute laugh about something that was totally irrelevant, nothing to do with the ward and afterwards I said to the doctors and trained nurses that were there, that it didn't really work out as it was supposed to, we were really supposed to be talking about how we felt and our problems and we all agreed that what we really needed was to sort of sit down as a group and *know that* we were all finding it difficult, we had acknowledged that.

Nurses believed that when individuals flagged, the structure of the ward would respond to provide the required support through re-allocation of duties and on site support. Nurses thus envisaged that when necessary, support would be provided on an *ad hoc* basis – hence regular formalized support sessions were inappropriate:

> If one was going to have counselling sessions every Wednesday from 2–3, (a) nurses might not be feeling perplexed by anything anyway and (b) we might be too busy. So it should be, I think, spontaneous.

> I think a group would have seemed strained. I think if you want to talk about something it must be spontaneous. I think organising something like that would be a total waste of time because I don't think you're letting your feelings show really. I think setting aside a certain time like that is creating an artificial situation. I think if you want to talk about something, you talk about it whether it's to other members of staff or to friends.

Nurses established their own private support networks. Unlike nurses in Bond's (1982) study some talked to their peers and found it cathartic:

> I've got the two sisters to talk to ... I would talk to them and all the qualified staff should support each other.

> Depends what it is, if it's about another student then I'd probably talk to my setmate, if it's generally about the ward, then any student.

> You identify people who are good listeners

Many nurses derived support from out of work contacts. Some spoke to their boyfriends, parents or flatmates about troublesome work issues. Other nurses suggested that they compartmentalised work issues, separating them from their private lives. They found the distraction of out of work activities therapeutic. Nurses generally felt that they did not want to be forced to discuss their feelings with colleagues or superiors.

CONCLUSION

Nurses in this study perceived that as nurses, they had a particularly useful role to play *vis-à-vis* dying patients; one which no other profession could provide. With adequate staffing levels and sympathetic nursing management sharing similar goals and perspectives about nursing, nurses of all grades could strive to provide good nursing care and rehearse all the components of basic nursing care. Good nursing encompassed all spheres of patients' needs including responding to emotional concerns. The shared worldview of nurses on this ward enabled them to confront and deal with pressures and stresses which nurses caring for dying people in other studies, have found debilitating and undermining of their skills.

11 Police Coping with Death: Assumptions and Rhetoric

Margaret Mitchell

POLICE DUTIES IN RELATION TO DEATH

Police officers, in their work with the community, are exposed to death and dead bodies and attend what are called 'sudden deaths'. These are defined as deaths which are 'not preceded by illness, or where illness is present for only a short time before death'(Scottish Police College Training Notes, 1991). The function of this duty, in legal terms, is to investigate the possibility of suspicious circumstances surrounding the death. More generally, the purpose is to ascertain whether the death requires a report to the Procurator Fiscal in Scotland (for whom the police act as agents), or in England, to the Coroner.

Media representations of the police fuel the public perception of their involvement in death as primarily occurring in dramatic or traumatic circumstances. Yet the most common sudden death the police have to attend is that in which a person, most often elderly, is found dead at home. To be certified dead, a certificate must be issued by a doctor, although in many cases involving old people, the family doctor may not have seen the person for months or even years. Having no recent medical history there is insufficient information on which to base a death certificate. Mostly, these cases are subsequently dealt with quite quickly because further investigation is not required and the person is deemed to have died of 'natural causes'.

Police officers are also involved in deaths which result from homicide or manslaughter, suicide, drug misuse, alcohol or poison, road traffic fatality, domestic accident, neglect, industrial accident or disease, or various surgical procedures. In addition, and essentially because of the lack of clinical knowledge about the cause, the police are also involved in Sudden Infant Death Syndrome (SIDS) or 'cot death'. Certain deaths, particularly deaths in custody, require investigation by the police and a mandatory public enquiry in the form of an Fatal Accident Inquiry in Scotland, or Inquest in England and Wales.

Police involvement in sudden death is not simply a paper exercise with limited direct or 'hands-on' experience. On the contrary, it is evident from Police Training Notes that when officers are called to a sudden death there is both considerable exposure to the dead body and contact with the relatives of the deceased.

At the scene, or 'locus', the officer must first ascertain that the person, from all outward appearances, is dead or whether an ambulance should be called. Before a person officially can be deemed dead, the body must be examined by a doctor to pronounce 'life extinct'. In some cases the doctor will be prepared to sign a death certificate giving the cause(s) of death; if a certificate is provided and there are no suspicious circumstances, the police are no longer involved in any formal procedures, other than a brief report. If further investigation is required, the police 'take possession of the body' (although the situation is somewhat different in some areas in England), and inform the Procurator Fiscal (or Coroner) and then arrange for post mortem examination. This is obviously a situation which relatives find difficult to understand, and to bear.

As an overriding frame of reference, police officers are required to think about any death as potentially suspicious, because, a 'death caused through violence, or in suspicious circumstances, may appear to have been a death by natural causes, and vice versa. It is, therefore, important that officers keep an open mind, view the evidence objectively, and avoid the use of mere supposition' (Scottish Police College Training Notes, 1991: 2). For evidential purposes, the officer must take careful note of the 'position of the body, description of the deceased's clothing and any features which may assist the inquiry at a later stage' (ibid). Since the 'locus' is potentially a scene of crime it must be preserved for possible criminal investigation purposes. This can pose difficulties for all concerned; when there are relatives in the house, there is a tendency for them to search through the deceased's personal effects thus disturbing potential evidence.

It is also the responsibility of the police officer to arrange for a funeral director to take the deceased to the mortuary. There the officer will conduct a full search of the body. Dependent upon the mortuary arrangements prevailing in the geographical area, the officer who was initially called to the sudden death will strip and note the condition of the body and, where appropriate, take clothing as evidence. This aspect of police work in Scotland is contentious. There is considerable debate about whether it should be part of police duties and whether it is essential for the appropriate collection of evidence. Should this task be carried out by police officers or undertaken by a more specialised organisation? In some urban areas, the officer obtains the evidence from the body but the actual task of stripping the body is carried out by mortuary attendants. It is noteworthy that these 'hands-on' tasks were required of police officers at the site of the Lockerbie air disaster of 1988 where several hundred police officers worked in the mortuary.

The police also make arrangements for the relatives to be informed of the death (delivering 'death messages' as it is known in the police service). Particularly in the case of people living in social isolation, the whereabouts of the next of kin are often unknown and the home needs to be searched for information about relatives. Often, a friend or neighbour – who may have been the initial informant about the death – will offer to tell the family. In quite the opposite situation, the home may be full of relatives who are emotionally distressed. Either way, the officer must ensure that this is done. From the perspective of the officer coping with this duty, distress can be associated both with exposure to the dead body and with the need to communicate with relatives.

It is often thought that in the course of their normal duties police officers are frequently exposed to sudden death (Brown 1994). However, obtaining actual exposure rates per officer is difficult: Brown and Forde (1989) found that sixty-five per cent of the constables they surveyed in the Hampshire Constabulary had attended a sudden death during the previous six months. Further estimates can be obtained from the number of sudden death reports to the Procurator Fiscal. In 1992, in the Strathclyde region (when there were 5204 constables) 4365 sudden deaths were reported to the Procurator Fiscal: these included 213 suicides, 188 accidental deaths, 64 murders, 382 manslaughter, and 52 culpable homicides – 899 violent deaths in total.

According to these figures, exposure might be at the rate of approximately one or two sudden deaths per year, although individual exposure will vary greatly according to geographical location and assigned duties. Calculating likely exposure per officer from reports to the Procurator Fiscal can also be misleading because the police attend many sudden deaths which are not subsequently reported to the Fiscal. Writing of American police activities, Williams (1987), noted that only six per cent of calls for police assistance bring the officers in contact with highly stressful situations and that by far the majority of police time is spent in more routine performance of duty. While the exposure of police officers to death and dead bodies may be greater than that in other occupations, it is likely that individual officers could go through several years of service without any exposure. Whatever the level of exposure to death and dead bodies, the question arises as to how police officers cope with such work.

COPING WITH DEATH

Compared with the amount of research on disaster work, surprisingly little research exists on how police officers deal with routine exposure to death (Duckworth 1986; Mitchell *et al.* 1991). Yet there seems to be an implicit assumption that officers are tough, and cope well with more routine exposures (Joyce 1989). When this latter perspective is discussed in police writing it is often anecdotal, and it seems that the cultural assumptions both within and outwith the police have blocked more careful examination. Identifying and critically examining assumptions about police practice is of psychological interest.

As will be discussed later, my own study of public and police perceptions concerning vulnerability to emotional distress uncovered quite clear expectations about coping (Mitchell 1994). From a list of 'categories' of people (presented in no particular order), the study sample were asked to rate which groups of people they thought would be vulnerable to emotional distress as a result of witnessing a traumatic incident, and who they thought would be least vulnerable. In Table 11.1 the numbers refer to a mean rating on a six point scale where a low score implies a perception of that type of person as unlikely to experience emotional distress. Overall, workers in the emergency services were seen as significantly less vulnerable to emotional distress.

Old people and females were seen as most likely to experience an emotional reaction; children (pre-adolescents), adolescents, middle aged people and young adults were seen as rather less vulnerable; and males, unemployed people and working people were regarded as even less vulnerable. People working as police officers, fire fighters or in the ambulance service were seen as relatively invulnerable, obtaining the lowest rating overall.

Table 11.1

Lay (public) perceptions of the likelihood of experiencing an emotional reaction to witnessing a traumatic incident

police officers; fire fighters; ambulance workers	2.7
working people	3.5
young adults; middle aged people; males; unemployed people	4.0
old people; females	4.6

This exercise was repeated with a sample of forty-four police inspectors with an average length of police service of twelve years. They, too, perceived emergency service workers as being least vulnerable. In particular, police and other emergency workers were seen as protected compared to other 'working males'. So from this data it is clear that both for the public and within the police service, there exists a perception that police officers cope well with their exposure to death on the job. Furthermore, there is a clearly perceived hierarchy of vulnerability in which police and other emergency service workers are considered immune to distress.

Habituation

What explains these findings? Outside of the police, there may exist views that police work is tough and that police officers deal with trauma and death as an everyday occurrence. It might be argued that their exposure leads to their becoming habituated, and hence to emotional 'hardiness'. This is often referred to as 'habituation' and is used in the same sense and analogously with its use in physiology. In the context of police work it is a persuasive idea; for example, in Brown's (1994) review of stress in policing it is an explicit assumption. The social perception that exposure leads to hardiness seems to have infiltrated police thinking or may, indeed, have originated there – it is hard to disentangle the source.

Much of the argument is tautological, however, and is also based on a misconception of what habituation constitutes, so some explanation of the concept in psychological and physiological terms is needed. Habituation is a physiological process by which repeated exposure to a stimulus results in a waning of the usual response, to the point that it is extinguished (Hayes 1994). By analogy to a physiological response, the dead body is seen as the stimulus and the emotional reaction as the response. Through exposure, it may be believed that the officer becomes habituated and this dulls and then extinguishes the potential emotional response. But it is only through consistent and repetitive exposure that habituation would occur because it depends on regular and repeated presentation of the stimulus. It is very likely, however, that this does not happen in the course of routine police duties. Furthermore, the concept of habituation refers to low level physiological responses (for example, a snail pulling back within its shell when touched); the analogy may be stretched beyond meaning into the domain of a cognitively and emotionally complex reaction such as distress in response to a dead body or a traumatic incident.

How true is it that the more exposure to death an officer has, the more inured he or she is to the experience? There has been barely any systematic research to answer this question. When a police officer has seen one dead body, do all dead bodies thereafter seem the same (as in 'seen one, seen them all')? Research on the response of police officers to work at civilian disasters suggests that individual officers may continue to be profoundly affected by their experiences. This was clearly established at Hillsborough (Hayes 1992), at the Bradford Football Stadium fire (Duckworth, 1986) and at Lockerbie (Mitchell *et al.* 1991).

What accounts for individual variation? A number of explanations can be forwarded including the officer's personal disposition or attributes, the work context, and their previous training or personal experience. Most likely, individual vulnerability is the consequence of a combination of several of these factors. But whatever the explanation, the basic finding that individual officers can react badly to demanding work fundamentally questions the assumption that immunity necessarily goes 'with the territory'. By extension, the emotional immunity to death work noted in some officers is not simply explained by the accumulation of their experience with death on the job (the frequency of which would in any event seem to be overestimated. Despite this, and in the face of statistical evidence to the contrary, Joyce, a serving UK police officer, in a rhetorical piece states that, 'death by accident or design, mutilated bodies, evidence of suffering and pain are part of every police officer's routine experience' (Joyce 1989: 380).

Training

It seems, then, that the assumption that regular exposure results in immunity is not well founded; yet elements of this thinking are found in the way recruits are trained. Brown (1992) believes that while methods of training may eventually become more responsive to contemporary thinking, the police culture is essentially resistant to change and so perpetuates beliefs about itself. One of these cultural elements is that officers are *ipso facto* emotionally tough and resilient. In the context of training police recruits to deal with death, Joyce (1989) writes that formal police training is designed to provide 'the legal and practical means for dealing with death. In addition, recruits might visit a local mortuary to witness a post mortem. While this is not necessarily a requirement of training most recruits still fear making fools of themselves in front of their colleagues and will go' (Joyce 1989: 381). This suggests that it is probably true that the culture of the police, variously described as 'masculine', 'aggressive' or 'tough' (Brown 1994: 151), may lead to a further obfuscation to thinking. Video films of road traffic accidents and other sudden deaths are also shown during most police training programmes; on the same basis, the visit to the mortuary is accompanied by neither preparation nor debriefing. While the visit or video is a controlled introduction to the practicalities of identifying bodies, Joyce states that the 'handling of the recruits own emotions is totally ignored' (Joyce 1989: 381).

It is significant for the training and acculturation of probationers that they are routinely taken out on calls with tutor constables to attend sudden deaths: quite explicitly to see how they manage. Probationers' exposure to such work is higher than that for serving officers and higher ranks, and this is reflected in a survey conducted by Brown and Forde (1989). They found that eighty-three per cent of probationers had attended sudden death in the previous six months, compared to sixty-five per cent of constables and fifty per cent of sergeants and inspectors. Clearly, this reflects the idea that exposure is 'good for' probationers and is part of their initiation. Furthermore, the advice that colleagues and tutors give on dealing with exposure or on personal coping is not known but it most likely reflects the social culture of the police. It would appear then, that the informal aspect of training which takes place during on the street experience allows an opportunity for the 'tough culture' to be passed on. In contrast to this seemingly rough handling of probationers, the Report of the Chief Constable of Strathclyde (1992) states that in terms of the public: 'tact and compassion are primary requirements in the investigation and reporting of sudden deaths' (Strathclyde Regional Council 1992: 7).

Further evidence that attending sudden death calls is part of the socialisation of younger officers learning the ropes is reflected by Stratton (1984), speaking of the training of police officers in the United States. He refers to the police officers', 'macho image, their need for non-emotional responses and their penchant for seeking out the most life threatening and violent assignments' (Stratton 1984: 281). The theme that younger officers hold or adopt this cultural stereotype is reflected thus: 'New inexperienced police officers tend to exaggerate their abilities and emphasise physical strength and ruggedness. Young officers have a need to believe that they are invulnerable and can handle any kind of danger' (Stratton 1984: 281). However, Williams, in a similar context, acknowledges that recruits are not disabused of the idea and that, 'training and peer response reinforce this behaviour' (Williams 1987: 269).

Black or gallows humour

A further belief about coping within the police service is the notion that so-called 'black humour' is used as a strategy. In the most explicit statement of its use, Joyce (a British police officer), in his article, 'Why do police officers laugh at death?', posits that, 'any potential for a joke may be seized on however black the humour' (Joyce 1989: 380). He goes on to list several lame jokes as examples of how police officers interact with each other, and provides only anecdotal support for the idea that black humour is a strategy frequently used by officers. Here again, the fact that it is perceived by police officers to be a common strategy seems to imply that it is effective. The focus of the previous section, that police recruits absorb a specific cultural style is also reflected here. This is reinforced by Joyce: 'recruits to the service, witnessing the emotionless, light hearted way in which colleagues confront deaths and other tragic events, quickly learn how to adopt similar disguises' (Joyce 1989: 380). Such assertions are not based on research, but reflect only the writer's point of view or personal recollections. As such they do not help us to know whether black humour is actually used, or whether it is an effective prophylactic.

However, there is some reason to think that this strategy might be useful. For example, Kahn (1989) states that humour can serve a coping function by allowing individuals to become 'detached from threatening aspects of the situation they find themselves in' (Kahn 1989: 57). He then points out that emergency service workers use humour, 'in a way that appears to outsiders to be callous, but which in reality allows them to cope with things that are happening' (Kahn 1989: 59). This notion of 'outsiders' who observe this seemingly inappropriate behaviour, and 'insiders' (for example, the police) is also reflected in the following: 'Outsiders to the law enforcement culture frequently deplore police officers' seemingly indifferent or irresponsible behaviour, but they don't understand how important it is for self preservation . . . gallows humour is common to those dangerous occupations; it reflects a need to distance oneself from the emotional intensity of experiences' (Williams 1989: 269). It is thus held that not only is black humour used, but also that members of the public observe and disapprove of this behaviour. But when do members of the public ever witness this behaviour? Since only anecdotal rather than empirical evidence is provided, issues of interest are: first, what is the degree to which black humour is actually used; second, if it is used, what function does it serve; and third, why is there an apparent necessity in writing on the subject to separate the needs and perceptions of 'outsiders' and 'insiders'?

The Lockerbie study

Recent data on the use of black humour and other strategies for coping with sudden death calls, became available in my own empirical research into the experiences of officers who worked at the site of the Lockerbie air disaster of 1988.[1] This civilian disaster, occurring as a result of a jumbo jet being blown up by a terrorist bomb, resulted in the deaths of 270 people. Police officers from several constabularies in Scotland worked at the site, including almost 2000 from Strathclyde Police. Significantly, for our present discussion, no additional training or preparation was provided for the officers who attended. In this, one recognises a dependence within police management on the idea that the officers would be capable of coping with dead and mutilated bodies because of their having dealt with death at some time in the course of routine duties. The data collected, approximately six weeks after the disaster, provides evidence that the officers did not simply 'take it in their stride'.

As part of the study a questionnaire comprising both highly structured and open-ended questions was completed by 948 of the Strathclyde police officers who had been in attendance at the Lockerbie site. Not all officers completed the open-ended section which invited them to write whatever they wished about the experience. Amongst the 329 who took this opportunity, there was little evidence of the emotional hardiness so important a part of police cultural rhetoric. Indeed, none of the statements reflected a hardened approach to the work, nor did any reflect the use of black humour. The following fairly typical statements will illustrate these points:

> The fact that by the sheer number of casualties the deceased had been reduced to a mere number . . [and] . . on seeing the number of bodies, my initial reaction was I wonder what the relatives are thinking. I felt anger towards the perpetrators of this act and wished that they were doing the job in which me and my colleagues were involved.

> Discovering personal items such as a child's handbag, photographs and clothing. I experienced a feeling of hopelessness due to the fact that all the boys were doing was cleaning the countryside around Lockerbie.

> I felt saddened by the needless loss of human life.

> I look at the incidents I have dealt with and feel that they pale into insignificance compared to the Lockerbie disaster.

> I was reluctant to leave my baby daughter on going out as several of the bodies I handled were of a similar age and appearance.

> Seeing a small child on the slab at the embalming room it made me realise the senselessness of blowing up the plane.

> I was deeply affected by the scale and the cause of the disaster and not having been to such a situation either in my police service or personal life.
>
> I wondered if they were dead when they hit the ground.
>
> Due to the magnitude of the incident it was almost impossible to dissociate one's feelings. Amongst my workmates I do not believe there are any who have experienced a tragedy so immense. I feel that owing to the scale of the occurrence and the time of year, it was commented on by members of my family that I was not my 'usual self'.
>
> I tend to think of the passengers and what went through their mind the instant it happened. I came across various items of clothing which were bloodstained and these made me feel quite depressed at the time.
>
> I have never experienced death on such a large scale before and hope I never do again.

The various themes which emerge from these and other comments not only reflect the officers' shock and surprise at the scale of the task, but also the view that their previous experience of police work had not been adequate preparation for this work. Also reflected is the personalising of the material and bodies they were working with, and the inability of the officers to distance themselves from the real people who had been killed. The scale of the disaster and the nature of the injuries which had led to the deaths likely added a quite different dimension to the task and this may have stretched the officers' normal coping. Nevertheless there exists the implicit expectation, even by the officers themselves, that they would cope because of their previous experience, and that they are hardened to such tasks.

A second and more structured section of the survey questionnaire took a standard list of fourteen commonly used coping strategies to assess which were used by the officers. A particular question tested whether black humour was frequently adopted as a method of coping. The officers worked in three broad categories of duties: in the mortuary; on search and recovery; and on traffic and patrol. Amongst the data obtained, questionnaires were completed by one hundred and twenty four officers who had worked in the mortuary. Their exposure to mortuary duty was not lengthy: the majority of the sample (eighty-seven per cent) spent only one day at the mortuary; a further eight per cent were there for two days; and the remainder for periods of up to eleven days. It emerged that black humour was used either 'quite a bit' or 'a great deal' (two of the rating categories) by only thirteen officers in the sample. It was by no means the predominant strategy. Perhaps it was the extreme nature of the Lockerbie tragedy that resulted in the minimal use of this strategy. In more routine work, however, it may be that the incidence of black humour is overestimated. The majority of officers who are simply getting on with the job and keeping their feelings to themselves will not be noticed in the same way as someone who is trying to cheer themselves or other people up with off-colour jokes. The salience of the behaviour could well lead to an overestimate of its incidence in these settings.

It is not clear from this study whether those officers who acknowledged using black humour were themselves originators of the jokes or whether they were simply a party to other people's behaviour or statements. Perhaps there are humourists working in the police who set themselves up in that role, and indeed, there may be an in-group or out-group mechanism operating. Perhaps the use of humour is also situation specific, and its acceptability dependent on the nature of the death. It may not be acceptable, for instance, at the death of child. But at what time during or after the exposure is it appropriate? Perhaps not at the time, but it might be useful after the duty as part of a process of distancing from the work. A further question is whether certain strategies might be adopted at the time, but not in the longer term. It is quite likely that those which help to get the job done at the time are not necessarily the best for dealing with death experiences in the longer term. So the personal use, relevance or function of humour is unclear and, therefore, only a very limited interpretation can be made about the *function* of this particular strategy. But the fact that it is used *at all* provides the groundwork for a more thorough analysis of how officers cope with the different situations in which they have to face death.

CONCLUSION

The purpose of this chapter has been to consider and make explicit the assumptions upon which much of police practice and indeed police training is based. It is evident that the dependence on habituation is unfounded, particularly when this is carried over into extreme situations such as dealing with the scale and the carnage of death at the site of the Lockerbie disaster. Whilst the overriding assumption is that the police deal well and competently with death work, this study provides evidence which gives cause for concern.

In conclusion it can be said that workers in the emergency services do 'get on with the job' to the best of their ability and in accordance with the formal and informal training they have received. But the police service needs to be aware that the assumed prophylactic effect of on-the-job experience coupled with the macho culture, may be a myth. Equally, members of the public should not be surprised when this cultural rhetoric breaks down and it is found that officers have difficulty coping with death work. Simply signing up to do this type of work does not ensure appropriate responses. Police officers are individuals, and are not simply constituents of a homogeneous occupational group. As Wright (1988) points out, 'the main issues – grief, anguish and the realisation that we may have little or no control over our lives – are the same for us all'. Recent evidence suggests that to help police officers to cope they require something other than a tough attitude, and that programmes of intelligent, structured support are needed because the emotional protection afforded by becoming accustomed to death work may be more rhetorical than real (Braddan *et al.* 1993).

Notes

The assistance of Inspector David Thomson of Strathclyde Police Force Training Centre in discussing some of the ideas in this chapter, and in providing me with information on the training of police probationers is gratefully acknowledged.

1. This research into 'The Health Effects of Duty at the site of the Lockerbie Air Disaster' was funded by Strathclyde Regional Council.

Part 4

Social Implications of Legal and Medical Responses to Death and Dying

12 Death and the Disease: Inside the Culture of Childhood Cancer

Stephen J. Ball, Sarah Bignold and Alan Cribb

This chapter is about death, and the possibility and ever presence of death, as experienced by the families of children with cancer. It is about what we will call the culture of childhood cancer – those primary meanings and shared perspectives which develop in relation to the *trajectory of uncertainty* which underlies the social and emotional impact of the disease and its treatment. The *culture of childhood cancer* has both subjective and objective forms. The former, and most significant, are the meanings and experiences which are mobilised around the trajectory of uncertainty; they are founded upon the unpredictability inherent in the diagnosis and treatment of cancers. The latter are represented by particular professional sites and social relationships (with carers and other families) which families encounter in the trajectory of uncertainty. These are the bases for a community of cancer, within which the positive aspects of the culture are most fully developed. The distinction between the culture and community allows us to recognise and acknowledge that some families have little participation in the community of cancer (by choice or by default) and are only peripherally drawn into the culture (or at least its positive aspects).[1]

This culture has two sides or faces to it. On one side, is a cultural ensemble of fear and whispers, uncertainty and equivocation – these are the bases of tensions, doubt and misunderstanding (between families and professional carers *and* between those 'inside' the culture and those on the 'outside' and also sometimes within families). On the other side, there is an ensemble of hope, struggle and support – from here sharing, strength, gratitude and long lasting relationships emerge (between families and professional carers and families and friends and relatives). This double-edgedness is central to almost all facets of the trajectory of uncertainty. Thus, treatment both holds out the hope of cure and involves the pain and rigours of side effects. Check-ups can mean another clear result or the awfulness of recurrence. Every encounter with a doctor can mean good news or bad, or most often no firm news at all. The regional centre, the oncology ward, the radiography unit are sites of hope and fear, support and suspicion.[2]

CANCER AND DEATH

Despite the significant medical advances made in cancer treatment in recent years and particularly in the treatment of children with cancer, the disease remains strongly associated with death in the popular imagination. Many of the parents we interviewed began to anticipate the death of their child as soon as their illness became associated with the possibility of cancer.

> Yes, literally … I've never … I mean I've known him 15 years and I've never seen him cry up until that day and ... he just thought oh my god, she's gonna die, she's gonna die (Mrs Price talking about her husband).[3]

> ... and then they used the word chemotherapy and things, and operations and it began to fall into place – that was something I'd heard of – and then from then on I thought she's going to die, because cancer spelt death really ... I'd planned her funeral that weekend ... just in my mind that spelt a death sentence.
>
> (Mrs Woods)

Within our society *cancer, death and children* form a particularly powerful triangle of pain and fear. 'Children are not supposed to die, certainly not before their parents. In fact child death is not only emotionally, psychologically and physically the most painful experience one can encounter, it is also philosophically unintelligible in today's world; it defies the natural order of things' (Knapp 1986: 14). In some of our interviews the 'evil' of cancer is counterpointed to the 'innocence of childhood'.

> I couldn't believe … why Claire … such an innocent little girl, but now I think, oh it's just one of those things, you know … nothing you can do about it. And when her friend died, she was only three ... Claire used to sit with her every night when she was in hospital, and when she died I felt really … really bitter … because she was such a gorgeous little girl. You just can't believe why some make it and some don't.
>
> (Mrs Jones)

> I mean there's little enough known about the actual disease, that's bad enough, that it's so evil in that it's something that happens by itself ... nobody can explain to you why.
>
> (Mrs Coulby)

The point here is that the cause or origins of the disease cannot be lodged in or related to any behaviours or life style deficiencies of the child. It strikes randomly and mercilessly.

THE TRAJECTORY OF UNCERTAINTY

Child cancer is relatively rare, there are many varieties, many types of cancer are poorly understood by medical science; the diagnosis of cancer, especially in its early stages is difficult, malignancy and growth are not directly related in all cases; the rigours of treatment, side effects and secondary illnesses complicate prognosis. All of these factors constitute a material basis for uncertainty (McIntosh 1977). Discussions with parents about their children are set within this framework of doubt and unpredictability. Davis (1966) makes the point that uncertainty may be increased by deliberate withholding of information, 'other factors, interests and circumstances intrude in the rendering of medical prognoses' (1966: 318); for example he and McIntosh found the 'doctors had theories about the kind of patient who might "really" want to know and who would react well to being told' (McIntosh 1977: 32). Doubt, uncertainty and equivocation are never easy to deal with at the best of times; in a context where death is an ever present possibility uncertainty can become unbearable. The need to know; to know something, anything, is a key element of parents coping with their child's illness. As noted already the nexus of uncertainty and hope is one of the key axes of the culture of childhood cancer.

The trajectory (Glaser and Strauss 1968) of uncertainty in relation to child cancer has four major phases, elements or transitional statuses, each marked by key points of transition or status passages: from illness to diagnosis; from diagnosis through one or several rounds of treatment; from treatment to recovery or palliative care (becoming terminal); and death. Tragically uncertainty is only finally resolved for those families whose children 'become terminal', the recovery status is hedged around by continuing doubts and equivocations – for example, the possibility of greater susceptibility to new cancers in later life. In a sense no child is ever cured of cancer but they may experience prolonged remission and decreasing chances of recurrence. Ross (1978) uses a similar trajectory in her discussion of social work intervention with families of children with cancer.

FROM ILLNESS TO DIAGNOSIS

Child illnesses or parental unease about the health of their children tend to be responded to by GPs on the basis of their experience that almost all health problems are minor and treatable by relatively simple remedies. The major difference between GPs seems to be in the length of time and the degree of certainty with which they maintain this position. In our cases initial misdiagnosis by GPs (and sometimes by local hospitals) is almost the norm. Crucial, in relation to this, is the point that most GPs will only see one child with cancer during the whole of their working lives.

> She lost weight ... she was tired, she just kept complaining of being tired ... but she wasn't ill ... you know ... nothing ... that we could kind of say ... she was really ill with. She had a cough, she had a bad cough ... took her to the doctors, and he thought it was an ear infection ... and she just got worse from then on, for about a week she just laid on the settee and wouldn't eat, so I called him back out again and they took her into hospital and they found it through tests.
>
> (Mrs Jones)

But there are some exceptions.

> My local GP was absolutely wonderful ... he thought when he poked Andrew that he had something on his liver ... but he said because it was so big, and the child's liver and kidney are so close together ... he had rung St Mary's and said I think this child has got a tumour, so he was on the ball before we even arrived in St Mary's.
>
> (Mrs Green)

At the point of referral to a specialist centre cancer becomes a possibility or a definite diagnosis (one of the few moments of awful certainty). The child moves between statuses; from being a sick child to a child with cancer. (It is here that the initial associations with death, presented above, come into play.) While the specialist professional carers may not be certain, they do communicate an understanding of cancer and its effects which are normally totally absent in generalist settings. They speak the language of cancer. The families begin their induction into the culture of childhood cancer.

> On getting to the Infirmary eventually ... after the Hickman line had been put in and a needle biopsy had been done, because she was too poorly to have a full biopsy, and obviously the specialist nursing care made all the difference. I mean it was absolutely tremendous, because everybody treated you quite differently. We'd had a very unhappy time at Queen Anne's ... it was really quite awful.
>
> (Mrs Atkinson)

> Oh he's brilliant, he is such a lovely man. You see at Burgess you don't question them because they're doctors ... you know, but up there, I mean he's a consultant ... but I mean we're on first names ... and we sit there and have coffee and cake together, and talk about anything, and you can ask him anything and he tells you anything ... but at Burgess they're like in the 1960s, they're up here and you are not.
>
> (Mrs Kirby)

The counterpointing of general and specialist care runs strongly throughout our data. In a simple sense this is not surprising but the contrast involves a complex array of factors that do not solely rest upon expertise but also upon demeanour, philosophies of care, openness and relationships of trust. These are boundary features of the culture of childhood cancer. As the induction of families into the culture progresses, the gap between insiders and outsiders (both lay and professional) becomes more clearly marked. Parents begin to acquire language, skills and knowledge not even possessed by other professionals.

> ... it's horrible when you're talking to somebody that doesn't know ... cos you learn so much. I mean you learn so much about the Hickman line, and my doctor come out here one night to give Mark some anti sickness IV, cos I never had none at home, and we had to tell him how to put it into the Hickman line.
>
> (Mrs Baker)

FROM DIAGNOSIS THROUGH TREATMENT

Once diagnosis is established the first major period of uncertainty begins as treatment is embarked upon and its outcomes awaited. Parents are obviously keen to know how things look. What are their child's chance's? The professional response to this is to talk percentages. Based on experience of previous cases they can offer parents estimates of recovery.

> ... it was a sarcoma she had, and there was about four other children with the same kind of tumour, so I don't think it's one of the rarer ones. They gave her about a 50/50 chance ... the prognosis was ... so it was good really ... compared to some of them ...
>
> (Mrs Jones)

While percentages are intended to blend realism with hope, some parents, particularly mothers, identify their child's treatment with failure even when the percentages are 'in their favour'. The association between cancer and death is difficult to break despite reported success rates. But for other families, these percentages, no matter how bleak a picture they paint, are a source of faint hope, something to hang onto, an outside chance that is the only basis for not despairing, not giving up. Again this points up the double-edgedness of the culture. What seems a source of hope for some is interpreted as an indication of hopelessness by others.

For the professional carers the use of percentages and 'chances' are part of the language of prognosis and a way of blending uncertainty with hope, and equivocation with knowledgability. In a sense this is a tactic in the management of uncertainty both for themselves and for the parents. The most skilful communicators are able to convey a sense of 'ifs and buts' and medical realism, while still holding out the possibility of a successful outcome to treatment.

> He said, I think it's a Wilm's ... yes, we will give him chemotherapy, and if the chemotherapy works, then we will take the tumour, and if we can take the tumour then we should be on to a very good success rate. Now he wouldn't tell us that it would be alright forever and ever, and that was very different from the surgeon who'd said ... well we're going to do this, this and this, and all will be wonderful. Richard was much more ... much more indefinite ... and very much more reserved in his judgement.
>
> (Mrs Green)

The essential point is that there is no guarantee of recovery or cure. Treatment is an extension of uncertainty, or perhaps more accurately it is a series of uncertainties.

> ... in ITU, when everything was so awful, we all expected him to die two, three times a week ...
>
> (Mrs Coulby)

Nonetheless, in the absence of certain knowledge and clear prognoses the parents need to know continues unabated. Glaser and Strauss (1965: 53) make the same point: 'The patient's objective is to get true indicators of his suspected status.' The ever present possibility of side effects, of failure, of death means that information, authoritative or otherwise is at a premium. This leads to a situation of *heightened cue awareness* and what can be called *over-interpretation.* That is to say, a tendency to attribute meaning and significance to just about anything that is said and done by professionals.

The next two extracts from our data highlight very clearly the parents' dependence on, and susceptibility to, interpretation. Again, like almost all aspects of the culture of childhood cancer the role and effect of interpretation and heightened awareness is double edged – they are sources of hope and of despair. These phenomena feed upon the need to know something that might be positive *and* the constant fear of the negative. First, Mrs Green's account indicates how the demeanour and language of consultants and nurses are interrogated with great care and discussed at great length in the search for meanings and impressions that are subliminally conveyed. The assumption is that there is more to know than is said, more that is meant than is openly conveyed. She is talking about her child's consultant.

> ... he did visibly change to us, once Andrew had had the operation and it seemed to be successful. Up until then Richard had always said there was a good success rate ... suddenly he's saying things like ... this is so good, I am very pleased ... Richard would never say things like that ... and I can remember we used to analyse this, the first time Richard said ... I am very pleased, we came down the motorway on cloud nine ... because he doesn't say words like that. He will say nothing rather than say anything ... and then when we had the op, we were feeling really on top of the world.
>
> (Mrs Green)

But there are other signs and indicators which assume significance. In particular the development of patterns and routines becomes important. Anything that seems different, non-routine, can quickly assume awesome proportions to parents and dire interpretations are brought into play. To some extent the professional carers are aware of this. But only to some extent.

> ... so we go for a chest x-ray, and the x-ray operators are very nice. The only thing was, I panicked one day, Andrew said he'd go in on his own, so I sat in the waiting room and Andrew went in and had it done, and we sat there and waited for it to be developed, and she came out and

> very straight faced said ... I need to do another one Andrew. Andrew went back in and had this other plate done ... I started to panic ... she came out, and it was all sealed up, and she just handed it to me and she said, are you going up the ward, and I said yes ... well by the time I got up the ward, I was convinced there was all sorts on that picture ... and they had to take me in the office and give me hot sweet tea ... while they rang x-ray to see what was going on, and the message came back up ... they hadn't got a very clear print, so they wanted another print ... and the operator did come up and apologise, she said it hadn't dawned on her, but she said she would bear that in mind in the future ... with everybody.
>
> (Mrs Green)

This heightened awareness also applies to the parental surveillance of their child, looking both for signs of improvement and more importantly signs of deterioration or recurrence (see below). This often extends well beyond the period of treatment.

Treatment is marked by a series of points of crisis and transition, an ebb and flow of emotions around a repeated sequence of treatment/-reaction/test. Throughout treatment, bad news and the possibility of death are never far away. If not for this child then for others: as parents become part of a community of cancer, they are continually reminded of the reality of child death. Getting close to other insiders, other parents with a child with cancer, other parents with the same child cancer, provides mutual support based upon common experiences. It allows for conversations and relationships based upon a shared sense of tragedy, grief and hope. But such relationships extend the possibility of being touched by death. Insiders know and speak the language of death.

> You get very involved with others, it can't be helped ... when we went to the funeral, obviously we were absolutely broken hearted, but somebody said to me, when you look at that little white coffin you wondered when it would be your child ... there isn't any good news anywhere ... There seemed to be an awful lot of children die.
>
> (Mrs Goodson)

Those inside the culture can offer a form of support based on shared pain and a simple truth – 'I have been there I know'. The ever present possibility of death also leads to a striking short-termism. The future disappears, coping and hoping are about the immediate; about getting through the night, the next treatment, the next check up. This is about 'watching and waiting very day' (Mrs Coulby) as one mother put it, or simply, 'One day at a time' (Mrs Woods).

For most families the point of the end of treatment is a moment of great anxiety. While treatment continues it is always possible to believe in 'cure'. The very notion of treatment conveys the idea that the disease is being attacked, beaten back, or at the very least held in check. Thus, uncertainty can be held in check. When treatment (or a series of treatments) is completed, focus shifts from the immediate (the next treatment, the next reactions) to some kind of future. For many, this is a future of return to health but for others it is a future where death is the only certainty.

FROM TREATMENT TO RECOVERY OR PALLIATIVE CARE

(1) Continuing uncertainty

Typically, the professional carers retain their stance of equivocation even when treatments appear successful.

> Yes, I mean we're gradually spacing out the visits sort of ... every three months at the moment ... but I think that she'll still want me to go in another year's time, because really ... until he's been off treatment three years, we can't say definitely that he's not going to relapse.
>
> (V. Bains, Macmillan nurse)

For the parents the markers of recovery – time elapsed and check ups – are faced with a mixture of hope and trepidation. Every check up brings with it the possibility of a relapse.

> You do, you're frightened, as much as you want him to be alright and everything ... you've got about five years at the end of the treatment to get through, haven't you, so you're living on a knife edge all the time.
>
> (Mrs Baker)

> ... and it all revolves round one clinic visit a week ... and a day either side ... like one day to get used to the idea of going to clinic, and then another day to actually wait and get the results and you only really have a few days in between.
>
> (Mrs Williams)

Uncertainty remains the primary feature of recovery. Parents must somehow come to terms with long term living with the possibility of recurrence.

> It's still with us ... I think ... when Claire doesn't feel well you start to worry that way, but I think as time goes on we do feel more positive that she is going to be cured, I mean they never actually say that they're cured, they just say the longer time goes on the better the chances are. They're looking at five years ... well Claire's got another year to go, so I still think well ... you know ... could it come back?
>
> (Mrs Jones)

> ... every morning you get up, you think, will this be the day that we'll see his legs buckle under him or he'll have a fit or, he'll do something, show some symptoms, another head tilt, and it'll be back.
>
> (Mrs Coulby)

For families with children with cancer these uncertainties become part of the process of growing up. Any illness may be an indicator of recurrence. Two very important codicils in relation to treatment and recovery have to be entered here. Both further complicate the relationship between cancer, the treatment of cancer and the ever present possibility of death.

(1) When treatment is worse than death. In the case of some radical treatment regimes some parents begin to feel that the suffering caused to the child may be worse than the release offered by an acceptance of death. In some cases parents are faced with desperate decisions – to commit their child to further damaging and painful treatments with little or *very* uncertain hope of success or to make the best of the time for life remaining.

(2) When survival is worse than death. For some parents the ravages of cancer can render the recovery of their child a dubious outcome.

> I don't wish him dead, it's not what I'm saying at all. I do wish him more peace than I think he's going to have, should he survive ... I've lost him, I've lost the child I had for two years ... Its all gone ... his eyes are dull ... there's five per cent of him left the way he was ...
>
> (Mrs Coulby)

Added to the sense of loss is the sense of fear for the child who survived: a fear for the child's future and the sort of life that is possible.

(2) The child becomes terminal

One of the key aspects of child cancer is that the vast majority of children who die of cancer die at home. Palliative care is organised in the home. And in many cases the family become the primary carers. The balance of control over care and over the mechanics of death is weighted in favour of the family. Medical skills and technical knowledge are acquired by the family and some are able to make important decisions about treatment and care with little input from professional carers.

> Just about everybody you could name offered to come, so it was a question of knowing who you wanted to have. I said no to all the junior doctors ... because ... rightly or wrongly, it's a bit like refusing students at the birth of your child. I just thought they were coming for the experience, and they had nothing to offer us as a family.
>
> (Mrs Atkinson)

> We decided that he didn't really need the morphine and I started to wean him off it and then I started to reduce the muscle relaxants that he was on ... he was on sort of double what he should have been having, in an effort to control his pain ... so I just suggested it to Ann (Macmillan Nurse) and she said okay ... let's give it a go, we'll do it gently and so I did and I got him off almost everything.
>
> (Mrs Kingsbury)

In many cases there is an exact reversal of power and priorities as compared to institutional dying. In the institution as Glaser and Strauss (1968: 61–2) note, 'The patient himself may have little control over management of his dying'. For families with a dying child at home there is the possibility of asserting their own management concerns. But other new tensions arise. The certainty of death is replaced by other uncertainties. How long does the child have to live and what will be the nature of their death? For some families this phase is dominated by the positive axis of the culture, the support and care, sharing and warmth are very much to the fore. These new uncertainties are typically jointly managed. But this depends very much on the nature of the previous relationships established with the professional carers. For other families tension and conflict and misunderstanding are to the fore. The management of the child's death becomes a focus of struggle. It was clear that some families were more able than others to assert their need or desire for independence in this phase. Some were more trusted by, or were more able to convince professional carers of their competence.

DEATH

Palliative care in the home provides for the laizisation or de-professionalisation, and (in a sense) naturalisation of death. Death is no longer a technical matter (Giddens 1991). All of this is quite anomalous in the context of the medicalisation and sequestration of death elsewhere in modern society (Mellor and Shilling 1992). Within these families death is 'an ever-present facet of daily existence' (Turner 1991: 235); it is very much a social phenomenon (Ariès 1974 and 1981) within the family.

> I did feel when he went terminal that I might have to fight to keep him at home, that I might have to fight to keep him at home once he'd died ... I didn't actually have to fight, but I had the feeling I had to. I think for his sisters at six and two, the best thing to do was to have him at home ... for Jenny in particular, who was a very bright six and half year old ... I mean her examination and feeling that Harry had gone cold and so on, it allowed her to really accept the death.
>
> (Mrs Cooke)

> ... it's a bit like people having, you know ... bad experiences of high technology births in hospital ... I'm sure you can have bad experiences of high technology deaths in hospital as well, and I do think that if possible ... to be at home with non-intrusive support is best, but it is difficult, cos everybody feels ... they're doing their best, but I do feel that ... the less people ... particularly in a small child's bedroom ... there's just not enough space for everybody ... We kept Karen here that night ... she died about 6 o'clock on May lst in the evening, and I insisted, although the GP said it probably wouldn't be best ... and everybody said I don't think you should ... I said well the undertaker doesn't need to come now.
>
> (Mrs Atkinson)

> ... so he had both chicken-pox and shingles ... but we treated it at home, but the end result of the shingles was a lot of bottom pain, he called it bottom pain ... so it camouflaged what were probably terminal symptoms from liver and spleen ... and bless him, he made a sort of big moan, and I thought ah, this is it, and he sat up, and he said I need to go to the loo, and he walked to the loo at 1.30, walked back to bed, cuddled up and died at 4 o'clock that morning. Now we didn't call the doctors and Liz straight away.
>
> (Mrs Cooke)

Gradually over time the professional carers are marginalised and the dying child is taken back into the family; although clearly it is still salient to note, as Glaser and Strauss do, 'the importance of the mode of dying in determining whether the family can sustain the drama until its very end' (1968: 81). The 'terror of death' (Lasch 1991) can be overcome although its consequences, for some, remain terrible, burdensome and destructive. Nonetheless, when paediatric oncology nurses are available to families, they remain part of the scene, either in the background or as stage-managers. They keep in touch with the terminal course, ready to act when necessary or when required.

But not every family feels able to cope with the death of their child at home. The paediatric oncology nurses sometimes find themselves in the position of seeking to convince a family that this is the best course. When necessary the level of support is higher, paradoxically the laizisation is professionalised through the work of the paediatric oncology nurses.

> ... the parents were very adamant at the beginning that they wouldn't keep him at home, and that he wouldn't die at home, and I felt a real sense of achievement that he did die at home, and that they were very pleased that they kept him at home, and that was all down to the fact that we kept them well prepared and informed of everything that might happen, so that they weren't frightened of things happening, and that's when you really feel that you've achieved something.
>
> (V. Bains, Macmillan nurse)

SUMMARY

The family experience and the social and emotional construction of child cancer may be understood in terms of four main stages in an illness trajectory. The interactions between parents and medical professionals are different in each stage, each involving different degrees and kinds of uncertainty. The trajectory begins from illness to diagnosis, and thence moves from diagnosis through treatment, and from treatment to recover or palliative care (where in the latter case the child is considered to be terminally ill). Within and across the trajectory and the interactions, families contribute to and participate in a *culture of childhood cancer*. This culture centres upon the management of uncertainty, which involves parents and medical professionals in complex and difficult, but also supportive interactions and relationships. The culture is 'organised' around the ethos and commitments of specialist paediatric oncology centres and the common interests of different families. Its existence points up the dramatic contrast between sites of specialist and general care which is represented in the families' experiences.

The final paradox about child cancer, given the concern of this chapter with the ever presence of death, is that the majority of children with cancer survive. It is not a death sentence; although of course rates of mortality vary considerably between types of cancer. Nonetheless, it seems unlikely that the close association between cancer and death will be easily broken. Death is central to the culture of childhood cancer, it underpins the uncertainty, the fear and the dread which rips and tears at families and divides them from friends and other relatives. But it is also the basis of sharing and bonding and dividing, it forges a strong boundary between those it touches and those it does not.

Notes

1. We do not have space here to pursue the gender related aspects of cancer care, we intend to do that elsewhere, but it is important to note that mothers are typically more fully embedded in the culture of childhood cancer than are fathers.
2. This paper draws upon interviews with family members (35), paediatric oncology nurses, consultants, GPs, etc. conducted as part of a Department of Health/Cancer Relief Macmillan Fund funded research project: see Bignold, Ball and Cribb (1994).
3. For reasons of confidentiality, pseudonyms have been used throughout the text.

13 Euthanasia and Assisted Suicide: Are Doctors' Duties when Following Patients' Orders a Bitter Pill to Swallow?

Demetra M. Pappas

Approximately two years ago, in 1992, I was immersed in research for a master's dissertation considering whether the time had come for a review of criminal justice policy regarding physicians who perform active euthanasia. My initial area of interest was the movement for decriminalization of euthanasia in the United States, where I had been a criminal lawyer. It was my intention to consider the Dutch experience, where, after ten years of *de facto* decriminalization, euthanasia was widely, and presumably safely, practised, and to contemplate the arguments for and against changing standards in some of the United States.

This was, at that time, a nice, discrete topic. After all, the Dutch situation was fairly settled, the American unable to be so before my paper was due to be submitted. There was plenty of room for comment on an area with not too much risk of imminent change given that the American elections would be late in the year, no Supreme Court cases were pending, and there were no bills pending in any of the State legislatures. Clean, neat and impersonal.

Six months later, I wrote a dissertation on a topic which had turned nasty and burgeoned. It had become ugly because my partner almost died that summer, and, shortly before his heart surgery, he had me draft a document which would ensure I do *to* him what I had wanted him to do *for* me. I rued the day I showed him the aggressive (and currently unlawful) euthanasia clause I had written into my will and defiantly invited him to 'take it to the Supremes and have a party', where he would, unquestionably, prevail. I found it difficult to put my heart into euthanasia after his had been in anaesthesia. The first rule of (male) academia, 'never work on anything you are personally involved with', had been broken.

The topic had burgeoned because, at the last moment, a controversial trial was held in England which reignited the dying embers of the doctor-administered euthanasia controversy. Simultaneously, there came to life a national debate about a right to die case brought by the family of a young Englishman in a persistent vegetative state. Thus, the geography and topography of my dissertation were radically altered, as indeed was the paper. The second adage of academia, 'always know your freshest work is in imminent danger of staleness', had been unbroken, as it will no doubt be by the time this chapter is published.

The paper ultimately submitted (Pappas 1992) reviewed the then-current state of the law in the Netherlands, the United States and the United Kingdom. This review was set against a backdrop consisting of some of the theoretical issues and a brief discussion of the Nazi atrocities, with the paper concluding that the time was ripe for a change in the law and policy concerning physicians who perform active euthanasia. Of the three countries considered at that time, each has seen some radical measure or proposal of law reform with regard to physician-assisted euthanasia, thus rendering the initial paper, which had been on the cutting edge of emerging law, to be of historical interest. The 'emerging' nature of the topic became one of expansion to other jurisdictions, rather than exploration of a new theoretical issue.

Since writing the first draft of this chapter, which was to be a review of the then-contemporary criminal justice policy considerations regarding physician-assisted suicide and doctor administered euthanasia in the Netherlands, United Kingdom and United States, I repeatedly found myself personally involved in the issue.[1] My research was very heavily focused on (voluntary) assisted suicide of terminally and chronically ill patients. A seemingly innovative draft chapter, first penned in 1993, describing euthanasia (a restatement of the law) and assisted suicide (a new statement of the law), was in fact, as much a part of a twenty year personal odyssey, as a twenty month academic walkabout.

Born at risk of Huntington's Disease – a rather nasty and always fatal progressive degenerative illness with loss of mental and bodily control and function over a period of ten to twenty years – I decided to take part in the first non-linkage genetic testing program so as to know what the future held. The risk factor of this dominant gene left a fifty per cent probability that I would be afflicted, a fact which impacted upon 100 per cent of the major decisions I have made since age twenty-two, when my grandfather explained the facts of my life to me. Thus, a year after facing my partner's fate, I squarely faced my own.

In August of this year, I found myself facing a death once again. The year 1994 saw the expiration of my father, who has been afflicted with

Huntington's Disease for nearly twenty years. His illness and its effects upon him and others has been a source of sorrow, although not open discussion, for many years. While his death certificate would proclaim the cause of death to be pneumonia, he lost all but intermittent lucidity well over two decades ago, losing the rest over the next few years. Likewise, he lost verbal dexterity over the years and all speech approximately a decade ago, with ambulatory movement degenerating to a total loss not long after. A man of vision, he tried to starve himself to death when I was fifteen. I have often thought that those who stopped him should stand guilty of a capital offense, as it is the last truly autonomous act I recall him engaging in. The gods did him no favours keeping his heart beating and lungs breathing.

Asked during doctoral fieldwork and legal testimony what my views are on euthanasia, I answer that my experiences inexorably lead to the conclusion that both the right to life and the right to die should be protected. I suspect this to be true of most who have dealt with the issue and had an opportunity to reflect upon the implications arising from legally permissible euthanasia and assisted suicide. There are those who have referred to me (correctly) as ambivalent, (uncharitably) as confused, and (frequently) less than absolute in my position. I find myself in good company in this regard. The Baroness Flather, at the Debate of the Report of the House of Lords Select Committee on Medical Ethics held on 9 May 1994, observed that after her appointment to the Select Committee in March 1993, members of the House of Lords variously approached her noting that of course she was in favour of euthanasia *and* of course she was opposed to euthanasia. Of two eminent prosecutors on the Michigan Commission on Death and Dying, one, John O'Hair, was avidly pro-choice, while the other, Richard Thompson, was zealously pro-life; neither was any the less committed to exploring and considering *all* the issues raised by the literal question of life and death. A number of the doctors, lawyers, legislators and judges I have interviewed have had personal, and frequently conflicting, experiences which have influenced their views concerning assisted suicide, active euthanasia or both.

In the criminal arena, it is the 'doctor cases' which have precipitated the major changes in the law, starting in the 1980s in the Netherlands. The winds of change are now sweeping both sides of the Atlantic Ocean as a result of tempests created by doctor prosecutions in England (the conviction and suspended sentence of Dr Nigel Cox in Winchester Crown Court in September 1992) and America (repeated dismissals of murder and related charges were brought in Michigan against Dr Jack Kevorkian, who has assisted in some twenty assisted suicides beginning in 1990 but has, to date, faced but one trial. This resulted in an acquittal in May 1994). While one can argue that because new legal mechanisms are not yet in place, or are just emerging and being subjected to challenge, the usage of the past tense of the verb 'precipitate' is inappropriate. However, it is raining legislation and hearings in Parliament, and there has been a virtual hailstorm of litigation and legislation in Michigan, which has created further storms in several other states. So, for the most part, other than to clarify a few terms, this chapter begins where the Masters dissertation concluded and takes the need for clarification and review of the law (if not necessarily law reform) as a given.

THE LETHAL AID LEXICON

Euthanasia is an ancient concept, reaching back over the millennia; decriminalization and 'illegalization', particularly regarding physicians, are more modern notions, looking forward into the next millennium.[2] However, many writers, doctors, lawyers, judges and scholars use some of the key words and phrases differently or interchangeably, so that the definitional waters have become muddied. Thus, the vocabulary and phrasing used in this chapter will be expressly defined and clarified.

Euthanasia at its most basic level, is the acceleration, causing or hastening of death, particularly where the patient is incurably or terminally ill. The two basic forms of euthanasia are *active* and *passive*. *Active euthanasia* generally refers to a positive act by the physician which is intended to bring about the death of the patient, such as the administration of a lethal injection. *Passive euthanasia* denotes an act of omission or commission, whereby a patient's treatment, and/or nutrition and hydration are discontinued. As a general matter, cases of *double effect*, in which pain killers prescribed for the purposes of palliation or relief of discomfort, but have as a secondary effect the shortening of life, are not, as a matter of law, considered to be euthanasia.

Physician assisted suicide differs from euthanasia in that it is the patient, rather than the doctor, who commits the life-shortening act, although the physician provides the means (such as where a doctor prescribes lethal doses of painkillers or barbiturates, which the patient then takes, either orally or by injection). Thus, the doctor, while charged as a principal in the crime, is an accomplice to the patient's act.

Voluntary euthanasia is where a patient expressly asks to have euthanasia administered (for example, a cancer patient who requests death). *Non-voluntary euthanasia* is where the act is performed without consent (as in cases where the victim is in a persistent vegetative state and thus incapable of giving consent). *Involuntary euthanasia* refers to situations where the 'patient' neither consents nor wants death (the Nazi atrocities serving as a powerful example of this).

For the purposes of this discussion, patients are assumed to have attained the age of majority and to be competent, unless otherwise stated. Without detracting from cases of those in persistent vegetative states, this chapter focuses upon cases of *voluntary medical aid in dying*; a term which embraces both the terms of *euthanasia* and *physician assisted suicide*. Similarly, *mercy killing* will be distinguished from euthanasia, as non-medical in intent or cause of death, usually with a humanitarian or compassionate motive (for example, the case of a man or woman who shoots, suffocates or administers poison to a critically ill spouse, friend or child).

Finally, although there are those who would argue that all human beings are terminally ill, I would suggest that, among others, end-stage cancer, AIDS, Huntington's and Alzheimers Disease victims be considered terminal, particularly once the patient is in a state where there is either a projected survival period of one year or less, or where the patient has no control of mental or bodily functions. In this category, for reasons having to do primarily with the wording of the aid in dying initiatives recently presented in the United States, are frequently included individuals who have been in a persistent vegetative state for a period of more than six months, although they may be maintained indefinitely. It should, however, be noted that the House of Lords Select Committee, in its Report, used a one year standard for diagnosis of persistent vegetative state.

One possible reason why physician-assisted suicide and active euthanasia are of interest in legal fora, from the parochial to the international, is that the medical advances of the past few decades have made it possible for doctors to prolong the process of dying, as well as to lengthen the time of living. We live in an age where a man whose heart stops can receive a new one and thus be enabled to live to be 100 years of age; similar technological advances can result in a dead woman, whose brain function has stopped, receiving nutrition and hydration or technically induced biological functions so that she is 'dis-enabled' to die. These technological developments give today's medicine men powers previously reserved to the Gods – those of healing and judging who shall receive the gift of life or, at the other end of the spectrum, a life sentence.

How society should judge the acts of these doctors, and who should sit in judgment of them, is another matter. Although it is axiomatic that murder is morally and legally wrong, it is by legal construction that there can be no consent to murder. Additionally, while the Sixth Commandment intones, '[t]hou shalt not commit murder', the Roman Catholic legal philosopher Norman St John-Stevas (1961) noted that there were exceptions, including altruistic suicide. We must consider that to kill is not necessarily to murder, and a Biblical translation which prohibits murder does not prohibit all killing. Under a prohibition including the latter, war and judicial execution, both of which St John-Stevas acknowledges as permissible under Christian law, would not be allowed in a state whose law derives from the Judeo-Christian ethic.

THE NETHERLANDS

In the Netherlands, universally taken to be the pioneering jurisdiction of law reform concerning medical aid in dying, and contrary to popular belief, euthanasia remains a criminal offense. Indeed, medical (and non-medical) aid in dying is absolutely prohibited by Sections 293 and 294 of the Dutch Criminal Code, Wetboek van Strafecht. Under Article 293 WvS, euthanasia at the express and serious request of the decedent is punishable by up to twelve years in prison. Assisted suicide is a separate crime, punishable by a prison sentence of up to three years.

However, Article 40 WvS provides that anyone who is forced to commit an offence under irresistible compulsion is not punishable for a criminal act. In the 1984 *Alkmaar* case, the Supreme Court established a defense of necessity, to be interposed by doctors who are prosecuted for active euthanasia. Doctors who administer medical aid in dying should, under carefully enumerated guidelines, report to the office of the public prosecutor, and may then be exempted from the ordinary prohibitions against murder and euthanasia.

Awareness of the focus upon the need to report the act is crucial to understanding the Dutch experience and recent legislation. The aim is to increase reporting rather than to decrease practice.[3] In 1991, the laws concerning burial procedures were altered with regard to general medical reporting procedures. The immediately observable result was that during the calendar month of January 1992, a record 339 deaths by euthanasia were reported, as opposed to a total of 592 for the calendar year of 1991. The total figure of deaths by euthanasia and assisted suicide for the calendar year of 1992 was, according to the Netherlands Ministry of Justice Press Report (February 1993) over 1300.

Nonetheless, Bill 22572, amending the Burial Act 1955 (but not the Dutch Penal Code), was enacted in 1993 (with an effective date of

1 January 1994) to specify an extensive reporting procedure which doctors must follow where euthanasia is performed.

The Dutch almost universally exalt the concept of patient self-determination and minimize the concept of physician blameworthiness. Dr Herbert Cohen, a Dutch physician who has not only given evidence but has himself recently been acquitted of euthanasia (which he does not deny having administered to many patients), regularly lectures to doctors and Dutch police on how to handle euthanasia cases. He commented in interview that '[e]uthanasia is never the preferred option, but signifies that medicine has failed'. Like many Dutch doctors, lawyers and ethicists he is of the view that this is not an example of slippery slopes – where allowing euthanasia for terminal patients is then extended to the chronically ill, then the depressed, and so on until it is involuntarily administered in order to preserve assets or racial purity – but is sanctifying and honouring life by respecting the self-determination of the possessor (the person) rather than the theological owner (God).

THE UNITED STATES

The celebration of self-determination and autonomy has also been the focus of Dr Jack Kevorkian. Kevorkian, known as 'Dr Death', has assisted in some 20 suicides in Michigan, a vitalist (pro-life) state in the USA. Because America is federal in nature, and the law regarding murder and assisted suicide governed by individual states, state law has been in constant flux. However, a few statistics show the effect Kevorkian's efforts have had on his crusade.

In 1991, Washington State saw the narrow defeat of Proposition 119, intended to decriminalize physician aid in dying (by non-active mechanisms with no lethal injection).[4] A voter referendum, which had been immensely popular prior to the election, had the misfortune of taking place one week after Dr Kevorkian's (simultaneous) second and third assisted suicides of Sherry Miller (by lethal injection) and Marjorie Wantz (by carbon monoxide) on 23 October 1991. The video-taped statements of the women and the nature of the side-by-side assisted suicides[5] have been credited with swaying the vote from sixty per cent in favour to fifty-four per cent opposed in one week. A successful civil *federal* challenge[6] brought by the organization Compassion in Dying (*v*. Christine Gregoire, Attorney General of Washington State) had as plaintiffs terminally ill patients and medical school professors. One, Dr Tom Preston, a noted cardiologist, said in interview that the plaintiff group wanted established doctors with no association to Kevorkian.

Kevorkian himself is no great fan of legal interference with what he considers a fundamental right to self determination. However, while there is a constitutional right to die (by refusing unwanted medical treatment, as articulated by the Supreme Court in the case of Nancy Cruzan), and suicide is not against the law, there is no constitutional right (except, provisionally in Washington State) to commit suicide, let alone have assistance. Indeed, approximately three-fifths of the states have laws prohibiting assisting a suicide.

When Kevorkian began his crusade in 1990, Michigan had no assisted suicide law. However, repeated dismissals of murder and related charges and continued activity by Kevorkian galvanized the Michigan Legislature into action. Unable otherwise to stop this 65 year old retired pathologist, who had been stripped of medical license after medical license, and who literally thumbed his nose at the law, the Michigan Legislature passed a law temporarily criminalising assisted suicide. The multi-page document also established a Commission on Death and Dying, to examine the issues relating to euthanasia and assisted suicide and to consider three alternatives: making the temporary ban permanent; or assisted suicide lawful; or leaving the law silent. The dual nature of the Act was to give rise to contentious litigation on state constitutional grounds, as well as those of fundamental rights.

Following passage, but prior to the original effective date of 1992 Public Act 270, Kevorkian assisted in seven more suicides, driving the Legislature to hold an emergency vote to bring forward the effective date in 1993 Public Act 3. Since the law went into effect Kevorkian has assisted in five suicides, continuing, with one exception, to make video statements and hold post-mortem press conferences. When he was finally tried under the new law, he claimed exemption under the double effect clause, testifying that he had administered carbon monoxide to relieve the suffering of his seventeenth client, Thomas Hyde. Kevorkian was acquitted on 2 May 1994, after less than one day of deliberations. On 9 May, the assisted suicide ban was ruled unlawful (as was the Commission on Death and Dying[7]) by the Michigan Court of Appeals, which went on to hold that the earlier decision and dismissal of murder counts on the Wantz and Miller assisted suicides was wrong, thus reinstating the charges. The cases continue.

It is of some import that the only state actively to legislate was one which criminalised the conduct, a result almost universally attributed to the activities of Kevorkian. One might argue that a different doctor would precipitate a different result; certainly the doctor plaintiffs in Washington hold this belief. However, on the other side of the Atlantic, the evidence is even more compelling.

BRITAIN

The September 1992 conviction of Nigel Cox, a respected rheumatologist currently engaged in practice, who received a suspended sentence for the crime of attempted murder, provoked a public outcry for law reform. Cox was not tried for murder because the body of the deceased had been cremated. Thus, no autopsy could be done to determine the cause of the death of decedent, who died five minutes after receiving two injections of potassium chloride (a toxin used to stop the heart during open heart surgery). Had the body not been cremated, Cox might have been subject to a mandatory life sentence.

Shortly thereafter, a prospective case was brought by Airedale NHS Trust, which sought a declaration from the Family Court (which it received, and which was reaffirmed by the Court of Appeal and the House of Lords) that its doctors would not be prosecuted if they discontinued nutrition and hydration and any non-palliative medical treatment of Tony Bland. Bland had been in a persistent vegetative state for four years following the Hillsborough stadium tragedy.

The House of Lords Select Committee on Medical Ethics was constituted on the heels of these two cases. It is said that timing is everything. If that is true, consider the fact that the Select Committee on Medical Ethics was proposed on 16 February 1993, *twelve days* after the House of Lords rendered a decision which allowed for the termination and withdrawal of Tony Bland's nutrition, hydration and medical treatment, because it was in Bland's 'best interests' to do so. Further, the Select Committee first convened in March 1993, one month after the legal resolution of the *Bland* case and only six months after the conviction of Nigel Cox. The pace of these events is certainly telling as to how important the legal, medical, theological, ethical and social issues arising from euthanasia and assisted suicide are considered to be.

Just as the Michigan Legislature responded with speed and deliberation to the activities of Kevorkian, so too did the House of Lords. This is demonstrated by even the briefest glance at its mandate, which directed the Select Committee Members to consider 'the ethical, legal and clinical implications of first, a person's right to withhold consent to life-prolonging treatment, and the position of persons who are no longer able to give or withhold consent'. In other words, the Select Committee was to consider the right to self-determination by those who are competent and the implied right to die of those in a persistent vegetative state. Second, the group was to evaluate '*whether and in what circumstances actions that have as their intention or a likely consequence the shortening of another person's life may be justified* on the grounds that they accord with that person's wishes or with that person's best interests' (emphasis added). Whilst the Dutch had an awkward compromise for twelve years, other jurisdictions were seeking to resolve the issues (or at least articulate and consider them) in under twelve months.

Members of the Select Committee on Medical Ethics presented their own case study as to the social implications of legal and medical responses to death and dying. Of the 14 members, two were in ill health; indeed several subjects commented that the lengthy illness of one member was the major influence for that individual's desire to be on the Select Committee, so as to have a real voice. A careful balance was struck between pro-life and pro-choice advocates. A fascinating aspect of this was that there was at least one of each among doctors, lawyers and academics. One doctor was a palliative care specialist with interest in the disabled; one a neurologist. One of the Law Lords from the *Bland* case provided a unique perspective, as did a nurse, the Archbishop of York and Baroness Warnock (whose recent report on assisted conception was path breaking).

Many expected the Select Committee to come forward with some sort of guidelines for regulating aid in dying or withdrawal of treatment. The Select Committee expressly declined to do so. While endorsing the right of the competent patient to refuse consent to any medical treatment, it recommended against changing the law to permit assisted suicide or euthanasia, prominently citing fears of abuse regarding the elderly, dying or disabled (that is, the slippery slope argument). Additionally, the Select Committee strongly stated that treatment-limiting decisions should not be determined on the basis of resource availability and that there should be more research into and availability of palliative care, a conclusion also reached by the Michigan Commission on Death and Dying. Distinguishing itself from its American cousin, the Select Committee concluded that advance directives, also known as living wills, should not be legislated, although they were lauded.

One change which *was* advocated, and was undoubtedly derivative of the *Cox* case and of the fear that other 'good' doctors would continue to walk in the shadow of the law, risking liberty as well as profession, while acting in good faith, was that the mandatory life sentence for murder should be abolished. This recommendation was the only one which the Government reply disagreed with, and was not embraced following the Debate at the House of Lords on 9 May 1994.

CONCLUSION

In an area of such rapid change in socio-legal and medico-legal circles, one could take weekly snapshots of life, as well as of law, and create a pictorial flip-pack. Whether doctors have a duty to follow patients' orders and risk the bitter pill of denunciation (and incarceration) by the legal system (as did Nigel Cox), the medical system (as did Kevorkian in losing his licenses) or by society, is a question not likely to be resolved in the near future. Confessing guilt while claiming exoneration, as is the practice in the Netherlands, is hardly an easy compromise. Alternatively, flouting the law, like Kevorkian, and becoming a pariah (even a famous one) is not in the best interests of the patient and undermines the doctor–patient relationship. The other course open to doctors in their enjoyment of the exalted palliative care, and claiming double effect (where potassium chloride is not the pharmaceutical in question), is intellectually (and otherwise) dishonest.

All that is certain is that the roles of patients and doctors will continue to evolve; that technology will become more advanced; and that changes in the demographics of illness are likely to precipitate more discussion and further debate in the field of medical aid in dying. At some point, the question of how to give life to a patient's right to die, while safeguarding against potential abuse, must be answered, for it is of no aid to a patient to have that right, either as an expression of his or her best interests (as in the United Kingdom) or in his or her liberty interests (as articulated in the US), if s/he must remain in a cage built by a legal system which may incarcerate the doctor if s/he complies with a request for medical aid in dying.

POSTSCRIPT

In keeping with the academic adage discussed in the introductory section, path-breaking changes have taken place since the 'final deadline' for this chapter.

In America, both the Pacific Northwest and the Midwest have underscored their prominence in the lively debate about assisted death. On

8 November 1994, Oregon, a state noted as a forerunner of emerging (and progressive) law, became the first to enact a provision allowing for medical aid in dying. Ballot Measure 16 was passed by a fifty-two to forty-eight per cent majority. The measure, to become effective on 8 December 1994, allows doctors to prescribe lethal doses of drugs to terminally ill patients. Requirements include certification by two doctors that the illness is terminal; two oral (or other) requests separated by at least fifteen days; a third request in writing; and that the patient administer the fatal dose him/herself.

In other news, the assisted suicide ban (if found to have been lawful by the Michigan Supreme Court) in Michigan expired on 25 November 1994. Within *hours* Kevorkian 'attended' his twenty-first assisted suicide; that of Margaret Garish, a seventy-two year old Oakland County resident, who suffered from rheumatoid arthritis and other illnesses. The Oakland County Medical Examiner has ruled the death a homicide and the county's pro-life prosecutor is considering charges. Meanwhile, and contrary to the recommendations of the Michigan Commission on Death and Dying, the Michigan Legislature is convening to consider extending the ban.

Finally, in England, in considering the case of an unidentified man who 'killed' his terminally ill wife by means of 'acute morphine poisoning', the Crown Prosecution Service has declined to prosecute because it was not considered to be 'in the public interest'. *The Observer* reported on the front page of its 4 December issue that a spokeswoman for the CPS stressed that 'there had been no change of policy governing the treatment of alleged "mercy killers"', adding that, '[e]very case is looked at on its own merit. This one is exceptional.' Curiously, EXIT, the Voluntary Euthanasia Society, expressed 'serious concern' over the decision because there was no evidence of either a request or consent.

References

Cases

Airedale NHS Trust v. Bland [1993] A.C. 789.

Compassion in Dying v. State of Washington and Gregoire, No. C94-119R (W.D. Seattle May 3, 1994).

R v. Cox (unreported), September 1992.

Cruzan v. Director, Missouri Department of Health, 497 U.S. 281, 100 S. Ct 2841, 111 L.Ed.2d 224 (1990).

People v. Kevorkian, 1994 Mich. App. LEXIS 237.
Hobbins, et al.. v. Attorney General, State of Michigan, 1994 Mich.App. LEXIS 232.

Legislation

Bill 22572, *amending* the Burial Act 1955, *as discussed* in the Report of the House of Lords Select Committee on Medical Ethics, Appendix 3.
House of Lords Select Committee on Medical Ethics, HL Paper 21–I, London: HMSO, Volume I (Report) (1994).
House of Lords Debate of the Medical Ethics: Select Committee Report, *Hansard* 9 May 1994 1344–1412.
Section 40, 293, 294 Wetboek van Strafrecht (WvS) Dutch Criminal Code, (as cited and translated in the Parliamentary Press Release of the Twede Kamer, February, 1993).
Special Report from the Select Committee of the House of Lords on Medical Ethics, HL Paper 67, Ordered to be Printed 9 March 1993.
California State Terminal Illness Assistance in Dying Initiative (1992).
Washington State Initiative Measure 119 (1991).
1992 Public Act 270, as amended by 1993 Public Act 3, MCL 752.1021 *et seq* (formerly Enrolled House Bill No. 4501)(State of Michigan, 86th Legislature).

Books, Articles and Pamphlets

Michigan Commission on Death and Dying, Freedom of Information Act Document A–902, Final Report of the Michigan Commission on Death and Dying, also known as a Report by a Group of People, June 1994.
Netherlands Ministry of Justice Press Report, Dutch Parliament Supports Government Proposal – EUTHANASIA REMAINS A CRIMINAL OFFENSE IN THE NETHERLANDS, REPORTING PROCEDURE ESTABLISHED IN LAW, February 1993.
New York State Task Force on Life and The Law, 'When Death is Sought: Assisted Suicide and Euthanasia in the Medical Context', May 1994.
D.M. Pappas, 'Patients' Orders and Doctors' Duties When Healing Hands are Requested to Render Lethal Aid: Should There be a Review of Criminal Justice Policy Regarding Physicians who Perform Active Euthanasia?' Document A–128 Michigan Commission on Death and Dying 1993.

Notes

1. I have since been assured that this is methodologically legitimate in circles of both feminist jurisprudence and feminist sociology.

2. Although it would be fascinating to consider also development of civil 'rights to die' law and patient autonomy, these questions are beyond the space and scope of this chapter., which solely regards its criminal law counterpart. Likewise, the focus of this paper is upon the current state of the law and potential future developments. Thus, the discussion of theoretical issues and the historical development of the law in the various countries must, for the most part, be deferred for other occasion. An exception to be noted, however, is one American case, in the 1950 prosecution in New Hampshire against Dr Hermann Sander, which is virtually identical to the September 1992 *Cox* prosecution in England; both of these cases were unreported, the former because it resulted in an acquittal, the latter because the one year suspended sentence which follow the conviction were unappealed.
3. This fact had a profound impact upon the deliberations of the House of Lords Select Committee on the Medical Ethics during its deliberations, which concluded that there was substantial evidence of a slippery slope effect in Holland. A further concern repeatedly raised during hearings conducted by this Select Comittee, and an oft-repeatedly critique of the so-called Dutch compromise, was that doctors had to commit the 'crime', say, 'I did it, I confess', and then answer (literally) twenty-eight questions explaining why the criminal conduct should be deemed not.
4. In 1992, Californis State had a more aggresive proposition, 161, on the ballot for the voter referendum; this initiative, which showed a 68 per cent positive poll a week before the election, was narrowly defeated. It is noteworthy that the referendun, which *would* have allowed for active euthanasia by lethal injection, was very heavily sponsored by the AIDS lobbies in California. This group of young, educated, affluent individuals who are now-healthy but potentially facing a degenerative fatal illness by which they will lose both their mental and physical capacities, has traditionally been one of the most progressive and aggressive proponent groups advocating lawful medical aid in dying.
5. Kevorkian now stands accused of murder, a charge which is being constitutionally challenged, *pendente lite*, and is currently pending in the Michigan Supreme Court. The charges, initially dismissed, were reinstated by the same Michigan Court of Appeals panel which struck down the law of assisted suicide, a case which will be discussed at length. Curiously, the Court of Appeals rendered its decision one week *after* Keverkian's trial.
6. This is currently under review by the United States Circuit Court of Appeals for the Ninth Circuit.
7. As a result, the Final Report of the Michigan Commission on Death and Dying, which consisted of a majority report in favour of assisted suicide, proposed a draft statute, a consensus report regarding procedural safeguards, and a report opposing any law other than a permanent ban of the conduct is currently considered 'A Report of a Group of People' rather than an official document. Almost simultaneously, the New York State Task Force on Life and the Law. an advisory group reporting to the governor, filed a unanimous report recommending against lifting New York's ban on assisted suicide; while this body does not have the ability to elect legislation, its clearly articulated reasons constitute persuasive authority.

14 The Donation of Organs for Transplantation: the Donor Families[1]

Margaret Robbins

INTRODUCTION

The transplantation of human organs is now a well-established procedure in the fields of cardiac, hepatic and renal surgery. The ability to exchange a malfunctioning organ with a healthy one has been hailed as one of the major achievements of modern medical science (Department of Health 1988). Renal transplantation in particular, is regarded as a cost-effective procedure that vastly improves the quality of life of people requiring renal replacement therapy, while the symbolism and poignancy of heart transplantation cannot be emulated by other medical and surgical therapies. Even though transplant operations are relatively common nowadays (currently about 400 heart and heart/lung, and 2000 kidney transplants are performed per year in the United Kingdom), the procedure still resonates of a 'Brave New World'.

A unique characteristic of organ transplantation, however, is that there is a limited supply of human organs, whether from living or deceased people. At least 70 per cent of kidney transplants involve cadaver organs. No other clinical therapy depends for its raw material so predominantly on the death of other patients, and perhaps few other therapies are carried out in such emotionally charged contexts: sudden death in intensive care units and the 'retrieval' of donor organs, followed by transplantation into chronically ill people who may have been on tenterhooks for months 'waiting for the phone-call'.

Transplantation raises a host of issues concerning the rationing of expensive high technology interventions and the technical and ethical limits to medicine. It is also questionable whether the treatment is available to all who need it and desire it on a fair and equitable basis. While these are important health policy issues, this chapter will focus on some of the more sociological questions raised by organ donation. In the first section, the development and current state of transplantation will be described. This will be followed in the second section by the presentation of material from a series of interviews with bereaved families of organ donors. This account illustrates a number of themes relating to issues of consent and adaptation to the idea of organ donation. The final section goes on to consider the social and cultural implications of transplantation with regard to disposal of the body after death, and suggests that the therapy involves an attempt by the medical scientific community to introduce a new moral discourse on body ownership.

THE EMERGENCE OF TRANSPLANTATION

Historical overview

The concept of tissue transplantation has clearly intrigued physicians and scientists for many centuries. The idea that injured bodies could be patched up and restored to wholeness with skin, gland and organ grafts has often been put into practice, although until recently, almost always with disappointing results. The modern era of transplantation in Europe can be traced back to the late 1590s, when a surgeon in Bologna started experimenting with skin grafting. He began with auto-grafting, that is, using the patient's own tissue (Hamilton 1982). This technique was again used in the nineteenth century. Meanwhile colonialists in India found evidence that this technique was already well-known, and was one of several ancient plastic surgical procedures still in use there (Hamilton 1982). Most attention was focused on skin grafting, and the rather chequered history of the various forms of experimentation only came to an end when the principles of histocompatibility (immunological rejection) were demonstrated.

The second world war accelerated progress on at least two fronts: one was a search for surgical techniques which would treat the extensive burns of fighter pilots; and the other was the observation of renal failure as a result of mismatched blood transfusions. The late 1950s and early 1960s saw the establishment of the principles of acquired immunity, antibody formation and eventually tissue typing techniques to allow a close match between transplanted tissue and recipient. With these advances in tissue matching also came an advance in immunosuppression therapy. To begin with patients undergoing kidney transplants in the late 1950s were treated with irradiation, or by cortisones, or antihistamines. Later, the drug azathioprine (Imuran) was discovered to have a pronounced effect on the immune response, and together with steroids, azathioprine became the routine therapy for immunosuppression in patients with transplanted organs, from the 1960s to the early 1980s. In the late 1970s however, a new drug, cyclosporin (Cyclosporin A, or CYA), was developed. This was hailed as a major advance and has subsequently been credited with huge improvements in the survival rates of transplant recipients (Morris 1984; Bos 1991). Cyclosporin, almost more than any other ingredient in the process, has helped to bring organ and tissue transplantation out of the realm of the experimental into the therapeutic.

Current practice and future developments

Transplantation activity as we know it today is thus the result of a succession of factors: effective immunosuppressive regimes; the development of micro surgical and anaesthetic techniques; developments in organisational structures to facilitate the notification, retrieval and tissue typing of organs; and developments in organ preservation techniques. In order to inform and satisfy public sentiment, numerous international and national agencies and networks have been set up to foster, co-ordinate, and regulate organ retrieval. Although many countries have now introduced legislation to regulate the use of human tissue in clinical science, particularly for the purposes of organ donation, the role of governments and health care delivery agencies has been relatively low key in the more general promotion of transplantation. The prime research stimulus has come from within transplant centres, kidney foundations and other private or semi-public organisations (Bos 1991).

Living and post-mortem 'donations'

Over the years a variety of human fluids and tissues have come to be regularly donated for the benefit of others, for example, giving blood or plasma, donating excess milk to a milk bank, providing sperm or ova for infertility treatments and so on. Most of these human products are replenishable, and donation is a very conscious act. These types of living donations appear to be relatively uncontroversial. Extracting human products from what is essentially a corpse, can on the other hand invoke the feelings of violation and mutilation which formed the substance of the public outcry against the body snatching activities of Burke and Hare (Richardson 1987). Under the demands of transplant surgery, the body is seen essentially as a resource for the benefit of others.

Of course a certain amount of unacknowledged extraction of tissue has often been carried out by pathologists and morgue attendants, sometimes for specific research purposes but also for routine purposes such as the regular extraction of pituitary glands (although this practice has largely discontinued). Also the motivation of leaving ones body to science is not that uncommon – many medical schools will attest that there is little difficulty in obtaining corpses for dissection. However, the demand for organs for transplantation is high and waiting lists are constantly growing. Thus the question of human tissue and organ use has been brought more into the open, and has become an issue for a greater range of health care professionals, for example, the nurses and doctors caring for potential organ donors in intensive care units.

Popularising organ donation

Proponents of transplantation can draw on a rich vein of public altruism and utilitarianism to support the donation of human organs: '*Don't take your organs with you to heaven – heaven knows we need them here*', '*make it your duty ... help us to help other live*', '*Help someone to live after your death*', and '*Will you be a hero in someone else's eyes*'. The current legal position in the United Kingdom is that the next of kin of a potential organ donor have to give their permission for organ retrieval to take place. Consequently, campaigns are directed at raising the general awareness of organ donation in the population so that at the time of a sudden death in the family when the deceased is a potential organ donor, their wishes regarding organ donation are well known, either from carrying a donor card, or from prior discussions within the family. Media coverage of transplant recipients, or of severely ill people (generally children) who need a life-saving transplant, keeps the profile of transplant surgery high and underlines the promotion of organ donation as a matter of gift-giving and moral duty.

Media coverage focuses upon the family as a unit of decision-making – partly because the next of kin are popularly assumed to be the legal possessors of the body and are responsible for its disposal. It is also because it is the surviving relatives who have to live with whatever decision is made.

DONOR FAMILIES

Research issues

Transplantation is the preferred treatment for patients requiring renal replacement therapy, and is often the only life-saving option for patients with liver and cardiac failure. Consequently, there is a high and unmet demand for transplants. Furthermore, there is a number of procedural steps during which organs may be 'lost': failure by hospital staff to identify potential organ donors (primarily people who have suffered a catastrophic injury to their brain); failure to approach the next of kin regarding permission; failure to co-ordinate the surgical teams for the organ retrieval; and failure to transplant the organs. These aspects are essentially under the control of health professionals, generally helped by specialist transplant co-ordinators. However, even with a completely efficient system, the actual supply of organs is always less than the potential because a considerable proportion of relatives does not give permission for organ donation. These rates of refusal to donate stubbornly persist at around the 30 per cent level. There has, therefore, been considerable interest as to why relatives refuse consent, and to what can be done to meet any information or educational needs which might have encouraged their consent.

Families of potential organ donors in South Wales

The material presented in this section relates to a larger study carried out on the availability of organs for transplantation in Wales, in the late 1980s (Salih *et al.* 1991). A series of interviews was conducted with bereaved families – who had either consented to organ donation, or who had refused – in order to examine how organ donation appeared to people who are asked about it when a relative had died (often extremely suddenly and traumatically) in hospital.

The sample of interviewed families derived from an examination of all cases of death in twenty-one acute care hospitals in South Wales over a twelve month period. By a process of applying varying criteria, cases of death were identified where the patients satisfied certain conditions for organ donation. The details of 186 deceased patients were followed up with the staff who had cared for them and with their next of kin as identified in the nursing or medical notes. The families of about thirty per cent of the deceased patients agreed to be interviewed. The material presented here is derived from a smaller subset of this thirty per cent: from fifteen interviews with families who gave their permission for organ donation, from eight interviews with families who refused donation, and from three interviews with families who had discussed organ donation in hospital, although it had not in fact taken place.

The interviews were usually conducted with families at about 3 to 4 months after the death. They were intended to explore: why relatives had agreed to organ donation or had refused it; how they felt hospital staff had discussed organ donation with them; and what they felt about their decision at the time of interview, that is, a number of months after the event.

Permission granted

The most common reason why families allowed organ donation was because it was something they had thought about and had agreed was a good thing to do. In six cases the donors had carried a donor card at some point in their lives and so the decision was a relatively easy one to make. The families talked in terms of making 'sense out of a senseless death', and making the death less 'worthless'. There was also the aspect of the donor living on in other people. In answer to the question 'how do you feel about your decision now ?' the sister of one donor said,

> Oh no regrets at all, no and its helped my mother tremendously. Oh yes, she says Oh its great because part of Kevin[2] is still going on. He's helped someone, he didn't die in vain.

The families who did not know if their relative had signed a donor card or not but who still agreed to donation because they were generally in favour of it, tended to emphasise that the donor had been a very giving person and would have done anything to help other people. They felt the donation was simply an extension of this. Two families gave consent for organ donation principally because of their familiarity with renal failure in another family member. They hoped that if they agreed to this donation, then another family would agree to donation at another point in time in order to help them. There was one exceptional case. The daughter of one donor allowed donation although it was something that the rest of her family was not keen on, and also something which she thought her father would not have wanted either. In answer to the question 'what do you feel about your decision to donate his organs? she replied,

> Well I don't know ... my brother didn't want it to happen ... I think it helped me to accept the fact that he was dead ... I felt that it was wrong to take the decision to donate, so what I said to my brother was that I wasn't asking him to agree with something he disagreed with, what I was asking him to do was to think about what had happened. Do you know what I mean and to think that OK dad had died but through his death somebody else had lived.

What this lady went on to explain was that her father had always been a busy man and she felt that he had never had enough time for herself and her brother when they were children, so what she hoped was that the organs would go to another family man who might then have more time for his children.

Permission withheld

The families who had refused organ donation divided into two camps. On the one hand were the three families who said that they did not know the wishes of their relatives and so they couldn't agree to it, and on the other hand were the families who knew that organ donation was against the wishes of their relative. The families who said that they had refused donation because they had not known the wishes of their relative, said that if their relative had expressed a wish for organ donation, they wouldn't have stood in the way. Nevertheless, there was some antipathy on their part towards organ donation. The wife of one of these potential donors said,

> Well I suppose we didn't discuss it before ... I suppose if we did discuss it then I would have gone by his wishes ... but I just didn't know. I just wanted him to be left alone ... sort of rest in peace.

In response to the question as to what she thought about organ donation, the wife of another potential donor said,

> I didn't like the idea. His mother wanted me to donate but I couldn't bring myself to it ... I don't know what it was ... my husband used to say, uhm, I'm gonna be a donor, my body's going to science. But he never signed one of these cards or put it in the post box like ... I think that's what I had in the back of my mind as well ... I thought if he was really genuine about being a kidney donor or whatever he'd have signed one of those cards.

Four of the families interviewed said that at some time their relative had definitely expressed a wish not to donate their organs. The husband of one potential donor was not surprised when the question was raised in the hospital but organ donation had been something he and his wife had discussed quite a lot. He said,

> Well my wife didn't like the idea, taking things out of a body and putting into someone else's. She didn't think it was right ... I don't like

> the idea myself ... There's something wrong with it, it's hard to say what it is, but its not right. You've got to save lives any way you can really, but doing that is something very unusual. For the person that receives these organs I don't know how they feel.

In contrast, the wife of another potential donor was very much in favour of organ donation herself but her husband had ripped up her donor card and had said he did not believe in it. So she carried out his wishes not to allow donation.

Something which was mentioned by many of these families was the feeling that their relative had been through enough, had been 'messed around' enough, and that they didn't like the idea of them being cut up. Quite clearly there are those who when approached about organ donation know very clearly the wishes of the potential donor, either in favour or against. There are also those whose own feelings about organ donation are instrumental in the decision. There are also a small number of families who find it very difficult to decide and who can find the request agonising.

Information issues

When the suggestion of organ donation is raised in hospital, most staff hope that it is a subject which has been thought about prior to admission and on which there is some kind of family consensus. It must be a matter of considerable relief to the medical and nursing staff when it is clear that the relatives know the wishes of the donor, or even when they suggest organ donation themselves. For this to happen, organ donation and transplantation needs to be a relatively high profile subject in the media – something that has been achieved with varying degrees of success for most of the 1980s. Life-saving transplant operations, particularly heart or heart/lung transplants, still make local if not national headline news. However, the contemplation of organ donation requires a contemplation of one's own death and this is something that many people still find very difficult.

However, tied in with this idea of public and private debate on organ donation is the problem of information about what organ donation actually entails. The interviews revealed that very little actual information was given to relatives both of donors and potential donors, about organ donation and about what was required of them. A great deal of confusion and distress was caused. Many relatives waited around in hospitals thinking that they had to sign consent forms, or they were kept waiting for up to 24 hours after the final set of brain stem death tests before the donor was taken to theatre. Some went home and were not contacted when the donation had been completed and were then upset at not being with their relative when life support had been withdrawn. Many were worried about whether the organ removal would disfigure their relative; whether s/he would be sewn up afterwards and treated with dignity; and, if the corneas were to be removed, what the effect would be afterwards. For some, the experience of donating the organs of their relative had left them feeling uncertain about their own wishes. The family of one organ donor felt that the experience had been so traumatic and distressing that they had all decided they were against organ donation in the future. In their relative's case, they claimed that they had not been told which organs would be taken and they were shocked when they went to view the body afterwards. They had not realised that the corneas would be taken: their relative's eyes had been enucleated and the sockets had not been repaired with due aesthetic consideration.

The timing and implications of withdrawal of life support are another matter. These were raised by one family with whom organ donation had been discussed, although in the end it was not a possibility. Initially in favour of organ donation, the parents regretted that it had not been possible and afterwards tried to find information as to why organ donation had not occurred after their child had 'died' (come off the ventilator). Accepting that someone is actually dead while appearing warm, perfused and 'breathing' is one of the mirages of medical science. When the parents realised that ventilatory support was extended to the time of organ removal they were relieved that organ donation had not taken place as it was not something they would have agreed to with any comfort. These parents intuitively could not accept that it was right to remove organs from such a person.

How much information hospital staff give to relatives is a problem. The need for information obviously varies from person to person and if details are glossed over in the hospital some families will be concerned enough to find out as much as possible about organ donation afterwards by doing their own library research. They may subsequently find out details which might have affected their decision.

Staff attitudes

It has been asserted that staff attitudes to organ donation are important determinants in the likelihood of families being approached about possible organ donation. Most interviewees (donor and non-donor families) reported hospital staff to have been excellent and sympathetic in their approach and in general there few dissatisfactions with the way that organ donation had been discussed. Some reported that a few doctors appeared ill at ease or did not seem to like the job of mentioning organ donation and that they seemed relieved when the relatives suggested it first. In reply to the question, 'did staff mention organ donation to you?', the sister of one donor said,

> No we did ... I think they were going to but we jumped the gun. I suggested it. They were very grateful to us, for, sort of approaching them, because it saved them from what is obviously not a very nice job.

However, given that the subject of discussion was organ donation, relatives did not seem to blame the doctors for being ill at ease or embarrassed by it. Many saw it as a job the doctors had to do and most of the families were half expecting that the question would be asked at some point. While the question itself did not seem to be a cause of resentment, what it represented in terms of their relative's death was harder to accept. For many families the shock came when the request for organ donation was made because they then had to confront the fact of death. The parents of one donor said,

> Even though we were prepared for the question it still came as a bit of a shock. I don't think we wanted to accept that Paul was dead. With the fact that the doctor was asking for the organs made it final. We knew then that he was dead because unless he was they wouldn't ask. It's not a thing you want to accept anyway.

The actual timing of the request for organs seemed to vary in the sample hospitals, not only between hospitals but also between staff. In some, the subject was raised before the brain stem death tests had been done. In others it was raised between the two sets of brain stem death tests; while in others still, the subject was not mentioned until brain stem death had been demonstrated after the second set of tests. There was also variation in the time when death was certified. Sometimes this was done on completion of the second set of brain stem death tests and sometimes on withdrawal of ventilation in theatre at the time of organ retrieval. The comments of the families on these issues underlined the need for a clear conceptual separation between the death of the person and the request for organ donation. Knowing that death had been certified may for some families bring home the fact that their relative had died and that the ventilator is performing a purely mechanical function. Postponing the certification of death until withdrawal of ventilation brings into question the status of brain stem death as a diagnosis of death.

Living with decisions

Finally, families were asked how they felt about their decision relating to organ donation, at some months after the event. Those families who gave their consent were mostly happy about the decision itself although there were other things which they were less happy about. Several had wanted more information about the recipients, although one family described being jolted into intensified grief at being told that the recipient of their son's heart was 'doing well and living in north-east England'. Four families reported being troubled with nightmares following the organ donation, three of these cases particularly were connected with the removal of corneas. At the time of interview these families said they were no longer having the bad dreams but that they had been troubled for the first few weeks and they had seriously wondered if they had done the right thing. Conversely, another family felt that donating organs had really helped them over the first few months of bereavement and were most positive with no regrets at all. Many families linked their feelings about the donation with the fate of the recipients. They felt it was all worth it as long as the organs had been transplanted with good results and that the recipients were doing well. All felt that agreeing to the donation had put themselves to extra stress and put their relatives through possible indignity. They accepted this, for the sake of the recipients.

Families who had refused organ donation all felt they had made the right decision. Those who did regret the absence of organ donation were some family members who were not actually responsible for the decision, for example, two mothers of adult men whose wives had been given the ultimate veto.

MEDICAL SCIENCE AND 'THE BODY'

Current concepts

Leaving aside the therapeutic and life-saving claims of the transplant community, and the fact that many people do agree to organ donation, transplantation raises other questions about the way we approach death; how we dispose of our bodies; how the health services deal with extracting body parts; and how decisions are made as to who does and who does not receive them. Commenting on the latter issue, West remarks, 'Transplantation challenges ethical precepts, but traditionally such reservations have taken a back seat to the temptations and incentives to perform innovative operations' (West 1991).

Some common themes concerning the nature of the body are apparent under the demands of transplant surgery. These themes are also implicit in the terminology used by medical professionals:

1. The body as a machine. Transplantation is a product of anatomical and symptom based medicine, depending on a mechanistic view of the body. The analogy with car maintenance is too clear to be laboured. Organs are 'extracted', 'salvaged' and 'replaced'.
2. The body as an ecological resource. The extraction and transplantation of organs from cadavers has been described as a rational form of recycling within the global biomass (Emson 1987). With the technology as it has been developed, healthy organs which would otherwise decay rapidly can instead be used to bring life back to others who are suffering major organ failure. Under this view, bodies are not goods to be bequeathed but are part of the larger biomass and should therefore be at the disposal of the wider public good. Organs are 'harvested' and 'retrieved'.
3. The body as a potential gift. Under this view, ownership of the body is important and organ 'donation' is encouraged by appealing to ideas of altruism/gifting (Gerrand 1994). Organs are 'donated', 'gifted' and 'received'.
4. The body as a commodity. Ownership of the body is important as a profitable resource. In various countries 'rewards' (monetary and non-monetary) have been paid to donor families and to hospitals that have participated in organ donor programmes. The parallels with body snatching for dissection are apparent, and as Richardson suggests, the body can become dangerously close to being a commodity in death as well as in life (Richardson 1987). Organs are 'procured' and organs from living donors are bought and sold.

These themes appear to be extremely potent in the presentation of transplantation. They emanate from the rational and scientific biomedical explanatory model of illness. This explanatory framework, with its Cartesian adherence to the mind/body divide has been subjected to recent critique and discussion (Turner 1992, Morgan and Scott 1993, Shilling 1993).

From the interviews with families of potential organ donors, evidence however, points to a shifting sand of sentiment regarding the proper disposal of bodies after death: a multi-layered concoction of religious, quasi-religious, and superstitious beliefs that contradict the mind/body dichotomy and assert that the body is more than simply the sum of its physical parts. This finding attests to the prevalence of other accounts which explain responses to health, illness and ultimately death (Stainton Rogers 1991), and which confirm the importance of recognising the *embodiment* of social, cultural and spiritual values.

CONCLUSION: THE DISCOURSE OF TRANSPLANTATION

Although transplantation is a major scientific achievement which has brought life and hope to many individuals, organ donation, the necessary corollary of transplantation, challenges conventional concepts of life and death. This work suggests that for some people, organ donation reduces the feeling of 'waste' that surrounds the untimely death of a young person, while for others it is an idea that cannot be accommodated, such are the feelings of 'unnaturalness' that it evokes. To reach a decision on organ donation involves a contemplation of death (one's own and one's loved one's) which is something that many people still find very difficult.

An aspect of organ donation that was mentioned during the course of interviews with families and with health professionals was the idea of putting oneself in the place of someone needing a transplant. If one were to desire a transplant either for oneself, or for a member of one's family, then one should allow the retrieval of organs from one's own body or that of a family member. The logic of this is deeply persuasive and it is here that the regulatory nature of medical discourse becomes most apparent and most problematic. Advances in medical science have a momentum of their own, and take place in a rarefied environment, often displaced from everyday life. High technology medicine (with its own science-driven agenda) presents marvellous opportunities for *individuals* (if they are lucky or wealthy enough). Indeed, denying individuals these benefits runs against many aspects of popular culture in 'high modernity which puts such high premium on the *individualisation* of the body' (Shilling 1993).

Analytically, buying into the apparent benefits of high technology medicine also implies the incorporation of a mechanistic view of the body as the dominant *modus operandi*.

The material presented here, however, suggests that public attitudes are not that clear-cut. If generalisation is possible from these data and other studies which have demonstrated a refusal rate of about thirty per cent (West 1991), then it can be concluded that there are strongly held feelings about the proper disposal of the body which counterpoint the dominant biomedical model. The implications of this for transplant surgery have been recognised over the last few years and it has become accepted that there will always be a proportion of families who will not allow organ retrieval from a dead relative. However, promotion campaigns continue to keep the benefits of transplant surgery uppermost in the public mind, while the media is quickly criticised when it chooses to dwell on the darker side of transplantation.

Meanwhile, recognising that the supply of human organs is imposing a ceiling on transplant rates, scientists see future developments in terms of non-human organs, particularly organs from genetically modified swine. This is currently stimulating enthusiastic research into 'the immunologic mechanisms of xenogenic rejection and the method of immunosuppression' (Nishimori *et al.* 1994). Far from resolving some of the ethical questions that have been 'camp followers' of the early and recent advances in transplant surgery, this field of medical science looks set to keep challenging ideas of body boundaries and self-identity.[3]

Notes

1. The fieldwork on which this chapter is based was financially supported by the Medical Research Council. I would like to acknowledge the contribution of other members of the research team –Debra Coupe, Stephen Frankel, and Ian Harvey.
2. All names have been changed.
3. I would like to thank Glennys Howarth, Peter Jupp and Ben Totu for their helpful comments on this chapter.

15 Facing Death without Tradition

Tony Walter[1]

In this chapter, I compare and contrast three different kinds of death. The first I term *traditional* and it corresponds to Ariès (1981) 'tame death' which he illustrates in the death of an old French peasant in times past:

> She contracted a summer cholera. After four days she asked to see the village priest, who came and wanted to give her the last rites. 'Not yet, M. le curé; I'll let you know when the time comes. Two days later: 'Go and tell M. le curé to bring me Extreme Unction'.
>
> (Ariès 1981: 10, quoting Guitton 1941: 14)

The woman was dying at home; she knew she was dying; she saw death as a spiritual passage, calling not the doctor but the priest who lived and was known in the community. Afterwards, doubtless a funeral would have been held in the local church and a period of mourning adhered to by the family. Tradition and religion dictated the scripts each actor played.

The second death I term *modern*; Ariès terms it hidden, or forbidden. Three quarters of the British now draw their last breath in hospital or in other institutions, away from home and hidden from society. The central character is no longer the dying person but the doctor, who relies not on prayer but on surgery, drugs and medical knowledge: the dying member of the community has become the dying hospital patient. Knowledge about dying is no longer held by the patient but has become the property of doctors who may or may not hand some of it down to the patient. When death itself comes, the patient may well have been sedated into unconsciousness for some hours or days. Seventy per cent of deaths in Britain are now followed by cremation and for most of these the only religious service consists of a few minutes in the crematorium which, like the hospital, is a high-tech, mass turnover institution organised on bureaucratic lines. In the months that follow, family and close friends keep their grief to themselves. Most modern people want to keep their dying and grieving 'd to hand control over to professionals and to leave ind. We die as we live, with private feelings separated tic procedures (Berger *et al.* 1974).

term *postmodern*, in the sense that it represents an progress beyond the modern way of death. Professional proce-s on the one hand, and the private experience of the dying and the grieving on the other, are no longer separated. In the hospice philosophy the ideal is for the dying person to regain control of the process, making informed choices about medical or spiritual techniques as s/he thinks appropriate. The feelings and preferences of the dying person are to take precedence over standardised nursing regimes; dying at home is encouraged if that is what the person and their family want. After death, the postmodern funeral celebrates the unique life of the deceased, and is followed by a period in which those who grieve are able to express and talk about how they feel. This is the good death eulogised in a thousand and one books criticising the modern way of death (Albery *et al.* 1993; Elias 1985; Illich 1977; Saunders 1990; Walter 1990), but only rarely achieved in practice.

I present the three ways of death as what sociologists refer to as *ideal types*. An ideal type is not ideal in the sense of being desirable[2] but in the sense of being an abstract idea in the head of the sociologist that is rarely if ever found in pure form in the real world. Ideal types have the same function as primary colours – red, blue, green – for the physicist: in the real world, hardly anything is pure red or pure blue, but these pure types help the physicist understand the infinite diversity of colours in the real world. So my three types help us understand the complexity of dying in the twentieth century. In particular they help us understand how ways of dying have changed historically, for there has been a tendency for the traditional type to give way to, or more accurately to be complemented by, the modern type, and the modern by the postmodern. Many deaths contain elements of all three, which can lead to tension and contradiction. Indeed, I sometimes refer to the types as historically succeeding one another, sometimes as co-existing today.

The three types of death are represented in Table 15.1.[3]

If we may characterise traditional death as essentially religious and modern death as essentially medical, then postmodern death is essentially personal. Its hallmarks are choice and personal expression. In this chapter I will look at the first two ways of death in a bit more detail before concentrating on the third – what is involved in facing death without tradition? How much choice can people exert when the body is finally winding down?

Table 15.1

	Traditional death	*Modern death*	*Postmodern death*
Authority	Tradition	Professional expertise	Personal choice
Authority figure	Priest	Doctor	The self
Dominant discourse	Theology	Medicine	Psychology
Coping through	Prayer	Silence	Expressing feelings
The traveller	Soul	Body	Personality
Bodily context	Living with death	Death controlled	Living with dying
Social context	Community	Hospital	Family

THE AUTHORITY OF TRADITION

Traditional societies (both those existing today, and in Europe in the past) are characterised by a high death rate and usually by a religious culture. Infant mortality is high, and death may come quickly and unannounced to any adult; without modern drugs, people can succumb to infectious disease within a few days. In such a society, as the burial service of the 1662 Prayer Book puts it, 'In the midst of life we are in death: of whom may we seek for succour, but of thee, O Lord?' The doctor, by contrast, is of little succour. If the society is stable, its members are likely to look to the faith of the old and the ancestors rather than to the new and the young; indeed, the rituals of burying and mourning the ancestors are central to how religion articulates society's sense of itself (Durkheim 1915). Religion provides an authoritative language and ritual to prepare the soul for its ongoing journey (see the chapters in this volume on Sikh and Hindu practices), and controls disposal of the body.

As Hockey observes in her chapter, traditional religious death rituals do not – contrary to fashionable opinion – necessarily meet the criteria of psychological health. In the Middle Ages, for example, death rituals were premised on anxiety about the Last Judgement and may have induced terror as often as hope. Death came with little warning and the dying moments could be delirious, leaving neither time nor clarity of mind to utter the required deathbed formula to assure entry to heaven (McManners 1981; Ariès 1981). Even given time, the poor very often could not afford the requisite rituals.

THE AUTHORITY OF EXPERTISE

The shift from the authority of traditional religion to the authority of the medical expert is associated in the West with changes in the bodily and social context in which both the dying and the living find themselves. Due as much to improved nutrition and clean water as to curative medicine (Illich 1977; McKeown and McLachlan 1971), the death rate has dropped rapidly over the past century and a half. We now expect each baby to live to adulthood and once in adulthood to live out the biblical span (which in biblical times people did *not* expect to attain). Death is no longer in the midst of us; it appears to have been controlled.

Whatever the actual role of curative medicine in improving life expectancy, it has been given most of the credit. Dying is no longer seen as a spiritual transition but as a medical condition. Death has been diversified from the single medieval image of the scythe-wielding skeleton to hundreds of specific diseases, each identifiable and potentially treatable by medicine (Bauman 1992a). The succour of the dying is no longer the Lord, but the doctor and his pain-killing drugs. Not only has dying been medicalised, but so too have disposal and grief. In the mid-nineteenth century, cemeteries were re-organised on the recommendation of experts in public health and the legislation of this period still provides the framework for disposal in the UK. The focus has shifted from a soul to be transported to the next world by faithful prayer, to a body that has a right to die without pain and to be disposed of without contaminating the living. In the twentieth century, grief too has come within the domain of medicine, with psychiatrists now defining what is normal and what is abnormal grief (Engel 1961, Parkes 1972) – previously community norms defined appropriate mourning.

Trust is now placed not in traditional knowledge held within the community but in the medical, paramedical and other professionals and institutions to whom and to which the body – before and after death – is handed over: the doctors who prescribe it drugs; the nurses who care for it in life and wash it in death; the funeral directors who remove it and (as they say) 'care' for it until the funeral; the high-tech crematoria that do the work once done by humble worms. We have placed our deaths, like our lives, in the hands of experts and expertise. The rise of the individual and the collapse of community have undermined the authority of tradition; we no longer know how to deal with death when it comes, so we pay professionals (either directly or through taxation) to handle it for us. In a de-traditionalised society, the expert rules.

Where does this leave the dying person and his or her family? With little authority and even less knowledge. Thankfully, having a parent or sibling die is no longer a normal part of growing up, but this means that knowledge about death and dying is no longer handed down from generation to generation as a normal part of socialisation. Most adults now know little about death, so must wait for doctor's orders and accept with deference the advice of the undertaker.

THE AUTHORITY OF THE SELF

Control of death by doctors and other experts has been welcomed by the vast majority of modern people, but there has been a price: the exclusion of the dying person. The dying patient, lying in the hospital bed stuffed full of drugs and tubes, visited by family at the bureaucratically determined visiting hours, is hardly a person (Elias 1985). Nor is the personality of the deceased present at the routinely impersonal funeral of the standard British crematorium (Walter 1990). The grieving have to keep a stiff upper lip and pretend that they feel fine, because death is supposed to have been abolished. Public provision and social expectation trample over private experience.

In response to all this, what Lofland (1978) has called 'the happy death movement' has attempted to personalise death and dying. The hospice movement, the life-centred funeral and bereavement counselling – still involved in as yet only a small percentage of deaths yet representing a significant trend – aim to put the experience of the individual centre stage. In this new order, private experience informs public provision. The key themes are personal choice and the celebration of personality (Walter 1994).

Patients with cancer or HIV are increasingly informed about not only their condition (Seale 1991b) but also the range of possible treatments; many pick and choose combinations of treatment, conventional and complementary. In many hospitals and in all hospices, visiting hours are designed to suit patients and their families rather than to suit nursing routines; the feelings of all concerned (doctors and nurses as well as patients and families) are publicly acknowledged (Wouters 1990).

After death, there is mounting criticism of impersonal funerals (Walter 1990; Young 1994). After a lifetime fighting the impersonality of the mass society and trying to carve out a sense of personal identity (Berger and Kellner 1964; Giddens 1991), a funeral that does not affirm this unique identity is experienced as less than satisfactory. Though more personal funerals are still far from the norm, this is the direction in which both popular and expert opinion is moving.

After the funeral, traditional community norms for mourning have been rejected. By the beginning of this century the British middle classes began to notice that death rates were declining and felt less need to ritualise death (Howarth in press); some women began to comment that mourning restricted them far more than men (Taylor 1983); in any case, extensive mourning could not be continued between 1914 and 1918 when there was a war to fight (Gorer 1965). For some decades after this the middle classes no longer quite knew how bereaved persons should behave, except that they should keep their grief to themselves. Recently, however, a new framework is emerging, called 'the grief process', in which the bereaved move through grief by talking about and/or directly expressing feelings, if not in the supermarket or at the bus stop at least with a trusted friend, professional counsellor or bereavement group (Wambach 1985). Personal feeling, not public expectation, sets this postmodern agenda. In the working class, death – especially infant death – remained an obvious part of life for longer, and the de-ritualisation of death has therefore lagged a couple of generations behind (Howarth in press). In some immigrant groups ritualised death is still the norm. The current revival of interest in death and dying is still very much a phenomenon of the middle class, especially of the 'expressive' professions (Martin 1981), less so of the commercial middle class.

One underlying reason for the revival of interest in death and the discovery of the dying or grieving person has been pointed to by Lofland (1978). Whereas in traditional societies people die in a matter of days from first receiving a wound or infection, the postmodern experience is very different. Consider cancer, coronary heart disease and HIV. Early diagnosis of these life-threatening conditions together with treatments that prolong life but cannot remove the condition, cause many people now to take not a few days to die, but months, years or even decades. Most adults of middle age or beyond either have, or know close family or friends with one of these conditions. Many dying people are better informed medically because they now have time to be. If the traditional human condition is that of living with death, and the modern condition one of death denied, the postmodern condition is more one of living with dying – embodied in the motto of one cancer relief agency *Living with Cancer* and the similar motto *Living with HIV*. Those with a life threatening disease are no longer being advised to turn their face to the wall and say their last prayer but to get on with living in the light of their mortality. As Lofland puts it, ours is no longer a brief encounter with death but a prolonged affair. Consequently, a new craft of dying is being developed – and the new craftsmen and women are none other than the dying themselves.

A revival of tradition

Lofland also observes that the 'happy death movement', like any social movement, needs an enemy. The enemy it has chosen, which is ritually denounced at the start of movement publications, is the modern way of death. These publications provide wholesome examples of traditional dying which highlight the deficiencies of impersonal modern death – the archetypal example being the death of a Swiss farmer which Kübler-Ross witnessed in childhood and which she recounts near the beginning of her best-selling *On Death and Dying* (1970). Most references to traditional death in the now huge literature on death and dying are therefore ideological, their purpose being not to provide scientific description of traditional death but to challenge the institutionalised modern way of death (Walter 1995b). In traditional deaths documented by historians and anthropologists, the dying or grieving person is the chief actor but not the writer of the script. Ideological references to traditional death, however, gloss over the script provided by tradition because this would not appeal to postmodern people who want to write their own scripts (see Hockey's chapter in this book, and Walter 1995b). Postmoderns are just as averse as moderns to being controlled by a narrow-minded traditional community.

I therefore cannot emphasise enough that, despite the glowing references in current death literature to the benefits of traditional ways, the postmodern way of dying, disposing and grieving, does not entail a return to traditional authority. The references are highly selective. What is authoritative is not tradition but the postmodern individual who picks and chooses from traditional deathways what s/he fancies. Jencks (1986) argues that this kind of 'double coding' in which modern expertise and traditional style are combined is typical of postmodern architecture. Bits and pieces of the past are chosen for their ability to make the building look good and the viewer feel good: this is certainly a revival of tradition, but not of the authority of tradition. The same is true of postmodern death – the only authority is the postmodern consumer. An example is *The Natural Death Handbook* (Albery *et al.* 1993) in which the world is scoured for examples of good dying, good burial practice and healthy grieving from which the Briton of the 1990s may construct his or her own exit. Another example is the chemotherapy unit of a major London hospital where in addition to the expertly tailored cocktail of sophisticated drugs the patient may choose aromatherapy, massage, counselling, spiritual healing and other complementary forms of healing. After death, as Bradbury argues in her chapter, bereaved people draw from a range of representations which they adapt to make sense of their own experience. In all this, experts still select what are 'good' forms of traditional medicine or 'healthy' kinds of ritual, so postmodern choice does not dispense with modern expertise. But whereas moderns reject tradition, postmoderns concoct their own personal mix of perceived tradition and modern expertise.

A Divided Authority

The new focus on the dying, dead or grieving person contains two strands. Each is often found within the same agency or even within the same individual, often in considerable tension.

The radical strand is associated with the view that there are as many ways of approaching death as there are individuals, or at least cultures: death can be endowed with meanings of all sorts, and it is not for experts to prescribe what this death means to this person, or how that person should express their grief (Wortman and Silver 1989). The radical strand therefore not only puts the dying, dead or bereaved person centre stage, but gives them authority to write their own script. No-one can tell them how to die or how to grieve, but carers can be 'with them' as they tread their own path.

> It should be your objective as friend and supporter to let your friend let go of life *in his own way*. It may not be your way, and it may not be the way you read about in a book or magazine, but it's his way and consistent with the way hes lived his life.
>
> (Buckman 1988)

In this strand, one is likely to hear less talk of psychological theories which prescribe the stages of healthy dying or grieving, and more likely to hear talk of 'spirituality. Spirituality is usually defined here as the process by which the individual makes sense of his or her own life and death, that which gives him or her spirit and courage; it is the postmodern replacement for religion, in which meaning is sought within the self rather than revealed through a church (Carson 1989; Saunders 1988; Walter 1995a).

The expert strand is convinced that death and loss are inherently traumatic, especially in a modern world which has lost touch with older rituals. The expert strand therefore replaces priests and doctors with counsellors and therapists who are believed to have the experience and the skills to assist the person through this difficult passage. (The priests and doctors may themselves learn counselling skills and present these as qualification for working with people who are dying or bereaved.)

Although the focus of these new experts is no longer the soul or the body but the self, the experts retain authority.

From the research of sociologists such as Armstrong (1984), Arney and Bergen (1984) and Rose (1989), one might conclude that there is no such thing as a radical strand. The holistic approach of modern medicine expands the realm of medical expertise. When professionals gaze into the heart of the dying or bereaved person, control is given not to that person but to the professional. The more the patient talks about inner feelings, the more complete is the doctor's surveillance of the patient. Now the doctor sees into every part of the person – every part of the person is now a patient. Likewise the expansion of nursing care to include emotional and spiritual concerns of dying patients has enhanced their professional status *vis-à-vis* doctors and more especially *vis-à-vis* paramedics such as social workers, counsellors, therapists and chaplains (Walter 1994). The result is the further professionalisation of death.

I do not think, though, that the radical strand can be completely dismissed as a smokescreen for professional aggrandisement, though undoubtedly there is an element of this. Many workers in palliative and bereavement care make genuine efforts to enable their patients and clients to die or grieve in their own way.

At best, the two strands co-exist creatively in the same person or agency: the hospice that enables the patient to die according to his or her own preference, in the meantime offering expert pharmacological and psychological help as requested. At worst, the expert strand veers into manipulation of distressed people, imposing on them expert definitions of reality and dogmatically reifying fashionable psychological theories. Even non-professionals can get hooked into expert definitions, as one participant observer of a bereavement self-help group in Arizona noted:

> Typical first statements widows would hear at widows' groups were 'Have you heard about the grief process?' and 'There's such a thing as a grief process, you know' ... Both widows and professionals took it seriously, and there was much concern if a widow was not 'moving through grief' as expected.
>
> (Wambach 1985: 204)

Likewise, there was a tendency in the decade after publication of Kübler-Ross' book for American nurses to *expect* patients to move through her five psychological stages – which she originally formulated not as prescriptions but as descriptions (Germain 1980).

The radical strand has a different weakness: it can be unrealistic in its vision of individual choice. With a low death rate and most people dying in old age and in hospital, few who are dying have direct knowledge of how others have died. They have therefore had little 'experience' of dying, which makes it hard for them to know what might constitute their own preference. (One oft-observed feature of near-death experiences is that the experiencers become much more relaxed about dying: they have been there already and know there is nothing to fear. Most people have not had such practice.) One small hospice study found that terminal cancer patients who had already experienced a hospice room-mate die were less fearful for their own death (Honeybun *et al.* 1992). Patients in hospital coronary care units might find that witnessing others deaths makes them *more* fearful, because of the frantic and violent resuscitation assault on the body undergoing cardiac arrest, but the point is the same: most of us have little idea of what it is to die. Patients therefore look around anxiously at other patients; they ask staff what it is going to be like when they get near the end; they read articles in magazines cut out by friends and relatives. People who are dying look to experts for help. Likewise people who are grieving read bereavement autobiographies (Holloway 1990) and join bereavement groups to listen to the stories of others who are further down the path of grief.

Not only do people who are dying or grieving look for help, modern palliative and bereavement services – even the most radical ones – actively teach ideals of the good death and of healthy grieving (Walter 1994). Hospices portray the good death as peaceful, and engage in 'hope work' (Perakyla 1988). Bereavement groups are concerned to normalise feelings, to assure members that what they are feeling is okay. We should observe that these are the values of the 'expressive' professional class (Martin 1981) and may conflict with, for example, the Hindu prescription to die on the floor; with Dylan Thomas' injunction 'Do not go gentle into that good night'; or even with scientific findings (Wortman and Silver 1989). Patients and clients are encouraged to 'be themselves' in certain ways but not in others.

CONCLUSION

The new authority in death and dying is not, therefore, the authority of the autonomous individual or of the postmodern consumer but the authority of persons who negotiate with each other and are influenced by what they see, hear and read. I will conclude by illustrating how this process of negotiation occurs in dying, disposal and grief.

Although most draw their last breath in a hospital or other institution, much of the time spent dying may well be at home. As Kellehear (1990) has shown in his study of a hundred Australians dying of cancer at home (many of whom went on to draw their last breath in hospital), family members negotiate the dying role, drawing on past experiences, family traditions and current needs. Here at home, the expertise of the doctor and the therapeutic concern with expressing feelings may have a place, but only within a pattern of family interaction in which the dominant concerns may be to sort out the person's practical affairs and to cater for the well-being of survivors.

After death, even the most individualised and original do-it-yourself funerals (Albery *et al.* 1993; Spottiswoode 1991) are not invented *de novo*. Rather there is a learning process in which more personal funeral traditions develop. The arranger of the apparently highly original funeral turns out to have had previous experience of personalised funerals or has seen one on television or was involved in highly personal care of the person as they were dying and decided to continue this care for the body after death.

Likewise, grief is negotiated. Though popularly believed to be a natural process deep within the individual, the grieving experience is socially influenced. The words we give to feelings affect the feelings themselves, and if a bereavement group is anything it is a process through which my feelings this week are affected by your account of your feelings last week. There can be conflict within families over who deserves support as the chief mourner, especially where a young married adult dies and both spouse and parent stake a claim for support from the other. There can also be conflict within a family between generations and between the sexes as to the 'proper' way to grieve (Littlewood 1992). When traditional mourning rituals are lost, we are not left simply with a natural psychological process called grief. We are left with an arena of at worst conflict, and at best negotiation, as to how each individual should behave and feel.

I am not disputing the genuineness of sorrow – all I am saying is that the emotion felt is socially influenced. Bereavement agencies often quote Shakespeare's 'Give sorrow words: the grief that does not speak / whispers the o'er fraught heart, and bids it break'. (Macbeth IV.III) Indeed. Grief has a language, and that language is like any other – continually evolving, its words influencing our concepts and feelings.

The interpersonal nature of dying, disposing and grieving has been obscured by the rather successful claim of psychologists and therapists to be the experts in this field. They have turned our gaze within the psyche of the dying or grieving person. In this chapter, however, I have argued for a more social understanding of dying and grieving. From this I conclude that dying, disposing and grieving according to personal choice, picking and choosing from tradition rather than being dictated by it, is indeed possible, but not without encouragement, negotiation and legitimation. Authority rests, in even the most postmodern death, not with the autonomous individual, but with negotiating and mutually influencing persons. Dying without tradition is possible, but only in the company of, and with the support of, others and with reference to emerging traditions and emerging expert definitions of what is 'natural' (Walter 199b). There are many ways in which human beings can approach their own and others' mortality, but no one chooses their approach independent of others. Some individuals may be able to die or grieve without religion and without tradition, but they still look to others for help, guidance and affirmation. True, we each die alone. But we also die as we live, as social beings.

Notes

1. Earlier drafts of this chapter were presented in 1993 at the Oxford conference 'Death, Dying and Disposal'; at the Lancester University conference 'De-traditionalisation: authority and self in an age of cultural uncertainty'; and to the sociology department of Plymouth University. I gratefully acknowledgee the insights and critisms given on these three occasions and also comments on drafts given by David Field, Valerie Levin and Clive Seale. I elaborate the arguments of this chapter in Walter (1994).
2. Personally, I am as reliant as the next person on professional expertise (type 2), I value personal self-determination (type 3) and I am glad I belong to the twentieth century though I respect the wisdom built up over centuries in settled communities (type 1). None of this should affect the analysis of this chapter.
3. This summaries a fuller table presented in Walter (1994: chapters 3 and 4), where the pros and cons of using the term 'postmodern' are also discussed.

Bibliography

Ahmedzai, S. (1993) 'The medicalisation of dying: a doctor's view', in D. Clark (ed.), *The Future for Palliative Care* (Buckingham: Open University Press).

Albery, N., Eliot, G. and Eliot, J. (eds.) (1993) *The Natural Death Handbook* (London: Virgin).

Ariès, P. (1974) *Western Attitudes Towards Death: From the Middle Ages to the Present* (Baltimore: Johns Hopkins University Press).

Ariès, P. (1981) *The Hour of Our Death* (London: Allen Lane).

Armstrong, D. (1984) 'Silence and Truth in Death and Dying', *Social Science & Medicine*, 24: 8, 651–7.

Arney, W.R. and Bergen, B.J. (1983) 'The anomaly, the chronic patient and the play of medical power', *Sociology of Health and Illness*, 5: 1–24.

Arney, W.R. and Bergen, B.J. (1984) *Medicine and the Management of Living* (Chicago: University of Chicago Press).

Association for Palliative Medicine of Great Britain and Ireland (1993) *Palliative Medicine Curriculum* (Southampton).

Baider, L. and Porath, S. (1981) 'Uncovering fear: group experience of nurses in a cancer ward', *Internation Journal of Nursing Studies*, 18, 47–52.

Baldwin, A. (1981) 'Changing Work Stress: Use of nurse-to-nurse consultation', *Nursing Administration Quarterly*, 5 (2) 42–7.

Ballard, R. (1989) 'Differentiation and Disjunction amongst the Sikhs in Britain', in N.G. Barrier and V.A. Dusenbery (eds), *The Sikh Diaspora* (Delhi: Manohar Publications).

Barbieri, F. (1992) 'The Two Faces of Beauty', *FMR*, 57: 62–8.

Basham, A.L. (1967) *The Wonder that was India* (Fontana-Collins).

Batson, C.D. and Ventis, W.L. (1982) *The Religious Experience* (Oxford: Oxford University Press).

Baudrillard, J. (1990) *Seduction*, translated from the French by B. Singer (New York: St Martin's Press).

Baudrillard, J. (1993) *Symbolic Exchange and Death* (London: Sage).

Bauman, Z. (1992a) *Mortality, Immortality and Other Life Strategies* (Oxford: Polity).

Bauman, Z. (1992b) *Intimations of Postmodernity* (London: Routledge).

Beauvoir, S de. (1974) *The Second Sex*, translated and edited by H.M. Parshley (New York: Vintage Books).

Beier, L.M. (1989) 'The good death in seventeenth century Great Britain', in R. Houlbrooke (ed.), *Death, Ritual and Bereavement* (London: Routledge).

Benoliel, J.Q. (1983) 'The historical development of cancer nursing in the US', *Cancer Nursing*, 6: 4, 261–8.

Benoliel, J.Q. (1988) 'Health care providers and dying patients: critical issues in terminal care', *Omega*, 18: 341–63.

Benton, T.F. (1985) 'Medical education and training in palliative medicine: Medical undergraduates', *Palliative Medicine*, 2: 139–42.

Berger, P. and Kellner, H. (1964) 'Marriage and the Construction of Reality', *Diogenes*, 46: 1–25.

Berger, P., Berger, B. and Kellner, H. (1974) *The Homeless Mind: modernization and consciousness* (Harmondsworth: Penguin).

Bhachu, P. (1985) *Twice-Migrants: East African Sikh Settlers in Britain* (London: Tavistock).
Bhattacharyya, N.N. (1975) *Ancient Indian Rituals and Their Social Context* (London: Curzon Press).
Biswas, B. (1993) 'The medicalisation of dying: a nurse's view', in D. Clark (ed.), *The Future for Palliative Care* (Buckingham: Open University Press).
Blauner, R. (1966) 'Death and social structure', *Psychiatry*, 29: 378–94.
Bloch, M. and Parry, J. (eds) (1982) *Death and the Regeneration of Life* (Cambridge: Cambridge University Press).
Bloch, M. (1982) 'Death, Women and Power', in M. Bloch and J. Parry, (eds), *Death and the Regeneration of Life* (Cambridge: Cambridge University Press).
Bloch, M. (1992b) *Prey Intó Hunter: The Politics of Religious Experience* (Cambridge: Cambridge University Press).
Bloch, M. (1992a) 'What Goes Without Saying', in A. Kuper (ed.), *Conceptualizing Society* (London: Routledge).
Boas, F. (1965) [1911] *The Mind of Primitive Man* (New York: Free Press).
Bond, S. (1982) 'Communications in Cancer Nursing', in M.C. Cahoon (ed.), *Recent Advances in Cancer Nursing* (London: Churchill Livingstone).
Bos, M.A. (1991) *The diffusion of heart and liver transplantation across Europe* (London: Kings Fund Centre).
Bowker, J. (1991) *The Meanings of Death* (Cambridge: Cambridge University Press).
Bradbury, M. (1993a) *The Social Construction of Death: A London Study*, unpublished PhD thesis, University of London (LSE).
Bradbury, M. (1993b) 'Contemporary representations of 'good' and 'bad' death', in D. Dickenson and M. Johnson (eds), *Death, Dying and Bereavement* (London: Sage).
Brain, R. (1979) *The Decorated Body* (London: Hutchinson).
Bronfen, E. (1992) *Over Her Dead Body* (Manchester: Manchester University Press).
Brown, C. (1992) 'A Revisionist Approach to Religious Change', in S. Bruce (ed.), *Religion and Modernization* (Oxford: Clarendon).
Brown, J.M. (1992) 'Changing the Culture', *Policing*, 8: 307–321.
Brown, J.M. (1994) *Stress and Policing: Sources and strategies* (London: Wiley).
Brown, J.M. and Forde, P. (1989) 'Occupational Stress amongst Hampshire Constabulary Officers', unpublished report, Hampshire Constabulary Research and Development Department.
Buckman, R. (1988) *I Dont Know What to Say* (London: Macmillan).
Buckman, R. (1993a) *How to Break Bad News – Guide for Health Care Professionals* (London: Macmillan).
Buckman, R. (1993b) 'Communication in palliative care', in D. Doyle, G. Hanks, and D. MacDonald (eds), *Oxford Textbook of Palliative Medicine* (Oxford: Oxford University Press).
Calman, K.C. (1988) 'Medical training – the early post-graduate years', *Palliative Medicine*, 2: 143–6.
Cannadine, D. (1981) 'War and Death, Grief and Mourning in Modern Britain', in J. Whaley (ed.), *Mirrors of Mortality* (London: Europa Publications).

Capra, F. (1982) *The Turning Point* (London: Wildwood House).
Carson, V.B. (1989) *Spiritual Dimensions of Nursing Care* (Philadelphia: W.B. Saunders).
Carstairs, G.M. (1958) *The Twice Born: a Study of a Community of High Caste Hindus* (Bloomington: Indiana University Press).
Carter, A. (1992) 'The Wrightsman Magdalene', *FMR*, 54: 17–22.
Cederoth, S., Corlin, C. and Lindstrom, J. (1988) *On the Meaning of Death* (Uppsala: Acta Universitatis Upsaliensis).
Chambers, G. (1979) *The Almost Complete Irish Gag Book* (London: Star).
Charlton, R. (1992) 'The philosophy of palliative medicine: a challenge for medical education', *Medical Education,* 26: 473–7.
Christian, W.A. (1972) *Person and God in a Spanish Valley* (Princeton: University Press).
Clark, K. (1959) *The Nude* (Garden City, New York: Doubleday Anchor Books).
Cleiren, M.P.H.D. (1991) *Adaptation After Bereavement* (Leiden: DSWO Press).
Clifford, J. and Marcus, G. (1986) *Writing Culture* (Berkeley: University of California Press).
Cooper, D.K.C. and Lanza, R.P. (1984) *Heart Transplantation* (Lancaster: MTP Press).
Corr, C.A. (1993) 'Coping With Dying: Lessons We Should and Should Not Learn From the Work of Elizabeth Kubler-Ross', *Death Studies*, 17, 1, 69–83.
Crichton, I. (1976) *The Art of Dying* (London: Peter Owen Limited).
Danto, A.C. (1994) *Embodied Meanings: Critical Essays and Aesthetic Meditations* (New York: Farrar Straus Giroux).
Davey, B. (1993) 'The nurse's dilemma: truth telling or big white lies?', in D. Dickenson and M. Johnson (eds), *Death, Dying and Bereavement* (London: Sage).
Davie, G. (1994) *Believing and Belonging* (Oxford: Blackwell).
Davies, C. (1990a) *Ethnic Humor Around the World: a Comparative Analysis* (Bloomington: Indiana University Press).
Davies, C. (1990b), 'Nasty Legends, Sick Humour and Ethnic Jokes about Stupidity', in G. Bennett and P. Smith, (eds), *A Nest of Vipers* (Sheffield: Sheffield Academic Press).
Davies, D.J. (1985) 'Symbolic Thought and Religious Knowledge', *British Journal of Religious Education*, 7, 2.
Davies, D.J. *et al.* (1990) *Rural Church Project Vol IV: The Views of Rural Parishioners* (Cirencester: Royal Agricultural College).
Davies, D.J. (1991) *Cremation Today and Tomorrow* (Nottingham: Alcuin/GROW Books).
Davies, D.J. (1993) 'The Dead at the Eucharist', *Modern Churchman*, xxxiv, 3, 26–32.
Davies, D.J. Watkins, C. and Winter, M. (1991) *Church and Religion in Rural England* (Edinburgh: T. and T. Clark).
Davies, J. (1994) *Ritual and Remembrance: Responses to Death in Human Societies* (Sheffield Academic Press).
Davies, J. (1995) *The Christian Warrior in the Twentieth Century* (The Mellen Press).
Davis, F. (1966) 'Uncertainty in Medical Prognosis, Clinical and Functional', in W.R. Scott and E.H. Volkart (eds), *Medical Care* (New York: Wiley).

Dent, T.H., Gillard, J.H., Aarous, E.J., Crimlisk, H.L. and Smyth-Pigott (1990) 'Pre-registration house officers in four Thames regions: I. Survey of education and workload', *British Medical Journal*, 300: 713–6.

Department of Health (1988) *Health Services Management: Provision of donor organs for transplantation* (London: Department of Health).

Dijkstra, B. (1983) *Idols of Perversity* (New York: Oxford University Press).

Douglas, M. (1966) *Purity and Danger: An Analysis of the Concepts of Pollution and Taboo* (London: Routledge and Kegan Paul).

Doyle, D. (1993) 'Palliative medicine – a time for a definition?', *Palliative Medicine*, 7: 253–5.

Doyle, D., Hanks, G. and MacDonald, D. (1993) 'Introduction', in D. Doyle, G. Hanks and D. MacDonald (eds), *Oxford Textbook of Palliative Medicine* (Oxford: Oxford University Press).

Duckworth, D. (1986) 'Psychological Problems arising from Disaster Work', *Stress Medicine*, 2: 315–323.

Duffy, E. (1992) *The Stripping of the Altars: Traditional Religion in England c. 1400–1500* (New Haven and London: Yale University Press).

Durkheim, E. (1919) *The Elementary Forms of the Religious Life* (London: Unwin).

Durkheim, E. (1951) *Suicide* (translated by J.A. Spaulding and G. Simpson) (New York: Free Press).

Durlak, J.A. and Riesenberg, L.A. (1991) 'The impact of death education', *Death Studies*, 15: 39–58.

Eisenbruch, M. (1984) 'Cross-Cultural Aspects of Bereavement II: Ethnic and Cultural Variations in the Development of Bereavement Practices', *Culture, Medicine and Psychiatry*, 8, 4, December, 315–347.

Elias, N. (1985) *The Loneliness of Dying* (Oxford: Blackwell).

Engel, G.I. (1961) 'Is Grief a Disease?', *Psychosomatic Medicine*, 23, 1, 18–22.

Ellman, R. (1988) *Oscar Wilde* (New York: Alfred A. Knopf).

Emson, H.E. (1987) 'The ethics of human cadaver organ transplantation: a biologists viewpoint', *Journal of Medical Ethics*, 13, 124–126.

Evans-Pritchard, E. (1972 [1937]) *Witchcraft, Oracles and Magic among the Azande* (Oxford: Clarendon).

Farr, R.M. (1987) 'Social representations: a French tradition of research', *Journal for the Theory of Social Behaviour*, 17, 4, 343–369.

Farr, R.M. (1993) 'Theory and method in the study of social representations', in G.M. Breakwell and D.V. Canter (eds), *Empirical Approaches to Social Representations* (Oxford: Clarendon).

Field, D. (1984) 'Formal teaching about death and dying in UK medical schools', *Medical Education*, 18, 429–34.

Field, D. (1986) 'Formal teaching about death and dying in UK nursing schools', *Nurse Education Today*, 6, 270–6.

Field, D. (1989) *Nursing the Dying* (London: Routledge/Tavistock).

Field, D. (1994a) 'Palliative Medicine and the Medicalization of Death', *European Journal of Cancer Care*, 3, 58–62.

Field, D. (1994b) *Education for Terminal Care in UK Medical Schools in 1994: Report to Respondents,* Department of Epidemiology and Public Health, University of Leicester.

Field, D. and Howells, K. (1988) 'Dealing with Dying Patients: Difficulties and Strategies in Final Year Medical Students', *Death Studies*, 12, 9–20.

Field, D. and James, N. (1993) 'Where and how people die', in D. Clark (ed.), *The Future for Palliative Care* (Buckingham: Open University Press).

Fiefel, H. (1963) 'Death', in L. Faberow (ed.), *Taboo Topics* (New York: Atherton Press).

Finke, R. (1992) 'An Unsecular America', in S. Bruce (ed.), *Religion and Modernization* (Oxford: Clarendon).

Firth, S. (1994) *Death, Dying and Bereavement in a British Hindu Community*, Unpublished PhD Thesis, London University (SOAS).

Flood, R. (1985) *The Book of Fascinating Christian Facts* (Denver: Accent).

Foltyn, J.L (1989) *The Importance of Being Beautiful: The Social Construction of the Beautiful Self* (Ann Arbor: UMI).

Francis, L. (1992) 'Male and Female Clergy in England', *Journal of Empirical Theology*, 5, 2.

Frazer, J.G. (1980) *The Golden Bough* (New York: Macmillan).

Freud, S. (1952) 'Beyond the Pleasure Principle', in R.M. Hutchins (ed.), M. Alder (gen. ed.), *Freud. Volume 54: Great Books of the Western World* (Chicago: Encyclopedia Britannica).

Garland, M. (1989) 'Victorian Unbelief and Bereavement', in R. Houlbrooke (ed.), *Death, Ritual and Bereavement* (London: Routledge).

Geertz, C. (1973) *The Interpretation of Cultures* (New York: Basic Books).

General Medical Council (1993) *Tomorrow's Doctors: Recommendations on Undergraduate Medical Education* (London).

Germain, C.P. (1980) 'Nursing the Dying: implications of Kübler-Ross' staging theory', in R. Fox (ed.), *The Social Meaning of Death*, Annals of the American Academy of Political and Social Science, Vol 447, special issue.

Gerrand, N. (1994) 'The Notion of Gift-giving and Organ Donation', *Bioethics*, 8, 127–150.

Giddens, A. (1991) *Modernity and Self-Identity* (Oxford: Polity).

Gillon, R. (1986) *Philosophical Medical Ethics* (Chichester: J Wiley).

Glaser, B.G. and Strauss, A.L. (1965) *Awareness of Dying* (Chicago: Aldine).

Glaser, B.G. and Strauss, A.L. (1968) *Time for Dying* (New York: Aldine).

Goodman, M. (1992) 'A Bardot Mystery', *People*, 30 Nov, 57–61.

Goody, J. (1993) *The Culture of Flowers* (Cambridge: Cambridge University Press).

Gorer, G. (1948) *The Americans, a Study in National Character* (London: Cresset).

Gorer, G. (1955) 'The Pornography of Death', reprinted in G. Gorer (1965) *Death Grief and Mourning in Contemporary Britain* (London: Cresset).

Gorer, G. (1965) *Death, Grief and Mourning in Contemporary Britain* (London: Cresset).

Goswami, U. (1992) *Analogical Reasoning in Children* (Hove (UK): Lawrence Erlbaum).

Grainger, R. (1988) *The Unburied* (Churchman Publishing).

Guitton, J. (1941) *M. Pouget* (Paris: Gallimard).

Hamilton, D. (1982) 'A history of transplantation', in P.J. Morris (ed.), *Tissue Transplantation* (Edinburgh: Churchill Livingstone).

Hamilton, E. (1942) *Mythology* (Boston: Little, Brown).

Harvey, D. (1989) *The Condition of Postmodernity* (Oxford: Blackwell).

Hatfield, E. and Sprecher, S. (1986) *Mirror, Mirror: The Importance of Looks in Everyday Life* (New York: SUNY).

Hayes, N. (1994) *Foundations of Psychology* (London: Routledge).

Hayes, P. (1992) 'Policing the Hillsborough disaster', paper presented at the National Institute for Social Work Annual Conference.

Heald, G. (1982) 'A Comparison between American, European and Japanese Values', paper presented at World Association for Public Opinion Research, Hunt Valley, Maryland.

Heron House Associates (1979), *The Book of Numbers* (London: Pelham).

Hershman, P. (1981) *Punjabi Kinship and Marriage* (Delhi: Hindustan Publication Corporation).

Hertz, R. (1960) 'A Contribution to the Study of the Collective Representation of Death', in *Death and the Right Hand*, Translated by R. and C. Needham (London: Cohen and West).

Higginson, I. (1993) 'Palliative Care: A review of past changes and future trends', *Journal of Public Health Medicine*, 15, 3–8.

Hinton, J. (1967) *Dying* (London: Penguin).

Hockey, J. (1992) *Making the Most of a Funeral* (Richmond: Cruse–Bereavement Care).

Holloway, J. (1990) 'Bereavement Literature: a valuable resource for the bereaved and those who counsel them', *Contact: Interdisciplinary Journal of Pastoral Studies*, 3, 17–26.

Honeybun, J., Johnston, M. and Tookman, A. (1992) 'The Impact of a Death on Fellow Hospice Patients, *British Journal of Medical Psychology*, 65, 67–72.

Hornby, P. (1978) *The Official Irish Jokebook, No.3 (Book 2 to follow)* (London: Futura).

Howarth, G. (1992) *The Funeral Industry in the East End of London: an ethnographical study*, PhD thesis, University of London (LSE).

Howarth, G. (in press) *Last Rites: The work of the modern funeral director* (Amityville, New York: Baywood).

Howells, K. and Field, D. (1982) 'Fear of death and dying among medical students', *Social Science and Medicine*, 16, 1421–4.

Howells, K., Gould, M. and Field, D. (1986) 'Fear of Death and Dying in Medical Students: The Effects of Clinical Experience', *Medical Education*, 20, 502–6.

Hull, F.M. (1991) 'Death, dying and the medical student', *Medical Education*, 25, 491–6.

Huntingdon, R. and Metcalf, P. (1979) *Celebrations of Death: The anthropology of mortuary ritual* (Cambridge: Cambridge University Press).

Illich, I. (1977) *Limits to Medicine: Medical Nemesis: The expropriation of health* (London: Penguin).

Jackson, K.T. and Vergara, C.J. (1989) *Silent Cities* (New York: Princeton Architectural Press).

Jalland, P. (1989) 'Death, Grief and Mourning in the Upper-Class Family 1860–1914', in R. Houlbrooke (ed.), *Death, Ritual and Bereavement* (London: Routledge).

James, P.D. (1988) *Devices and Desires* (London: Faber & Faber).

James, V. (1986) *Care and work in Nursing the Dying: a Participant Observation Study of a Continuing Care Unit*, Unpublished PhD thesis, University of Aberdeen.

James, N. and Field, D. (1992) 'The Routinization of Hospice: Bureaucracy and Charisma', *Social Science and Medicine*, 34, 1363–75.

Jamison, K.R. (1993) *Touched with Fire: Manic Depressive Illness and the Artistic Temperament* (New York: The Free Press).

Jaynes, J. (1976) *The Origin of Consciousness in the Breakdown of the Bicameral Mind* (Boston: Houghton Mifflin).

Jeffery, D. (1994) 'Education in Palliative Care: A qualitative evaluation of the present state and the needs of general practitioners and community nurses', *European Journal of Cancer Care*, 3, 67–74.

Jencks, C. (1986) *What is Postmodernism?* (Art and Design).

Jodelet, D. (1991) *Madness and Social Representations* (Brighton: Harvester Wheatsheaf).

Johnson, I., Rogers, C., Biswas, B. and Ahmedzai, S. (1990) 'What do hospices do?', *British Medical Journal*, 300, 791–3.

Jones, M.A. (1960) *American Immigration* (Chicago: University of Chicago Press).

Jones, L. (1993) 'The Hermeneutics of Sacred Architecture', *History of Religions*, 32, 3.

Joyce, D. (1989) 'Why do Police Officers Laugh at Death?', *The Psychologist*, September, 379–81.

Jupp, P.C. (1990) *From Dust to Ashes: the Replacement of Burial by Cremation in England 1840–1967* (London: Congregational Memorial Hall Trust).

Jupp, P. and Howarth, G. (eds) (forthcoming) *The Changing Face of Death: Historical accounts of death and disposal* (Basingstoke: Macmillan).

Kahn, W.A. (1989) 'Towards a Sense of Organisational Humour: Implications for organisational diagnosis and change', *Journal of Applied Behavioural Science*, 25: 45–63.

Kalsi, S.S. (1992) *The Evolution of a Sikh Community in Britain: Religious and Social Change Among the Sikhs of Leeds and Bradford* (Department of Theology and Religious Studies: University of Leeds).

Katz, J.T.S. (1989) *Context and Care: Nurses' Accounts of Stress and Support on a Cancer Ward,* Unpublished PhD Thesis, University of Warwick.

Katz, J.T.S. (1993) *Caring for Dying People – Workbook Three of K260, Death and Dying* (Milton Keynes: Open University).

Kellehear, A. (1990) *Dying of Cancer: the final years of life* (Chur: Harwood Academic).

Kessinger, T. (1974) *Vilyatpur – 1848–1968: Social and Economic Change in a North Indian Village* (Berkeley: University of California).

Killingley, D. (1991) 'Introduction', in S.Y. Killingley (ed.), *Hindu Ritual and Society* (Newcastle upon Tyne: Grevatt and Grevatt).

Klopfer, P.H. (1970) 'Sensory Physiology and Aesthetics', *American Scientist*, 58, 399–403.

Knapp, R.J. (1986) *Beyond Endurance: When a Child Dies* (New York: Schoken).

Kristeva, J. (1989) *Black Sun: Depression and Melancholia* (New York: Columbia University Press).

Kübler-Ross, E. (1970) *On Death and Dying* (London: Tavistock).

Lacan, J. (1986) [Seminar VII. The Ethics of Psychoanalysis] *Le Seminaire VII. L'ethique de la psychanalyse* (Paris: Seuil).

Lakoff, R.T. and Scherr, R.L. (1985) *Face Value: The Politics of Beauty* (Boston: Routledge and Kegan Paul).

Lansdown, R. (1985) 'The Development of the Concept of Death in Childhood', *Bereavement Care*, Summer, 15–17.

Lasch, C. (1991) *The Culture of Narcissism* (New York: Norton).

Le Goff, J. (1984) *The Pirth of Purgatory* (London: Scolar Press).

Leaney, J. (1989) 'Ashes to Ashes: Cremation and the Celebration of Death in Nineteenth Century Britain', in R. Houlbrooke (ed.), *Death, Ritual and Bereavement* (London: Routledge).

Lévi-Strauss, C. (1958) *Anthropologie Structurale* (Paris: Plon).

Lévi-Strauss, C. (1973) *Tristes Tropiques* (London: Jonathan Cape).

Lewis, E. (1976) 'The Management of Stillbirth: Coping with an Unreality', *The Lancet*, September 18, 619–620.

Lewis, I.M. (1986) *Religion in Context* (Cambridge: Cambridge University Press).

Lipset, S.M. (1964) *The First New Nation: The United States in Historical Perspective* (London: Heinemann).

Littlewood, J. (1992) *Aspects of Grief* (London: Tavistock/Routledge).

Lofland, L. (1978) *The Craft of Dying: the modern face of death* (Beverly Hills: Sage).

Luckman, T. (1969) 'The Decline of Church Oriented Religion', in R. Robertson (ed.), *Sociology of Religion* (Harmondsworth: Penguin).

McIntosh, J. (1977) *Communication and Awareness in a Cancer Ward* (London: Croom Helm).

McKeown, T. and McLachlan, G (1971) *Medical History and Medical Care* (New York: Oxford University Press).

McManners, J. (1981) *Death and the Enlightenment: changing attitudes to death among Christians and unbelievers in eighteenth-century France* (Oxford: Clarendon).

MacAndrew, C. (1988) 'On the Possibility of an Addiction Free Mode of Being', in S. Peele (ed.), *Visions of Addiction: Major contemporary Perspectives* (Lexington: Lexington Books).

Macauliffe, M.A. (1909) *The Sikh Religion* (Oxford: Oxford University Press).

Macklin, P. and Erdman, M. (1976) *Polish Jokes* (New York: Patman).

Maguire, P. and Faulkner, A. (1988) 'Communicating with cancer patients: 1. Handling bad news and difficult situations'; '2. Handling uncertainty, collusion and denial', *British Medical Journal*, 297, 907–9; 972–4.

Marenco, E.K. (1976) *The Transformation of Sikh Society* (New Delhi: Heritage Publishers).

Martin, B. (1981) *A Sociology of Contemporary Cultural Change* (Oxford: Blackwell).

Martin, D. (1978) *A General Theory of Secularization* (Oxford: Basil Blackwell).

Martins, H. (1983) 'Introduction Tristes Durées', *Journal of the Anthropological Society of Oxford*, November.

Mason, C. and Fenton, G.W. (1986) 'How successful is teaching on terminal care?', *Medical Education*, 20, 342–8.

Melia, K.M. (1987) *Learning and Working – the occupational socialization of nurses*, London: Tavistock.

Mellor, P.A. and Shilling, C. (1993) 'Modernity, Self Identity and the Sequestration of Death', *Sociology*, 27.

Middleton, J. (1982) 'Lugbara death', in M. Bloch and J. Parry (eds), *Death and the Regeneration of Life* (Cambridge: Cambridge University Press).

Miner, H. (1956) 'Body Ritual among the Nacirema', in Spradley and Rynkiewich (eds), (1975) pp.10–19.

Mitchell, M. (1994) 'Lay Perceptions of Post-Traumatic Stress Disorder', paper presented at the Northern Ireland British Psychological Society Conference.

Mitchell, M., McLay, W.D.S., Boddy, J. and Cecchi, L. (1991) 'The Police Response to the Lockerbie Disaster', *Disaster Management*, 3 (4): 198–205.

Mitford, J. (1963) *The American Way of Death* (New York: Simon and Schuster).

Montebello, P.de. (1983) 'Director's Note', in *Egyptian Art*, New York: The Metropolitan Museum of Art. (Originally printed in *The Metropolitan Museum of Art Bulletin* (Winter 1983/84.)

Morgan, D.H.J. and Scott, S. (1993) 'Bodies in a social landscape', in S. Scott and D. Morgan (eds), *Body Matters* (London: The Falmer Press).

Morris, P.J. (1984) *Kidney Transplantation: Principles and Practice* (London: Grune and Stratton).

Moscovici, S. (1984) 'The phenomena of social representations', in R.M. Farr and S. Moscovici (eds), *Social Representations* (Cambridge: Cambridge University Press).

Mulkay, M. and Ernst, J. (1991) 'The changing profile of social death', *European Journal of Sociology*, 32, 172–183.

Napier, D.L. (1986) *Masks, Transformation, and Paradox* (Berkeley: University of California Press).

Needham, R. (1986) 'Foreword', in D.L. Napier, *Masks, Transformation, and Paradox* (Berkeley: University of California Press).

Neimeyer, R.A. (1988) 'Death anxiety', in H. Wass, F.M. Berado and R.A. Neimeyer (eds), *Dying: Facing the Facts*, (2nd ed) (Washington: Hemisphere).

Neuberger, J. (1987) *'Caring For Dying People of Different Faiths'*, Lisa Sainsbury Foundation Series (London: Austen Cornish).

Nishimori, H., Suzuki, S., Kido, K. *et al.* (1994) 'Combination therapy with FK 506 and splenectomy may induce tolerance in cardiac xenografts', *Transplantation Proceedings*, 26, 3, 1064–6.

Oates, J.C. (1994) 'A Riddle Wrapped in a Mystery Inside an Enigma', *The New Yorker*, (12 Dec 1994), 45–6.

Oberoi, H.S. (1988) 'From Ritual to Counter Ritual', in J.T. O'Connell *et al.* (eds), *Sikh History and Religion in the Twentieth Century* (Toronto: University of Toronto).

Parkes, C.M. (1972) *Bereavement: studies of grief in adult life* (London: Tavistock).

Parry, J. (1982), 'Sacrificial death and the necrophagous ascetic', in M. Bloch and J. Parry (eds), *Death and the Regeneration of Life* (Cambridge: Cambridge University Press).

Parry, J. (1994) *Death in Banaras* (Cambridge: Cambridge University Press).

Parsons, T. and Lidz, V. (1967) 'Death in American Society', in E. Shneidman (ed.), *Essays in Self-Destruction* (New York: Science House).

Peberdy, A., Siddell, M. and Katz, J. (1993) *Death and Dying: workbook I, 'Life and Death'* (Milton Keynes: Open University Press).

Perakyla, A. (1988) 'Four Frames of Death in Modern Hospital', in A. and S. Gilmore (eds), *A Safer Death* (London: Plenum).

Phipps, W.E. (1987) *Death: Confronting the Reality* (Atlanta: John Knox).

Porter, R. (1989) 'Death and doctors', in R. Houlbrooke (ed.), *Death, Ritual and Bereavement* (London: Routledge).

Preston-Whyte, M.E. (1992) 'Doctor–patient communication', in R.C. Fraser (ed.), *Clinical Method: A General Practice Approach*, (2nd Edn.) (Oxford: Butterworth/Heinemann).

Quattrocchi, L. and Harvolk, E. (1987) 'Something Rich and Strange', *FMR*, 28, 91–104.

Quint, J.C. (1967) *Nurse and the Dying Patient* (New York: Macmillan).

Radcliffe-Brown, A.R. (1964) *The Andaman Islanders* (New York: Free Press).

Razavi, D., Delvaux, N., Farvacques, C. and Robaye, E. (1988) 'Immediate effectiveness of brief psychological training for health professionals dealing with terminally ill cancer patients: A controlled study', *Social Science and Medicine*, 27, 369–75.

Rensch, B. (1984) 'The Probable Neuronal Basis of Visual Aesthetic Effects', *Psychologische Beitrage*, 26, 608–615.

Richardson, R. (1987) *Death, Dissection and the Destitute* (London: Routledge and Kegan Paul).

Richardson, R. (1989) 'Why was death so big in Victorian Britain?' in R. Houlbrooke (ed.), *Death, Ritual and Bereavement* (London: Routledge).

Ressler, R. (1993) Interview: 19 February 1993, University of Redlands.

Riley, J.L. (1984) 'The psychology of bereavement: a personal view', *Update*, 179–183.

Rokeach, M. (1973) *The Nature of Human Values* (New York: Free Press).

Rose, N. (1989) *Governing the Soul: the shaping of the private self* (London: Routledge).

Rosenblatt, P.C., Walsh, R. and Jackson, A. (1976) *Grief and Mourning in Cross Cultural Perspective* (New Haven: Human Relations Area Files Press).

Ross, J.W. (1978) 'Social Work Intervention with Families of Children with Cancer', *Social Work in Health Care*, 3 (3), 257-972.

Rowell, G. (1977) *The Liturgy of Christian Burial* (London: Alcuin Club Collections and SPCK).

Salih (Robbins), M., Harvey, I., Frankel, S. *et al.* (1991) 'Potential availability of cadaver organs for transplantation', *British Medical Journal*, 302, 1053–5.

Saunders, C. (1988) 'Spiritual Pain', *Hospital Chaplain*, March.

Saunders, C. (ed.) (1990) *Hospice and Palliative Care: an interdisciplinary approach* (London: Edward Arnold).

Scott, J. and MacDonald, N. (1993) 'Education and training in palliative medicine', in D. Doyle, G. Hanks and D. MacDonald (eds) *Oxford Textbook of Palliative Medicine* (Oxford: Oxford University Press).

Scottish Police College Training Notes, 1991, Tulliallan, Kirkadly.

Seale, C. (1991a) 'A comparison of hospice and conventional care', *Social Science and Medicine*, 32, 147–52.

Seale, C. (1991b) 'Communication and awareness about death: A study of a random sample of dying people', *Social Science and Medicine*, 32, 943–52.

Shilling, C. (1993) *The Body and Social Theory* (London: Sage).

Singh, N.G.K. (1993) *The Feminine Principle in the Sikh Vision of the Transcedent* (Cambridge: Cambridge University Press).

Solomon, R.C. (1984) 'Getting Angry: the Jamesian theory of emotion in anthropology', in R.A. Schweder and R.A. LeVine, *Culture Theory* (Cambridge: Cambridge University Press).

Spencer Jones, J. (1981) 'Telling the right patient', *British Medical Journal*, 283, 291–2.

Sperber, D. (1975) *Rethinking Symbolism* (Cambridge: Cambridge University Press).

Spottiswoode, J. (1991) *Undertaken with Love* (London: Robert Hale).

Spradley, J.P. and Rynkiewich, M.A. (eds) (1975) *The Nacirema: Readings on American Culture* (Boston: Little, Brown).

Standing Medical Advisory Committee/Standing Nursing and Midwifery Committee (1993) *The Principles and Provision of Palliative Care* (London: HMSO).

Stannard, D. (1977) *The Puritan Way of Death: a Study in Religion, Culture and Social Change* (Oxford: Oxford University Press).

St. John-Stevas, N. (1961) *Life, Death and the Law: a Study of the Relationship Between Law and Christian Morals in the English and American Legal Systems* (Eyre and Spottiswoode).

Stainton Rogers, W. (1991) *Explaining Health and Illness* (Hemel Hempstead: Harvester Wheatsheaf).

Stevens, W. (1915) 'Sunday Morning' and 'Peter Quince at the Clavier', in *The Palm at the End of the Mind* (New York: Vintage Books).

Stokes, O. (1975) 'Women in Rural Bihar', in D. Jain (ed.), *Indian Women* (Delhi: Ministry of Information, Government of India).

Strathclyde Regional Council (1992) *The Chief Constable of Strathclyde's Annual Report.*

Stratton, J.G. (1984) *Police Passages* (Manhatten Beach, CA: Glendon).

Sundin, R.H., Gaines, W.G. and Knapp, W.B. (1979) 'Attitudes of dental and medical students toward death and dying', *OMEGA*, 10, 75–85

Taylor, L. (1983) *Mourning Dress: a costume and social history* (London: Allen and Unwin).

Thomas, L-V. (1976) *Anthropologie de la Mort* (Paris: Payot).

Thorpe, G. (1991) 'Teaching palliative care to United Kingdom medical students', *Palliative Medicine*, 5, 6–11.

Thorsen, J.A. and Powell, F.C. (1991) 'Medical students' attitudes towards ageing and death: a cross-sequential study', *Medical Education*, 25, 32–7.

Tierney, G. (1979) *Self-Portrait/Gene Tierney* (New York: Wyden Books).

Todd Report (1968) *Royal Commission on Medical Education 1965–1968* (London: HMSO).

Torrie, M. (1981) *Helping the Widowed* (Richmond: Cruse).

Trilling, D. (1973) 'The Death of Marilyn Monroe', in M. McCreadie (ed.), *The American Movie Goddess* (New York: John Wiley and Sons).

Trinkhaus, E. and Shipman, P. (1993) *The Neanderthals: Changing the Image of Mankind* (New York: Alfred A. Knopf).

Turner, B.(1991) *Religion and Social Theory* (London: Sage).

Turner, B. (1992) *Regulating Bodies: Essays in Medical Sociology* (London: Routledge).

Turner, V. (1978) *Image and Pilgrimage in Christian Culture* (Oxford: Blackwell).

Tylor, E.B. (1871) *Primitive Culture* (London: Murray).

Uberoi, J.P.S. (1975) 'The Five Symbols of Sikhism' in H. Singh (ed.), *Perspectives on Guru Nanak: Seminar Papers* Patiala: (Punjabi University).

Vachon, M.L.S. and Pakes, E. (1984) 'Staff stress in the care of the critically ill and dying child', in H. Wass and C. Corr (eds), *Childhood and death* (New York: Hemisphere).

Vachon, M.C.S. (1987) *Occupational Stress in Caring for the Chronically Ill, the Dying and the Bereaved* (Washington: Hemisphere).

Van Gennep, A. (1960) *Rites of Passage* (Chicago: University of Chicago Press).

Walter, T. (1990) *Funerals – and how to improve them* (London: Hodder).

Walter, T. (1994) *The Revival of Death* (London: Routledge).

Walter, T. (1995a) *The Eclipse of Eternity* (London: Macmillan).

Walter, T. (1995b) 'Natural Death and the Noble Savage, *Omega,* 30, 4, 237–48.

Walter, T. (1993) 'Dust Not Ashes, the American Preference for Burial', *Landscape*, 32, 1, 42–8.

Wambach, J.A. (1985) 'The Grief Process as a Social Construct', *Omega*, 16, 3, 201–11.

Warren, J. (1993) 'Dimming the Fatal Allure of Golden Gate Bridge', *The Los Angeles Time* (7 Nov 93), A3, 38.

Warrick, P. (1993) 'Choosing Not to Die Alone.' *Los Angles Times* (30 March 93) E1–2.

West, R. (1991) *Organ Transplantation* (London: Office of Health Economics).

White, S. (1995) 'Hindu Cremations in Britain', in P.C. Jupp and G. Howarth (eds), *The Changing Face of Death: Historical accounts of death and disposal* (Basingstoke: Macmillan).

Wilde, L. (1975) *More, the Official Polish/Italian Jokebook* (Los Angeles: Pinnacle).

Wilkes, E. (Chairman) (1980) *Terminal Care: Report of a Working Group* (London: Standing Medical Advisory Committee).

Wilkinson, A. (1995) 'Death and Two World Wars', in P.C. Jupp and G. Howarth (eds), *The Changing Face of Death: Historical accounts of death and disposal* (Basingstoke: Macmillan).

Wilkinson, S. (1991) 'Factors which influence how nurses communicate with cancer patients', *Journal of Advanced Nursing*, 16, 677–88.

Williams, C. (1987) 'Peacetime Combat: Treating and preventing delayed stress reactions in police officers', in T. Williams (ed.), *Post-traumatic Stress Disorder: A handbook for clinicians* (Cincinnati, Ohio: Disabled American Veterans).

Wilson, B.R. (1982) *Religion in Sociological Perspective* (Oxford: Oxford University Press).

Wilson, B.R. (1969) *Religion in Secular Society* (Harmondsworth: Penguin).

Woodward, R.B. 'An Eye for the Forbidden', *Vanity Fair* (April 1993) 190–5; 216–18.

Wortman, C.B. and Silver, R.C., (1989) 'The Myths of Coping with Loss', *Journal of Consulting and Clinical Psychology*, 57, 3, 349–57.

Wouters, C. (1990) 'Changing Regimes of Power and Emotions at the End of Life: The Netherlands 1930–1990', *Netherlands Journal of Sociology*, 26, 2, 151–67.

Wright, B. (1988) *Management and Practice in Emergency Nursing* (London: Chapman and Hall).

Young, M. (1994) 'Ashes to Hashes', *The Guardian*, 9 June.

Index